AGRICULTURAL DEVELOPMENT AND RURAL LABOUR

AGRICULTURAL DEVELOPMENT AND RURAL LABOUR

A Case Study of Punjab and Haryana

HARBANS SINGH SIDHU

CONCEPT PUBLISHING COMPANY, NEW DELHI 110059

The Indian Council of Social Science Research (ICSSR) gave financial support towards the publication of this work. However, responsibility for the contents of the book — facts, opinions, conclusions, etc. — is entirely that of the author and not of the ICSSR.

ISBN 81-7022-336-9

First Published 1991

Published and Printed by
Ashok Kumar Mittal
Concept Publishing Company
A/15-16, Commercial Block, Mohan Garden
NEW DELHI 110059 (India)

Lasertypeset by
Microtech Advance Printing Systems (Pvt.) Ltd.
H-13, Bali Nagar
NEW DELHI 110015

PREFACE

SINCE INDEPENDENCE Indian agriculture has witnessed substantial development and change in level of production, cropping pattern and level of input use. The adoption of new agricultural technology in mid-1960s consisting of high yielding varieties of crops, irrigation, fertilisers, methods for the control of weeds, diseases and pests along with modern cultural practices further accelerated the process of development. The areas where this new technology was successfully adopted recorded a significantly higher rate of growth of output and yields. Punjab and Haryana are pioneers in the field, and have thus recorded a phenomenal rate of growth of around five per cent per annum during the past two and a half decades or so.

Agrarian change of this magnitude is bound to have far reaching socio-economic consequences for various sections of the rural population involved directly or indirectly in agriculture and/or dependent on it for their livelihood. However, the literature on the subject reveals that only two major questions have engaged the attention of researchers and policy-makers. They are whether (i) the new technology has led to more rather than less inequality in the distribution of income and wealth in the country-side; and (ii) will it under the influence of factor price distribution encourage a form of mechanisation that is labour displacing rather than labour absorbing? The major limitation of these studies is that they are confined mainly to the cultivating classes. The agricultural wage labour and other non-cultivating sections of the rural population are brought into discussion only parenthetically, if at all.

A substantial section of the rural population works as agricultural labour which is directly involved in agriculture and is dependent upon it for its livelihood. Similarly, there is another section of non-cultivating rural households, consisting of carpenters, blacksmiths, weavers, potters, masons, plumbers, cobblers, barbers, milkmen and retailers, which, though not directly involved in agriculture, are yet largely dependent on agriculture. Any large-scale change in agriculture is bound to affect these sections of the rural population. It is likely to affect their employment prospects, patterns of employment, wage rates, income levels and consumption patterns. There is hardly any comprehensive empirical study dealing with all the aspects of the impact of agricultural growth on these sections of the rural population.

The present study is an endeavour to fill this gap. It deals with almost all aspects of the problem such as impact of agricultural growth on employment, unemployment, participation rates, employment status, wage rates, earnings, income levels of the household, consumption patterns and levels of living, extent of poverty and its correlates particularly the unemployment poverty nexus using appropriate statistical techniques. However, the success or otherwise of the endeavour is for the reader to judge.

I have pleasure in recording my deep sense of gratitude to Prof. G.S. Bhalla of J.N.U., New Delhi, under whose guidance and supervision this study was completed. Right from he genesis of the idea to the completion of the study he has been a constant source of inspiration. Prof. Moonis Raza, Prof. Aijaz Ahmed, Prof. Ashok Mathur, Prof. G.K. Chadha, Prof. Kusum Chopra, Prof. Amitab Kundu and members of the staff of Centre for the Study of Regional Development, J.N.U. were extremely helpful in my work. I am grateful to all of them.

Prof. S.K. Goyal, Director, Corporate Studies Group of the Indian Institute of Public Administration, New Delhi, with whom I worked for some time, inspired me throughout. I am deeply grateful to him. I am also thankful to Prof. Dharam Vir of Panjab University, Chandigarh, who was helpful at every stage of my work.

Discussions with friends and colleagues particularly Dr. Surendar Singh, Dr. R.K. Sharma, Dr. Iqbal Singh, Dr. H.S. Shergill, and Dr. Surjit Singh helped me to clarify my ideas. I am obliged to them for their helpful suggestions. I am also thankful to Mr. V.M. Dhar, Mr. B.M. Gupta and Mr. M.P. Goyal, Computer Programmers, for help in processing the data.

The members of the staff of the libraries of Jawaharlal Nehru University, Indian Institute of Public Administration, and National Council of Applied Economic Research, New Delhi were always helpful in meeting my persistent requests for material. I am hugely beholden to them for the help so readily rendered.

I am indebted to Prof. A.S. Dhesi, Prof. S.S. Hans, and Prof. Tejwant Singh Gill of Guru Nanak Dev University, Amritsar for several suggestions and act of kindness. S. Gang Singh typed the manuscript with diligence for which I am obliged to him.

The generous fellowship of U.G.C. was a timely help in my study of the problem. I record my acknowledgement for the publication grant of ICSSR without which the publication of the book may have been difficult if not possible.

I also express my sense of obligation to numerous persons not named who helped me in a number of ways. For the shortcomings of the work however I alone am responsible.

HARBANS SINGH SIDHU

CONTENTS

LIST OF TABLES

LIST OF APPENDICES

1

INTRODUCTION

The Problem

AGRICULTURE IN certain areas in India has witnessed an unprecedented change since mid-1960s with the evolution of high yielding varieties of crops and the adoption of modern and improved farm practices. The new agricultural technology consists of a highly complementary package of inputs which includes assured water supply, use of hybrid seeds, chemical fertilizers, pesticides, herbicides and a variety of mechanical equipments, like, seed drills, tractors and combine harvesters. The core of this package, however, is the hybrid seeds of some major crops which under appropriate circumstances have recorded substantially higher yields than traditional and locally improved varieties. Initially, this success was achieved through the large-scale adoption of high yielding varieties of Mexican wheat. This has been followed by a varitable rice revolution made possible by the Phillipene varieties of rice such as IR-8 and PR-106. The new agricultural technology or the "Green Revolution" as it is more commonly referred to, is not merely a package of inputs but it also incorporates a package of new agricultural practices and the two together form the technology of 'Green Revolution'. Given the short maturing period of new varieties and the possibility of multiple cropping, the new technology follows a distinctly different crop calendar. In the areas where this new technology has been successful it has accelerated the transformation of the agricultural economy from the one characterised predominantly by subsistence farming to the one in which cultivation is undertaken as a profitable farm business.

Since availability of irrigation is almost a pre-condition for the successful adoption of new varieties, certain areas like, Punjab,

Haryana, Western Uttar Pradesh, Coastal Andhra, Coastal Kerala, parts of Tamil Nadu and some parts of West Bengal which had some kind of assured irrigation, were more successful in adopting the new technology. Consequently growth performance of Indian agriculture has not been uniform, primarily because in certain areas, because of lack of irrigation, new agricultural technology could not be adopted equally successfully. The areas where the new technology has been successful have recorded a substantially higher rate of growth of output.

The new agricultural technology consists of two components, i.e., the bio-chemical component and the mechanical component. The bio-chemical component i.e., the irrigation-seed-fertilizer innovation is normally considered to be land augmenting and labour-using in nature. It is also thought to be capable of generating large increases in employment and also staggering these more evenly over the year, thus reducing the seasonal unemployment and poverty of the landless who largely depend on agriculture for their livelihood. The use of perennial groundwater for irrigation and the short maturing nature of new varieties have increased the intensity of cropping and in some areas there have been significant shifts in the cropping patterns also. As a result, the usually lean seasons have become more active over time. Along with the shifting production possibilities with the adoption of bio-chemical innovations, however, related technical changes have also been taking place. Some of these technical changes, like, mechanical tilling, sowing and harvesting, are labour saving in nature and thus modify the effect of bio-chemical innovations on employment.

Simultaneously the increased output in agriculture and increased income of the farmers are expected to give rise to higher demand for labour for various other services. Handling of increased marketable agricultural surpluses is one such example. Various improvements being affected in land and the creation of other infrastructural facilities, like, village roads, canals, water courses, increased demand for bricks on account of increased demand for better *pucca* houses, construction activities and various other developmental projects, which always accompany such a development, are expected to provide additional employment. At the same time, however, some of the traditional customary services, which were being provided by village artisans, are fast disappearing. This has caused some shift in the employment pattern of rural labourers. The net result of these developments, however, is expected to be an increase in the overall demand for labour. Because of increased overall demand and the importance of timeliness of each operation, the new technology is also expected to increase the bargaining power of wage-labour at crucial points of time.

Barring a Lewisian theoretical situation, where the supply curve of labour is perfectly elastic over a wide range, the large increases in demand for labour would normally be expected to have significant positive impact on both employment and wage rates for labour. What have the actual changes been like? Do the agricultural labourers in these areas, where new technology has been more successful, have more work availability in terms of number of days employed ? Do they get higher wages in such areas ? If so, does it reflect in their consumption patterns and levels of living ? How does the structure of wage rates and the pattern of labour employment change in response to the shifts in supply and demand ? In other words, have the gains of agricultural growth in such areas percolated down to agricultural wage labour and other non-cultivating rural labour households ? These are some of the questions to which the present study is addressed.

The area of our study is Punjab and Haryana. The choice of area is influenced by the fact that the new agricultural technology has been more successful in these two States than anywhere else in the country. Also, these two States put together have enough variations in the level of agricultural development across districts and regions and this makes it possible to correlate the impact of level of agricultural development with employment, wages, income and consumption of wage labour and other non-cultivating rural labour households.

Review of Literature

Here we shall briefly review only those studies which have been conducted in the context of recent technological change in agriculture and which directly or indirectly deal with the impact of this technological change on employment, wages, incomes or levels of living of non-cultivating rural labour households or rural poverty in general. A detailed review of general studies on the topics of employment/unemployment, incomes, wage rates and their determinants, consumption and rural poverty, etc., is given in the respective chapters.

The literature of the period of Green Revolution reveals that two major questions have been engaging the active attention of researchers and policy-makers. These questions are:

(i) has the new technology led to more rather than less inequality in the distribution of income and wealth in the country-side ? and
(ii) will it under the influence of factor price distortions encourage a form of mechanisation that is labour displacing rather than labour absorbing.

In addition to these, some other aspects, like, the impact of new technology on the wage rates and levels of living of agricultural wage labour, the relative share of labour in production growth in the context of switch from local to HYV production technology and the impact of agricultural growth on rural poverty, etc., have also been studied by some researchers.

Studies on the question of distribution of gains from new technology can be broadly divided into two categories. In the first category we can include those early studies which pointed out that the farm income distribution has become more skewed as a result of the adoption of new technology. This group which includes Ladejinsky (1969 A[1] and 1969 B[2]), Falcon (1970),[3] Wharton (1969),[4] Lewis (1970),[5] Frankel (1969[6] and 1970[7]), and Byres (1972),[8] saw trouble on the horizon. The possibility of acute social tension and indeed of the Green Revolution turning into 'red revolution'. The trouble, they maintain, is likely to stem from a number of sources. These include the effective exclusion of small peasants and landless labourers from the gains of the Green Revolution as their real income fails to rise and their employment prospects deteriorate with the advent of mechanisation; growing regional disparities with irrigated areas advancing steadily and dry areas languishing and strengthening the power of rich peasants in rural India. However, most of these studies are impressionistic in nature and the conclusions have been derived either on the basis of impressions gathered during the visits to the villages in the Green Revolution areas (as in the case of Ladejinsky) or by referring to historical parallels (as in the case of Byres). Very few of these studies are based on analysis of data collected from properly drawn reasonably large samples and using proper techniques.

However, there is another group consisting of a fairly large number of studies which includes Sen (1970),[9] Khaund (1970),[10] Sharma, Mehta and Single (1970),[11] Harrison (1972),[12] Parthasarthy (1973),[13] Bhalla (1974),[14] Rao (1975),[15] Singh (1977),[16] Bhalla and Chadha (1982)[17] and Sidhu (1984),[18] which is based on fairly large sample and uses proper techniques. A general conclusion of these studies is that while some have gained more than others, all groups have benefited from new technology. Some of these studies, like, Bhalla (1974), Singh (1977) and Sidhu (1984), have distinguished the effects of new technology on income distribution among adopters from that among the non-adopters and concluded that the adoption of new technology has helped to reduce the relative income inequality among the adopting sub-set. But these studies have two major drawbacks. First, these are based on the cross sectional analysis of income of adopter and non-adopter farmers and so fail to take into account the dynamics of change over a period of time. Secondly, the analysis in most of these studies is confined to the cultivating classes only and agricultural wage labourer and other non-cultivating sections of rural society have been brought into the discussion only parenthetically, if at all. Thus, these studies really do not throw much light on the impact of new agricultural technology on the incomes of non-cultivating rural labour households, the topic with which we are concerned in the present study.

Another aspect of the new agricultural technology, which interested a fairly large number of researchers and incidentally, also important for the present study, is its implications for demand for labour. Changes in labour demand have direct bearing on employment, income, wages and level of living of agricultural labourers. Therefore, we shall review these topics in greater detail. As already mentioned, the new agricultural technology has two components, i.e., the bio-chemical component consisting of the irrigation-seed-fertilizer innovations and the mechanical component, i.e., mechanical tilling, sowing, harvesting/threshing and transporting of farm produce. Perennial controllable irrigation is growth-inducing in two ways. First, it extends the effective cropping period, thus, increasing the productive absorption of labour on an acre of land. Secondly, it acts as a vehicle for introducing innovations embodied in new fertilizer-responsive seed varieties which raises productivity of labour on each cropped acre. Thus the bio-chemical component of the new technology is generally considered to be labour absorbing in nature. The mechanical component, however, is considered to be labour displacing in nature. When the effects of the mechanical innovation are not separated from those of the seed-fertilizer innovation, then the seed fertilizer technology might seem to be labour saving.[19] Hanumantha Rao (1975) using aggregate data for 265 districts for the year 1964-65 pointed out a lack of positive association between fertilizer use and number of agricultural workers per net sown acre, which he interpreted as an indication that use of fertilizer and irrigation might have, on balance, been labour saving. But this study relates to pre-Green Revolution period. Therefore, most studies on farm employment implications of technological changes make a distinction between effects of the water-based-seed-fertilizer innovation and mechanical tilling, sowing and harvesting. They have found that whereas the former is generally labour absorbing the same cannot be said about the latter.

Some estimates have been attempted in the Indian context regarding the effect of different types of mechanisation of farm employment of labour. They are, however, not very conclusive, partly, because the estimation procedures are not uniform and, partly, because of inadequate data and approximations used. The major micro-level studies, using farm-wise data, are Hanumantha Rao (1975),[20] Vashishtha (1975),[21] Sharma (1972),[22] Acharya (1973),[23] Lockwood (1972),[24] Rudra (1971),[25] Singh and Singh (1972),[26] Bell (1972),[27] Chopra (1974)[28] and Bina (1983)[29]. Some of the important macro-level studies on the direct employment effects of technical change in Indian agriculture are by Billings and Singh (1970)[30] and (1971),[31] Sethuraman (1971)[32] and Raj Krishna (1974)[33]. Apart from the direct employment effects, estimates of indirect employment effects have also been attempted by Sethuraman (1971)[34] and Raj Krishna (1974).[35]

In the micro-level studies which are based on the farm level data, the coefficients of labour input per hectare for different crop patterns and for different categories of farms, with or without the specific technical changes, are estimated. Then, with the help of these technical coefficients and taking into account the relative importance of different crop patterns, different categories of farms and the specified elements of technological change, macro-level coefficients are worked out. The technological coefficient which received the maximum attention in these studies is tractor. Thus, most of these studies end up in analysing the impact of tractorisation on farm employment.

Hanumantha Rao (1975) using farm level data for Ferozepur district of Punjab for 1954-55 to 1956-57, when use of tractor power was negligible, and for 1968-69, and 1969-70, when it was quite considerable, attempts an estimate of the employment effects of tractor use. First, he makes comparison between tractor farms and bullock farms of similar size and irrigation levels and finds that tractor farms have higher cropping intensity and employment per hectare. This being a combined effect of tubewell, irrigation, high-yielding seeds, fertilizer and tractor, he tries to separate out the effect of tractor use. Using a multiple regression analysis in which labour employment is a function of farm size, proportion of areas irrigated, proportion of area under HYV seeds, fertilizer per unit of area, investment in tubewells and two sets of dummy variables, one for tractor ownership and the other for thresher ownership, he tries to work out the influence of these variables on employment per hectare. His results show that tractor dummy is insignificant for both output and employment and on this basis he concludes that the technological displacement of labour, consequent on the use of tractor, is roughly compensated by positive employment effects of the change in cropping pattern and intensity associated with tractor use. But unless it is assumed that it is the tractor which is primarily responsible for higher cropping intensity and higher proportion of area under HYV seeds this conclusion, though plausible, is not quite established.

Vashishtha (1975), using the same 1968-69 data set for Ferozepur, estimates the effect of tractorisation on the intensity of cropping, on output per acre as well as on employment per acre. Using a variance-covariance method, he works out the adjusted mean levels of each of these three variables after standardising for the effects of farm size, irrigation intensity, inputs of seed-fertilizer-manure-pesticides, tubewell/pump-sets and thresher for farms with and without tractors. Comparing the adjusted mean levels with each other and with actual ones, he finds that tractorisation had no significant effect on either cropping intensity or output per acre. The observable difference between tractor farms and non-tractor farms were mainly the result of difference in irrigation and seed-fertilizer input rate. As far as employment per acre is concerned, while the effect of tubewell/pump sets per acre was found to be positive and that of threshers negative, the effect of tractor turned out to be neutral.

A major drawback of both these studies is that the analysis is carried out in terms of tractor ownership rather than tractor use. Thus, the intensity of tractor use and its distribution in various operations are ignored and this is likely to effect the stability of employment coefficients of tractorisation.

Sharma (1972) working on a cross-sectional data from a pilot study of HYV programme in Karnal district of Haryana and using the method of comparison between tractor and non-tractor farms, similar in terms of size and irrigation, concludes that the labour used per acre is about seven per cent higher for bullock farms. The difference, however, is not very large and it may well be because of differences in fertilizer use. The study of Sapre (1972) relates to a relatively backward region. The study was conducted in Dhulia district of Maharashtra. Taking output per hectare as an indicator of employment per hectare, he finds output per hectare to be higher in tractor operated farms. As for the tractor farm having higher output per acre and, therefore, higher employment per acre, is concerned, while it is perfectly possible that to the extent tractor use contributes to cropping intensity, notwithstanding labour saved on ploughing, it increases employment, because of the labour needed for more weeding, harvesting, threshing, etc., outweighs the labour saved, assuming, of course, that these operations are not mechanised with the help of tractor. But even then the main problem of separating out the effect of tractor use on cropping intensity from the effects of other related but independent factors, like, irrigation, remains unresolved. Acharya (1973) with farm level data from two districts of Rajasthan compared labour use per cropped acre between a tractor-operated HYV user and a non-mechanised HYV user, and found that it was higher for the first one.

Aggarwal (1983) uses data collected under the "Comprehensive Scheme for Studying the Cost of Cultivation of Principal Crops" from the principal wheat growing area of Punjab for the crop year 1971-72. She is of the view that the employment effect of tractorisation must be studied in terms of those farm operations only for which tractors are principally used. Secondly, she points out that unless the bullock farms are separated from tractor hiring ones, the labour displacement effect is likely to be biased in a downward direction. Therefore, in her study, she takes care of both these points. Her main conclusions are:

(a) In comparison with bullocks, the use of tractor substantially reduces the labour time required for ploughing and sowing both per gross hectare and per net sown hectare and;

(b) that labour time used per sown hectare is lower on tractor farms in spite of the higher cropping intensity associated with tractor farms relative to bullock farms.

All tractor farms taken together use on average 45.1 labour hours per sown hectare less than bullock farms. Among these tractor farms those owning tractor use 92.3 labour hours per sown hectare less than bullock farms and those depending on hired tractor services use 29.3 hours less. Thus, Bina finds that introduction of tractor displaces labour significantly.

Strictly speaking, Lockwood's study is not a study to measure the effect of tractor use on farm employment, but it is interesting for at least two reasons. First, the author studies the features of all tractor-using farms, irrespective of whether the tractors are owned or hired. Secondly, he discussed separately the employment effects of different operational uses of tractors. The study is based on a survey data collected by the Programme Evaluation Organisation of the Planning Commission during 1967-68 to 1969-70 for samples of farms using HYV seeds and those not using these in eight districts of Punjab, Haryana and western Uttar Pradesh. In the sample of HYV using farms, those who own tractors constitute only nine per cent while those who hire it or contract its services account for 40 per cent of the sample. However, those who hired tractors used these for a smaller proportion of the area than the tractor owners. Again in Lockwood's sample representing an initial phase of tractorisation, the tractors were actually being used mainly for land preparation including a good amount of contract work and were not used for many additional operations except for '*carting*' during harvest season and as "*automobiles*" during off season. Over time as the number of tractors increases and their owners apply it for more and more operations, the demand for labour is likely to be affected much more seriously.

The employment effects of tractorisation have not been uniform on all segments of rural labourers. It is of some interest to know the breakdown of the employment effect of tractorisation on family labour, hired casual labour and permanent farm servants. Studies by Rudra (1971) and Chopra (1974) deal with these issues. Rudra's study is based on a sample survey of large farms (20 acres and above) from 11 districts of Punjab for the year 1968-69 and it makes some interesting comparisons regarding the comparison of labour use. Rudra, by dividing these farms into three categories – (a) farms having tube-wells, pumps and tractor, (b) those having tube-wells and pumps but no tractor and (c) those having none – and considering relative frequency of these farms by the number of farm servants and the number of man-days of casual labour used, observes that the mechanised farms particularly falling in category (a) save some casual labour in per acre terms compared to the non-mechanised farms, but the intensity of use of permanent farm servants is more or less the same across these categories. Given a certain number of male family workers on a large farm, the addition of tube-wells and pumps reduces, at the cross-sectional level, the demand for permanent farm servants somewhat but increases that for casual labour. Further addition of tractors then increases the demand for permanent farm servant but remains unchanged for casual labour. Thus, pumps and tube-wells seem to displace permanent farm servants, who, perhaps, were earlier used for lifting water and maintaining the bullocks, and create demand for casual labour. The tractors, on the other hand, seem to raise demand for permanent farm servants. The net effect on total use of hired labour in farm category (a) is, however, not clear from Rudra's study.

Chopra (1974), on the other hand, on the basis of her sample of 130 households collected from 13 villages of Hoshiarpur, Ludhiana and Ferozepur districts of Punjab finds that intensity of cropping is higher by about 16 per cent on tractor owned farms as compared to non-tractor owned farms. Since intensity of cropping is the combined result of irrigation as well as tractor, she separates 52 farms which had constant irrigated areas before and after the introduction of tractor and finds that even in these farms intensity of cropping has risen by 13 per cent which she attributes to the use of tractor. As far as the employment effects of tractor are concerned, her sample shows an increase in the employment of labour at the macro as well as micro-level. But unlike Rudra (1971), Chopra (1974) comes to the conclusion that while tractor use has decreased somewhat the demand for permanent labour which was perhaps earlier used for seed bed preparations, it increased the use of family labour. The demand for casual male labourers on these farms has gone up by 38.47 per cent after the introduction of tractor.

Since the highest degree of farm mechanisation along with the irrigation-seed-fertilizer innovation has been witnessed in the north-western States of Punjab, Haryana and western Uttar Pradesh, it is only natural that most of the studies of the effect of farm mechanisation on demand for labour should relate to these States only. Bell's study is somewhat different in this respect insofar as it covers the Kosi canal area in Bihar. His conclusion is that although tractors used for land preparation alone could be called land augmenting, their overall net effect on labour use would be negative or positive depending upon whether the labour intensive inter-cultural practices are adopted or not. Comparing a paddy-jute rotation with a three-crop (wheat and two crops of paddy) rotation with high yielding seeds, he observed that the constraint for the switch is not labour shortage but shortage of drought power which is required for two more or less simultaneous and time-bound operations of threshing the harvested crop and preparing land for the next one. The use of tractor in such a situation is a concomitant of the labour using seed-fertilizer innovation. He does not, however, work out the net effect of tractorisation on employment.

Thus, the available evidence from micro-level studies on the effect of tractorisation particularly in the context of north-west India is inconclusive. But these studies relate to the initial phase when its use was confined mostly to seed-bed preparation. However, it seems to have had some effect on the casual-attached composition of hired labour.

The employment effects of tractorisation, experienced in the initial phase and analysed by micro-studies discussed above, are specific to the particular operational composition observed at that time. For projection of the total employment effects of tractorisation, one has to take into account the likely or planned operation-wise composition of tractor use. Given the official encouragement of tractorisation – through subsidised credit to buy it and the consequent rapid expansion of tractor population – its displacing effects are likely to become stronger as it is increasingly being used for more labour intensive operations. The basic procedure used in macro-level projections of the direct employment effect of tractorisation is to apply the coefficients of labour input for each crop, with the old and the new techniques of raising it, to the projected area under each crop grown with the traditional technique and with the new technique, respectively.

A major study of this type is by Billings and Singh (1971) who, on the basis of certain assumptions, concluded that over the period from 1968-69 to 1983-84 farm labour demand in Punjab would decline by 17 per cent. Their conclusion was based on the assumption that by 1983-84, 20 per cent of all cropped area would be tractor ploughed, the entire wheat crop mechanically threshed, all corn mechanically shelled, 50 per cent of wheat crop mechanically harvested and that tube-well and pump sets will cover 60 per cent of irrigated area. They estimated a 14 per cent increase in cropped area and a cropping pattern determined by past trends and optimality conditions. Of the total direct labour displacement in the model of Billings and Singh, about half would occur in the peak harvesting months on account of mechanised harvesting and threshing, thus effecting the casual labourers most. The remaining displacement, on account of pump irrigation and tractor ploughing, would be spread over the year. Although considerable degree of mechanisation has taken place in Punjab since 1968-69 there is no sign of a substantial reduction in demand for labour.

Another well known macro-level study of the effects of farm mechanisation on employment is by Raj Krishna (1974). Raj Krishna decomposes the direct employment effect in terms of the effects of cropping pattern, cropping intensity, specified items of farm mechanisation and the interaction element. Assuming a terminal year pattern of technology similar to that assumed by Billings and Singh, his model indicates for Punjab over 1968-69 to 1983-84 a sizable negative direct employment effect for wheat-rice combine which is composed of a larger negative one on account of the assumed rates of mechanisation, partially compensated by the positive effects on account of rise in cropping intensity and on account of change in rice-wheat mix. He then separates out the direct employment effect of tractors with their multiple uses. His conclusion is that the negative substitution effect of the technological change, though outweighed by the positive scale effect of growth, would mean a slower farm employment growth rate corresponding to a given agricultural production growth. It has been argued that the manufacture, servicing and operating of agricultural machinery increases non-agricultural employment which must be taken into account in evaluating the overall employment effect of tractor technology. Raj Krishna estimates these indirect employment effects also. His calculations indicate that growth in non-agricultural employment induced by something like five per cent rate of growth in agricultural production with labour-displacing technological change will not fully compensate for the slow growth in agricultural employment. Thus, to avoid rural unemployment, he argues, the policy-makers would have to adjust the growth innovations demand mix.

Thus, one finds that in the existing literature on the employment effect of tractor there remains a discrepancy between the macro-level direct effect (negative) estimated or projected on the assumption that tractor is used for the multiplicity of operations for which it is designed and the micro-level effect (more or less neutral) derived from its actual use in the early phase of tractorisation which from all available accounts consisted mainly of ploughing and very little of other operations. What will be the total effect of farm mechanisation on rural employment when harvesting, reaping, shelling and threshing are totally mechanised, however, remains to be seen. All the available evidence so far suggests that, in what has been an initial phase of diffusion of technological change in agriculture, the combined effect of controlled irrigation, high yielding seed varieties and fertilizers on farm employment has dominated over that of mechanisation.

Another important aspect in the context of technological change in agriculture covered by a relatively smaller number of studies, but what is relevant, from our point of view, is the issue of trend in money and real wage rates in agriculture. Among the early studies mention may be made to Bardhan (1970[36] and 1973),[37] Jose (1974),[38] Krishanji (1971)[39] and Lal (1976).[40] But these studies cover roughly a decade of pre-Green Revolution period and only the early phase of Green Revolution. Two other studies which cover almost the entire decade of 60s and 70s, but relate to the individual States of Punjab and Andhra Pradesh only, are by Bhálla (1979)[41] and Parthasarthy and Adiseshu (1982)[42]. The source of data used by Bardhan is the NSS specifically Labour Enquiries relating to 1956-57, 1963-64, 1964-65 and the 25th round of NSS relating to 1970-71. Jose and Krishanji's studies are based on *Agricultural Wages in India* (AWI) data which is published by the Ministry of Food and Agriculture. The study by Lall (1974) is also based on NSS data.

Using NSS data on agricultural wages and Consumer Price Index for Agricultural Labour (CPIAL), Bardhan (1970) compares Punjab (including Haryana and Himachal Pradesh) with Kerala in terms of the changes in money and real wage rates from 1956-57 to 1964-65. The average money wage rate for male agricultural labour rose in both the cases, but much more in Kerala than in Punjab, while the rise in cost of living was of a similar order. As a result there was a considerable rise in the real wage rate in Kerala over the period but a decline in Punjab despite the fact that production growth was higher in Punjab even at that time. In a subsequent study, Bardhan (1973) extended the comparison over a longer period between 1956-57 and 1970-71. It was found that the initial decline in real wage rates in Punjab and Haryana was temporary and there was a rise after the mid-60s. But still the rise was less than in Kerala. The higher rise in farm wages in Kerala was attributed by Bardhan to the organised bargaining power of agrarian trade unions.

Similarly, Jose (1974) using *Agricultural Wages in India* (AWI) data and covering roughly the same period, i.e. 1956-57 to 1971-72, which includes the initial phase of Green Revolution, also found that the disparity in the trend in real wage rates between Kerala and Punjab/Haryana was much less during the five years following 1966-67 than during the preceding five years. This is consistent with Bardhan's comparison based on NSS data. Bardhan, Krishnaji and Jose using different sources of data have computed changes in real wage rates for other areas also. The general conclusion which emerges from these studies is that over the total period of 15 years covered by these studies, in the initial five-year period real wages were more or less rising. Then there was a decline of varying degrees between 1961-62 and 1967-68 in most of the States except Kerala. In the later years, the trend has been upward except in a few agriculturally stagnant States, like, Orissa.

Using NSS data, Lal (1974) finds that between 1956-57 and 1970-71 real agricultural wages rose in all the States of India except West Bengal for which data are not available from the NSS for 1970-71. He divides entire period into two sub-periods, i.e., 1956-57 to 1964-65 and 1964-65 to 1970-71, and finds that in the first sub-period real wages rose in seven States and were constant or fell in the remaining eight. On the other hand, in the second sub-period, i.e., 1964-65 to 1970-71, they rose in all the States.

Bhalla (1979) studies the real wage rates of agricultural labourers in Punjab for the period 1961-77. She observes that during this period there was a race on between rising productivity pushing up wages, on the one hand, and increasing labour force and inflation, on the other, pushing down real wages. The outcome was often decided by inflation which periodically eroded real wages to the level below even those attained in 1961 as between 1965-68 and again in 1974, 1975 and 1977. For the period as a whole, whereas the agricultural output had gone up more than two and half times its level in 1961, real wages of male agricultural labourers registered a rise of approximately 15 per cent. As for the variation in wages is concerned, between 25 per cent and 43 per cent of the year to year variations in real wages for different operations are explained by farm output growth. While productivity per male agricultural worker explains about 50 per cent of the interdistrict variations in 1970s, it explains very little of inter-district variations in real wages during the early 1960s. From this, Bhalla concludes that in the labour market the forces of demand and supply seem to have acquired increasingly greater importance in the determination of real wage rate during the Green Revolution decade.

Taking agricultural wage data for individual districts of Andhra Pradesh from the Season and Crop Reports, Parthasarthy and Adiseshu (1982) analyse the trend in real wages between 1958-59 and 1978-79. They calculate the association between trend in real wages and trend in net per capita (rural) agricultural production. The long term trend in real wages is, however, one of stagnation whether the deflator used is the average retail prices or the Consumer Price Index for Agricultural Labourer. The value of regression coefficient though positive in both the cases is not significantly different from zero. Thus a comparison of 1978-79 real wages with pre-Green Revolution position shows a rise but there is no trend. Even when linear trends are fitted separately for the first 10 years from 1958-59 to 1967-68 and for the second 11 years, period, i.e., 1968-69 to 1978-79, the coefficients are not significant. Thus, the inference that there is stagnation in real wages applies not only to the entire period but also to the two sub-periods when taken separately. Thus, the main conclusion of Parthasarthy and Adiseshu is that:

> "the improvement in productivity of labour *per se* do not contribute to improvement in real wages unless they bring down the prices paid by agricultural labourers."[43]

The authors also examine the trend in real wages district-wise and find that there is a negative though insignificant trend in real wages even for a relatively well-developed district, such as West Godavari which is known to have experienced significant changes in technology. Parthasarthy and Adiseshu's findings notwithstanding, the general conclusion which emerges from these studies is that production increase did have positive impact on wage rate. The increasing differences in the yield per acre because of the success of new agricultural technology in certain States reflected itself in the widening regional disparity in rural labourers' level of living. However, these studies also point towards the fact that agricultural labourers' wages are poorly adjusted to and sometimes lag behind rise in their cost of living.

If increase in real wages, even where it took place, is only a fraction of the growth of output, the relative share of labourers in incremental output and growth must have gone down. Some researchers have explored this question in the context of new agricultural production technology. Here mention may be made to Hanumantha Rao (1975),[44] Parthasarthy and Prasad (1974)[45] and Mellor and Lee (1974),[46] to name only a few. Hanumantha Rao (1975) first compared labour's share in gross and net farm output for a random sample of farms in Ferozepur district of Punjab as between 1954-57 and 1968-70 and found that the labour share has declined over time. He then compared the labour share as between the local varieties and the high yielding varieties of Mexica Wheat and IR-8 rice separately for the latter period, i.e., 1968-70. He observed a tendency in the labour share to get smaller with the HYV although the absolute labour cost (including family labour evaluated at market rate) per acre is considerably higher for HYV paddy or wheat than for the local variety. The decline in labour's share was found to be much sharper in the case of large farms (above 50 acres) than for all farms taken together. The labour's incremental share in production growth over the period works out to 24 per cent for all farms and 13 per cent for the very large farms. The share as between local and Mexican wheat was 16 per cent and between local and IR-8 paddy 11 per cent for all farms.

The basic difficulty with Hanumantha Rao's study is that it includes in labour share the imputed value of family labour input also which has been imputed at market wage. But if the hired component of farm labour use rises with intensive cropping and production growth, which is actually true, then this procedure when used in inter-temporal comparisons would tend to over-estimate labour's share in the earlier period because the hired in labour is likely to be less than family labour withdrawn. Parthasarthy and Parsad's study is free from this problem as they compare wage bill for hired labour alone. Analysing data from East Godavari and West Godavari districts, their study shows that while the total wage bill goes up with shift from local to IR-8 paddy variety, but the relative share of labour in gross value of output gets smaller. This tendency is more pronounced for Rabi IR-8 paddy on which farmers in the area use more fertilizer than on Kharif. The incremental share of hired labour for a switch from local to IR-8 paddy works out to about 10 per cent on an average for these two Andhra districts.

Mellor and Lee (1973) using information gathered from a large number of small scale surveys, conducted by Agro-Economic Research Centre, programme evaluation organisation of the Planning Commission and individual researchers in different parts of the country, find that incremental share for hired labour in an increased production with switch to HYV was usually about 10 per cent for wheat and Kharif paddy and somewhat less than that for Rabi paddy. Thus, the common conclusion of all these studies on the question of relative share of labour in production growth in the context of new agricultural technology is that labour's share has gone down with a switch from local varieties to HYV seed-fertilizer production technology, the increase in absolute amount of wage bill notwithstanding.

Although the extent of change in agricultural labourer's level of living in the context of new agricultural technology since late 60s has not been adequately measured yet several attempts have been made to measure the time trend in incidence of rural poverty and the relationship between rural poverty and agricultural growth. Mention may be made of Bardhan (1973),[47] Rajaraman (1975),[48] Ahluwalia (1978),[49] Griffin and Ghose (1979),[50] Saith (1981),[51] Sinha (1981)[52] and Chadha (1983)[53]. About the temporal behaviour of poverty as well as its relationship with agricultural growth, different studies report conflicting results. For example, Bardhan (1973) found that incidence of poverty in Punjab (including Haryana) increased during 1960-61 and 1967-68. Similarly, Rajaraman (1975) reported that the incidence of poverty in Punjab (excluding Haryana) increased during 1960-61 and 1970-71. But the problem with both these studies is that these are based on comparison between two isolated and arbitrarily chosen years. Ahluwalia (1978) on the other hand built up a more or less comprehensive time series for all-India as well as for individual States spanning the period 1956-57 to 1973-74. On the basis of a single time trend fitted to the time series, he concludes that the Indian experience over the past two decades cannot be characterised as showing a trend increase in incidence of rural poverty in India as a whole. The same conclusion holds for all individual States except Assam and Bengal which show a significant trend increase in poverty. As for the relationship between agricultural growth and rural poverty is concerned, on the basis of his regression analysis, Ahluwalia comes to the conclusion that there is a clear evidence of an inverse relationship between rural poverty and agricultural performance. Thus, his results suggest that there is some trickling down of benefits from increases in agricultural production.

Chadha (1983), however, is not satisfied with Ahluwalia's methodology of fitting a single time trend to the time series of poverty figures for Punjab (including Haryana) and concludes on this basis that the incidence of poverty in rural Punjab remained unchanged between 1957-58 and 1973-74. He feels that it is not a happy practice to fit a single trend for the whole series from 1957-58 to 1973-74 especially when Ahluwalia himself perceives that "the incidence of poverty for almost all States declines up to the early 60s and then begins to rise again, reaching a peak in 1967-68 or 1968-69, and declining again thereafter."[54] The Punjab-Haryana scenario, according to Chadha, fits very well into Ahluwalia's perception; the 1960-61 figure being the lowest and that for 1967-68 being the highest. Accordingly, a single time trend fitted to the whole series seems inappropriate. Thus, Chadha feels that the best thing would be to consider the poverty graph by parts essentially because the agrarian scene in Punjab was qualitatively different after 1966-67 or 1967-68 and before it. Therefore, he extends Ahluwalia's figures up to 1977-78 and fits separate time trends for period prior to 1966-67 and after it and discovers the general trend for the incidence of poverty to decline steadily since 1966-67 when the Green Revolution in Punjab-Haryana had just begun. On the other hand, the earlier years show a stationary trend which is in conformity with Ahluwalia's results. Thus, Chadha's study supports the conclusion that rural poverty and agricultural growth are inversely related.

Griffin and Ghose (1979), however, refute the State level

conclusion of Ahluwalia (1978) and show that over the 1960-64 to 1970-74 period, poverty increased in 12 out of 13 States for which trend-line could be fitted for the period; only in Andhra Pradesh was there a trend towards diminishing poverty whereas in four of the remaining 11 States the positive trend coefficients were significant at five per cent confidence level. They also demonstrate that there is virtually no relationship at the State level between the incidence of poverty and agricultural performance over their truncated reference period, i.e., from the average of 1960-64 to the average of 1970-1974. Commenting upon the results of Griffin and Ghose, Sinha (1981), however, feels that "while the result may be statistically valid but it is in substance counter intuitive".[55] Sinha argues that it is possible that some other factors contributed to an increase in poverty incidence even though the increase in agricultural productivity had the partial effect of reducing it. In his opinion the class-specific differential in cost of living index could be one such factor. He argues that while the consumption of farm products of big farmers is met out of their own production, the small farmers and agricultural labourers have to depend on market purchase at least in the lean season. The purchasing power of the under-privileged classes is thus eroded in years when there is a rise in the cost of living, unless there are compensating variations in money earnings. He, therefore, introduces Consumer Price Index for Agricultural Labourers (CPIAL) as an additional variable in his empirical analysis. His results show that while agricultural performance has significant negative impact on the incidence of rural poverty in only six States, i.e., Andhra Pradesh, Bihar, Kerala, Punjab (including Haryana), Tamil Nadu and Uttar Pradesh, the coefficient of CPIAL is significant in 10 out of 14 States. On this basis, Sinha concludes that while agricultural growth has significant negative impact on rural poverty in some States, "it appears that there is an increasing cash component in rural wages and this is not sufficiently protected from erosion by rising cost of living in several States."[56]

Saith (1981) fitted a number of equations to the all-Indian series obtained from the weighted average of State specific poverty trends dropping alternatively two to three initial years and the terminal year. His general observation is that there is a positive and significant time trend even at the all-India level. He uses deviations of price index from trend level, deviations of production index from the trend level and time trend to explain Ahluwalia's all-India series and shows that the effects of price rise and time trend outweigh the poverty reducing impact of agricultural performance.

Thus, one finds that while there is no unanimity on the question of trend in rural poverty in India, there is more or less an agreement in the existing literature on the question of negative impact of agricultural growth on rural poverty. Therefore, the existing literature on the question of agricultural growth and rural poverty, by and large, supports the view that there has been some trickle-down of the benefits from increases in agricultural production.

The Present Study

We in the present study propose to explore the impact of agricultural development on the availability of work, attached-casual composition of wage labourer, extent of unemployment, income levels and its composition, wage rates and their mode of payment, consumption patterns, and levels of living of rural wage labour and other non-cultivating households in the heartland of India's Green Revolution, i.e,, Punjab and Haryana. Specifically, our main objectives are the following:

1. To estimate the extent of unemployment among wage labour households and compare and contrast these unemployment figures across districts and to analyse the impact of agricultural development on the availability of work to wage labourers.
2. To analyse the attached casual composition of rural wage labourers in different districts of Punjab and Haryana and to see how agricultural development of the region affects it.
3. To estimate the level of household and per capita income of non-cultivating rural labour households, to analyse its composition and to compare their income levels and its composition across districts and regions of Punjab and Haryana.
4. To estimate the wage rates and their mode of payments in different districts and to analyse the determinants of wage rates.
5. To determine the expenditure level and composition pattern of wage labour and other non-cultivating households and to explain the variations across regions.
6. To estimate the extent of poverty prevailing among wage labour and other non-cultivating households of different districts and

regions of Punjab and Haryana and to see its relationship, if any, with the level of agricultural development of the district.

Keeping in view the above objectives certain hypotheses regarding the relationship between unemployment among wage labourers, their attached-casual composition, rate of female participation, their income levels, wage rates, consumption patterns, levels of living, and the level of agricultural development of the district have been tested.

Apart from testing the various hypotheses an attempt shall also be made to explore the connection between poverty and unemployment. It is quite likely that all the poor families may not be the one's which are not getting work for a sufficient number of days because per capita income of a household, apart from the number of days its working members get work, also depends upon prevailing wage rate, the size of the family, its age-wise composition, the number of dependents and the resource position of the household. Our endeavour would be to find out correlates of poverty prevailing among wage labourer of Punjab and Haryana. The study relates to the year 1975-76 and covers all the districts of Punjab and Haryana.

After the introductory Chapter 1, Chapter 2, deals with the structure of Punjab and Haryana economies and analyses the pattern of agricultural development which took place in these two States since 1960-61.

Chapter 3 contains information regarding database, sampling design, methodology followed and concepts and definitions used in the present study.

The pattern of employment and extent of unemployment prevailing among wage labour households and its relationship with the level of agricultural development of the region are examined in Chapter 4.

Chapter 5 deals with the income levels and composition of income of wage labour and other non-cultivating households. Wage rates, their mode off payment and factors determining wage rates are also discussed in this chapter.

Chapter 6 analyses the expenditure pattern and consumption level of wage labour and other non-cultivating households and variations across regions are explained. Level of absolute poverty prevailing among wage labour and other non-cultivating households of different districts of Punjab and Haryana have been estimated and its relationship with level of agricultural development of the area studied.

Chapter 7 explores the connection between poverty and unemployment and tries to identify the factors which explain poverty prevailing among wage labour households of Punjab and Haryana.

A summary of the conclusions emerging from the study is given in the last Chapter 8.

NOTES

1. Wolf Ladejinsky (1969a): "The Green Revolution in Punjab: A Field Trip" *Economic and Political Weekly*, 4. June 28, pp. A73-A83.
2. ——— (1969B): "Green Revolution in Bihar – The Kosi Area: Field Trip" *Economic and Political Weekly*, 4, September 27.
3. Walter P. Falcon (1970): "The Green Revolution: Generation of Problems", *American Journal of Agricultural Economics*, 52, December, pp. 698-710.
4. G.R. Wharton (Jr.) (1969) "The Green Revolution: Cornucapia on Pandora's Box", *Foreign Affairs*, 47, April. pp. 464-76.
5. John P. Lewis (1970): "Wanted in India: A Relevant Radicalism", *Economic and Political Weekly*, Special Number, July.
6. Francine R. Frankel (1969): "India's New Strategy of Agricultural Development", *Journal of Asian Studies*, August.
7. ——— (1970): "Agricultural Modernization and Social Change", *Mainstream*, March 28.
8. T.J. Byres (1972): "The Dialects of India's Green Revolution". *South Asian Review*, 5, 2, January, pp. 99-116.
9. B.Sen (1970): "Opportunities in the Green Revolution", *Economic and Political Weekly* 5, March 28.
10. H.P. Khaund (1970): "Changes in Income Distribution Pattern and their Significance in a Society in Transition", *Indian Journal of Agricultural Economics* 25, Conference Number.
11. A.G. Sharma, Prakash Mehta and J.N. Single (1970): "Impact of High Yielding Varieties of Crops on Pattern of Income Distribution", *Indian Journal of Agricultural Economics*. 25, Conference Number.
12. J.G. Harrison (1972): "Agricultural Modernisation and Income Distribution", A Ph.D. Thesis submitted to the Princeton University.
13. G. Parthasarthy (1973): "Changes in Rice Farming and Their Economic and Social Impact: A Case Study of Delta Village in Andhra" (Mimeo).
14. G.S. Bhalla (1974): *Changing Agrarian Structure in India A Study of the Impact of Green Revolution in Haryana*, Meenakshi Prakashan, Meerut – Delhi.
15. C.H. Hanumantha Rao (1975): *Technological Change and Distribution of Gains in Indian Agriculture*, Macmillan Company of India, Delhi.
16. Surendar Singh (1977): '*Transformation of Agriculture in Ganganagar District of Rajasthan*', A. Ph.D. Thesis submitted to Punjab University, Chandigarh.
17. G.S. Bhalla and G.K. Chadha (1982): "Green Revolution and the Small Peasant: A Study of Income Distribution in Punjab Agriculture," *Economic and Political Weekly*, XVII, 20 & 21, May 15 and 22.

18. H.S. Sidhu (1984): "Technological Change in Agriculture and the Distribution of Gains — A Case Study of Haryana," *PSE Economic Analyst*, V, 1 & 2.
19. Y. Hayami and V.W. Ruttan (1970): "Factor Prices and Technical Change in Agricultural Development: The US and Japan 1880-1900", *Journal of Political Economy*.
20. C.H. Hanumantha Rao (1975): *op. cit.*
21. P. Vashishtha (1975): *An Econometric Study of the Effect of Tractorisation on Farm Output and Employment* (Mimeo).
22. R.K. Sharma (1972): *Economics of Tractor versus Bullock Cultivation: A Pilot Study of Haryana*, Agro-Economic Research Centre, Delhi.
23. S.S. Acharya (1973): "Green Revolution and Farm Employment" *Indian Journal of Agricultural Economics*, XXVIII, 3, pp. 30-45.
24. B. Lockwood (1972): "Pattern of Investment in Farm Machinery and Equipment", *Economic and Political Weekly*, 7, Review of Agriculture, September 30.
25. A. Rudra (1971): "Employment Patterns in Large Farms of Punjab", *Economic and Political Weekly*, Review of Agriculture, June 26.
26. R. Singh and B.B. Singh (1972): "Farm Mechanisation in UP", *Indian Journal of Agricultural Economics*, XXVII.
27. C. Bell (1972): "The Acquisition of Agricultural Technology: Its Determinants and Effects", *Journal of Development Studies*, 9,1, pp. 123-59.
28. Kusum Chopra (1974): "Tractorisation and Change in Factor Inputs — A Case Study of Punjab", *Economic and Political Weekly*, IX, 52, pp. A119-A127.
29. Bina Aggarwal (1983): *Mechanisation in Indian Agriculture: An Analytical Study Based on the Punjab*, Allied Publishers, New Delhi.
30. M.H. Billings and A. Singh (1970): "Mechanisation and Rural Employment — With some Implications for Rural Income Distribution", *Economic and Political Weekly*, 5, Review of Agriculture, June 27.
31. ——— (1971) "The Effect of Technology on Farm Employment in India", *Development Digest*, X, 2.
32. S.V. Sethuraman (1971): "Measuring Rural Unemployment to provide Guidelines to Policy-Makers", *Economic and Political Weekly*, 6, June 12.
33. Raj Krishan (1974): "Measurement of Direct and Indirect Employment Effects of Agricultural Growth with Technical Change" in Edwards E.O. (ed) *Employment in Developing Nations Report on a Ford Foundation Study*. Columbia University Press.
34. S.V. Sethuraman (1971): *Op. cit.*
35. Raj Krishna (1974): *Op. cit.*
36. P.K. Bardhan (1970): "The Green Revolution and Agricultural Labourers" *Economic and Political Weekly* V, 29-31, July.
37. ——— (1973): "Variations in Agricultural Wages : A Note", *Economic and Political Weekly*, VIII, 21, May 26.
38. A.V.Jose (1974): "Trends in Real Wage Rates of Agricultural Labourers", *Economic and Political Weekly*, IX, 13, Review of Agriculture, March 20.
39. N.Krishanji (1971): "Wages of Agricultural Labour" *Economic and Political Weekly*, VI, 39, Review of Agriculture, September 25.
40. Deepak Lal (1976): Agricultural Growth, Real Wages and the Rural Poor in India", *Economic and Political Weekly*, XI, June, pp.A47-A-61.

41. Sheilla Bhalla (1979): "Real Wage Rates of Agricultural Labourers in Punjab, 1961-77 — A Preliminary Analysis", *Economic and Political Weekly*, XIV, 26, Review of Agriculture, June 30, pp.A57-A68.
42. G.Parthasarthy and K. Adiseshu (1982): "Real wage of Agricultural Labourer in Andhra Pradesh: Two Decades of Stagnation", *Economic and Political Weekly*, XVII, 31, July 31.
43. *Ibid.*, p.1247.
44. C.H. Hanumantha Rao (1975): *Op. cit.*
45. G.Parthasarthy and D.S.Prasad (1974): "Response to and Impact of HYV Rice according to Land Size and Tenure in a Delta Village", *Developing Economies*. XII, 2, pp. 182-98.
46. J.W.Mellor and U.J. Lee (1973): "Growth linkages of the New Food Grain Technology", *Indian Journal of Agricultural Economics*, 26.
47. P.K. Bardhan (1973): "On the Incidence of Rural Poverty in India in the Sixties", *Economic and Political Weekly*, 8, February.
48. Indra Rajaraman (1975): "Poverty, Inequality and Economic Growth: Rural Punjab 1960-61 - 1970/71", *Journal of Development Studies*, XI, 4. pp. 278-90.
49. M.S.Ahluwalia (1978): "Rural Poverty and Agricultural Performance in India", *Journal of Development Studies*, XIV, III, April, pp. 298-323.
50. Keith Griffin and A.K. Ghose (1979), "Institutional Structure, Technological Change and Growth in Poor Agrarian Economies: An Analysis with reference to Bengal and Punjab", *World Development*, 7, 4/5 pp. 385-96.
51. Ashwani Saith (1981): "Production, Prices and Poverty in Rural India", *Journal of Development Studies*, XVII, 1, January.
52. J.N.Sinha (1983): "Full Employment and Anti-Poverty Plan: The Missing link", *Economic and Political Weekly*, XVI, 50, December 12.
53. G.K.Chadha (1983) *Dynamics of Rural Transformation — A Study of Punjab 1950-80* (Mimeo).
54. M.S. Ahluwalia (1978) *Op. cit.*, p.304.
55. J.N. Sinha (1981) *Op. cit.*, p. 2015.
56. *Ibid.*, p. 2017.

2

STRUCTURE AND GROWTH OF PUNJAB AND HARYANA ECONOMIES

IN ORDER to study the impact of agricultural development of the kind that took place in Punjab and Haryana in the recent past — on employment, income, consumption of wage labour and other non-cultivating household — it is necessary to understand, in the first place, the structure of Punjab and Haryana economies and the pattern of agricultural development that took place in the two States during the last two decades or so. This is the theme of the present Chapter. We shall first discuss the structure of the Punjab and Haryana economies and then study the growth of output since 1960-61 consequent to increased use of agricultural inputs and other supporting infrastructure. Our discussion is based on the secondary data obtained from various sources particularly the state Statistical Abstracts of Punjab and Haryana for various years.

This chapter is divided into three sections. In Section I, economic structure of rural Punjab and Haryana is examined. In particular, the changing structure of work force and growth performance of sectoral incomes in the two States are discussed in detail. In Section II, alongwith the infrastructural development in the two States during the last two decades, because of their specific importance, major inputs, like, irrigation expansion, use of fertilizers and tractors and role of co-operative credit and progress of HYV programme, etc., are discussed in detail. Section III examines the growth of agricultural output. The contribution of area and productivity or yield improvements towards the growth of output of two major crops, i.e., wheat and rice, are also examined.

I

Economic Structure of Rural Punjab and Haryana

The economic structure of an area can be broadly seen in terms of the relative importance of the various sectoral activities. The relative importance of a sector in turn depends upon its share in the total work-force and total income being generated. In this section, we shall analyse the economic structure of rural Punjab and Haryana in terms of work-force and employment structure and sectoral incomes.

Work-Force and Employment Structure

Tables 2.1 and 2.2 show the broad features of the population expansion in rural Punjab and Haryana. It is clear from these Tables that both Punjab and Haryana continue to be predominantly rural economies with Haryana being more rural than Punjab. The share of rural to total population, which was 76.94 per cent in 1961 in Punjab, came down slightly to 76.30 per cent in 1971 and fell further to 72.28 per cent in 1981. Similarly, for Haryana it came down marginally from 82.8 per cent in 1961 to 82.3 per cent in 1971 and finally stood at 78.0 per cent in 1981. In Punjab, during 1961-1971 rural population grew at a faster rate than total population while during 1971-1981 total population grew much faster than rural population which means a faster growth of urban population. In Haryana, while during 1961-1971, both rural and urban population grew at more or less the same rate, during 1971-1981 there was a definite trend towards urbanisation. Thus, in both Punjab and Haryana there was a pronounced trend towards urbanisation during the decade of 1970s.

There are significant variations in the share of rural population across districts in both the States. Districts which have industrial towns, like, Amritsar, Jalandhar and Ludhiana, in Punjab and Ambala and Faridabad, in Haryana, are having lower percentage of rural population compared to districts which have no industrial townships. Over a period of time these variations have got further widened.

Typical of all growing societies in the initial stages of development, the density of population in both the States have been increasing steadily since 1961. With 221 persons living in per square kilometre in 1961 in Punjab, the number increased to 269 in 1971 and 331 by 1981. Similarly, in Haryana it rose from 172 in 1961 to 227 in 1971 and 291

TABLE 2.1: Expansion of Population in Punjab: 1961-81

District/State	Percentage of rural population to total population			Decennial growth rate of population				Density of population (per square km)		
				1961-1971		1971-1981				
	1961	1971	1981	Rural	Total	Rural	Total	1961	1971	1981
1. Gurdaspur	80.40	79.70	78.33	22.6	21.7	20.0	22.2	279	346	422
2. Amritsar	69.80	70.80	67.06	17.9	19.5	11.8	18.1	300	365	426
3. Kapurthala	76.96	76.80	70.31	22.3	22.0	14.5	25.1	210	263	329
4. Jalandhar	71.55	69.90	64.58	17.1	14.9	9.4	18.5	355	428	507
5. Hoshiarpur	89.31	87.90	85.44	18.9	17.5	13.8	17.0	222	271	317
6. Ropar	82.40	85.20	78.11	18.9	16.4	19.2	29.7	224	263	342
7. Ludhiana	70.74	65.20	57.88	24.9	16.6	12.8	27.1	295	374	468
8. Ferozepur	77.30	77.80	77.46	16.7	17.1	23.8	24.5	160	176	224
9. Faridkot	80.41	80.20	75.97	17.1	18.2	17.3	23.9	—	200	249
10. Bhatinda	81.84	80.20	77.21	20.6	21.6	18.6	26.3	15.3	185	233
11. Sangrur	80.90	79.70	77.12	18.4	17.1	18.6	22.6	187	225	275
12. Patiala	73.90	73.60	70.39	23.5	23.6	22.9	29.0	206	259	341
Punjab	76.94	76.30	72.28	23.5	21.7	16.6	23.0	221	269	331

Source: Statistical Abstract of Pubjab for Various Years.

TABLE 2.2: Expansion of Population in Haryana: 1961-81

District/State	Percentage of rural population to total population			Decennial growth rate of population				Density of population (per square km)		
				1961-1971		1971-1981				
	1961	1971	1981	Rural	Total	Rural	Total	1961	1971	1981
1. Hissar	84.4	83.9	80.6	36.8	38.1	—	28.5	112	153	236
2. Rohtak	86.3	84.3	79.9	21.7	25.7	—	23.6	239	295	345
3. Gurgaon	83.4	81.5	79.9	33.7	37.6	—	26.0	206	278	310
4. Karnal	82.9	83.0	73.7	32.7	32.9	—	31.6	191	246	354
5. Ambala	66.0	68.6	60.9	26.9	24.0	—	27.5	235	287	365
6. Jind	87.8	86.8	86.2	35.7	37.6	—	23.1	174	238	283
7. Mahindergarh	90.3	89.8	86.8	23.4	27.3	—	24.7	160	200	316
8. Sirsa	—	—	79.6	—	—	—	32.7	—	—	166
9. Bhiwani	—	—	83.9	—	—	—	26.2	—	—	180
10. Faridabad	—	—	59.4	—	—	—	39.8	—	—	464
11. Kurukshetra	—	—	83.4	—	—	—	31.4	—	—	300
12. Sonepat	—	—	82.0	—	—	—	22.9	—	—	383
Haryana	82.8	82.3	78.0	31.6	32.2	21.4	28.1	172	227	291

Source: Statistical Abstract of Haryana for Various Years.

in 1981. The decade of 1971-81 witnessed much faster growth compared with 1961-71 in both the States. Over the entire period of 1961-81, population growth was faster in Haryana as compared to Punjab. This has narrowed the gap between the two States in terms of density of population. As regards inter-district variations, once again industrially important districts, like, Ludhiana, Jalandhar and Amritsar, in Punjab, and Faridabad and Ambala, in Haryana, are having higher density of population compared to other districts and over time density in these districts has risen faster, thereby increasing the inter-district gap. In Haryana, district Karnal has also caught up with Ambala in terms of density of population. On the whole, it is evident that districts with a higher share of urban population have witnessed a faster increase in the density of population.

Tables 2.3 and 2.4 show the district-wise percentage of working population to total population for Punjab and Haryana, respectively. A look at these Tables show that while in Punjab the rate of participation has been fairly constant over time, in Haryana there has been steep fall from 37.92 per cent in 1961 to 26.44 per cent in 1971 and it recovered a little bit to 27.92 per cent in 1981. It does not, however, mean that there has been such a drastic fall in the rate of participation in Haryana as the figures reveal in the first instance. Most of this difference is because of the changes in the definition of a worker in the successive Censuses. The changes in definition effected more the status of female labour. Since Haryana had much higher female participation rate as compared to Punjab, the change in definition effected total participation rate of Haryana more than that of Punjab. However, the male participation rate over time is roughly comparable. For that reason, male participation rate shows more stability over time for both the States. But even in the case of male participation rates there has been mild decline in the case of Punjab, from 53.09 per cent in 1961 to 52.01 per cent in 1981. The decline in the case of Haryana during the same period is of the order of four per cent, i.e., from 52.17 to 48.17 per cent.

It appears that both changes in the definition of workers and voluntary withdrawal from the labour-force by better off section of peasantry as a result of their economic betterment are responsible for the observed fall in rate of male participation in work. There are wide inter-district variations in the case of female participation rates but inter-district variations in the case of male participation are mild and there is no systematic trend.

TABLE 2.3: Percentage of Workers to Total Population (Punjab)

District/State	1961			1971			1981		
	Male	Female	Total	Male	Female	Total	Male	Female	Total
1. Gurdaspur	51.78	3.66	29.48	49.04	1.03	26.42	46.69	2.84	25.69
2. Amritasar	52.55	3.25	29.83	52.88	1.40	29.14	52.39	3.01	29.35
3. Ferozepur	55.18	9.61	34.27	55.00	1.06	29.91	54.91	3.77	30.81
4. Ludhiana	50.44	3.59	28.85	53.40	1.43	29.57	51.56	3.94	29.26
5. Jalandhar	50.25	3.97	28.68	49.79	1.41	27.10	50.31	3.08	27.95
6. Kapurthala	51.45	2.90	28.65	56.53	1.08	27.78	51.56	2.38	27.96
7. Hoshiarpur	50.99	11.22	32.16	48.77	1.10	26.19	47.37	3.23	26.00
8. Ropar	—	—	—	51.15	1.02	28.07	48.87	2.94	27.55
9. Patiala	53.69	3.34	30.86	50.02	1.43	29.36	52.59	3.61	29.84
10. Sangrur	56.20	11.74	35.91	56.95	0.82	31.32	56.53	2.60	31.52
11. Bhatinda	55.75	8.42	34.19	56.24	0.87	30.73	55.71	2.07	30.81
12. Faridkot	—	—	—	—	—	—	54.57	2.82	30.29
Pubjab	53.09	6.67	31.68	52.82	1.18	28.87	52.01	3.09	29.03

Source: For 1961 and 1971, *Census of India*, Series-17, Part ii-B. For 1981, *Statistical Abstract of Pubjab*, pp. 46-47.

TABLE 2.4: Percentage of Workers to Total Population (Haryana)

District/State	1961			1971			1981		
	Male	Female	Total	Male	Female	Total	Male	Female	Total
1. Ambala	53.04	4.49	31.08	49.47	1.67	27.38	51.56	2.77	28.74
2. Karnal	52.95	12.09	34.16	48.62	1.77	27.04	50.40	3.71	28.92
3. Rohtak	48.11	28.82	38.97	42.55	2.23	23.66	49.71	6.90	26.38
4. Gurgaon	51.41	23.57	39.30	46.55	2.37	26.12	41.38	4.80	24.10
5. Mohindergarh	50.04	27.13	39.00	44.91	4.17	25.61	42.19	2.45	22.85
6. Hissar	55.09	26.67	41.94	50.05	2.94	28.18	50.66	5.77	29.70
7. Jind	54.90	25.89	41.53	47.46	2.57	26.72	48.89	6.18	29.18
8. Sirsa	—	—	—	—	—	—	53.62	3.09	30.00
9. Bhiwani	—	—	—	—	—	—	45.39	8.53	27.89
10. Faridabad	—	—	—	—	—	—	50.08	3.75	29.30
11. Kurukshetra	—	—	—	—	—	—	51.18	2.36	28.56
12. Sonepat	—	—	—	—	—	—	45.65	7.74	28.05
Haryana	52.17	21.51	37.92	47.27	2.41	26.44	48.17	4.82	27.92

Source: For 1961 and 1971, *Census of India*, Series 6 Part ii-B, p. 4. For 1981, *Statistical Abstract of Haryana*, p. 39.

Tables 2.5 and 2.6 show the percentage of male agricultural workers in total rural male work-force and percentage of male agricultural labourers in the total male agricultural workers in Punjab and Haryana, respectively, between 1961-81. We have confined ourselves to male workers only because, as already pointed out, the number of female workers given by three Censuses, because of the definitional problem, are not comparable. A number of points need to be noted. Firstly, in Punjab proportion of agricultural workers in the total male work-force rose sharply during 1960s and declined marginally during 1970s. It shot up from 57.03 per cent in 1961 to 63.56 per cent in 1971 and finally stood at 60.30 per cent in 1981. In Haryana, on the other hand, it declined throughout the period. It declined marginally during 1960s and quite significantly during 1970s. In 1981, about 60 per cent of rural male workers in both the States are engaged in agriculture. The proportion of agricultural workers in total male workers is lower in industrially developed districts, like, Ludhiana, Jalandhar and Amritsar, in Punjab and Ambala and Faridabad, in Haryana, as compared to other districts. Secondly, the number of agricultural workers has risen by 47.81 per cent in Punjab and 41.38 per cent in Haryana during 1961-81. Thirdly, the most important point to be noted is that while the number of total agricultural workers during 1961-81, as noted above, has increased by 47 and 41 per cent, respectively, in Punjab and Haryana, the number of agricultural labourers registered a more than three-fold increase in Punjab and about three-fold increase in Haryana during the same period. The index of agricultural labourers with 1961 as 100 stood at 320.62 in 1981 in Punjab and at 297.18 in Haryana.

The proportion of agricultural labour in total agricultural workers in Punjab rose from 17.29 per cent in 1961 to 31.92 per cent in 1971 and 37.50 per cent in 1981. Similarly in Haryana, it rose from a mere 12.50 per cent in 1961 to 24.13 per cent in 1971 to 26.28 per cent in 1981. Thus, a fast agricultural development witnessed by Punjab and Haryana during this period as a result of new agricultural technology has been accompanied by a rising level of rural proletarianisation. However, this process was much faster during 1961-1971 as compared to 1971-1981. Whether this process of proletarianisation has also led to pauperisation of rural proletariat or not is not very clear because some empirical studies have shown that the per capita yearly earnings of agricultural labour households are higher than those of sub-marginal farmers even under the conditions of improved production technology.[1]

That being so the tendency among marginal farmers to opt out of cultivation to become full-fledged agricultural labourers has economic rationale and under such circumstances proletarianisation may not have led to pauperisation. In fact, it might have improved their economic lot. Yet the increasing proportion of agricultural labourers in total agricultural workers has some important implications in terms of its effects on employment and wage rates of agricultural workers because now more workers compete with each other for hiring out their labour power. The net effect on employment and wages, however, will depend upon the relative strength of demand increasing and supply increasing factors.

TABLE 2.5: Rural Male Workers in Punjab: 1961-81

District/State	Agricultural workers as percentage of total workers			Agricultural labour as percentage of total agricultural workers		
	1961	1971	1981	1961	1971	1981
1. Gurdaspur	50.29	59.64	61.11	16.20	32.49	40.64
2. Amritsar	47.62	56.74	55.54	20.40	36.26	40.42
3. Kapurthala	56.09	62.40	55.96	9.05	24.92	33.48
4. Jalandhar	43.65	51.65	47.65	18.28	35.35	42.75
5. Hoshiarpur	58.78	62.37	63.10	7.15	28.96	37.82
6. Ropar	—	63.96	34.47	—	25.48	32.76
7. Ludhiana	44.88	51.79	45.67	18.29	35.24	40.80
8. Ferozepur	64.98	74.05	70.10	21.08	29.77	33.91
9. Faridkot	—	75.12	70.45	—	35.44	39.28
10. Bhatinda	67.86	76.91	70.18	18.62	28.55	31.83
11. Sangrur	69.23	72.17	72.05	16.66	28.64	33.82
12. Patiala	59.06	64.17	59.53	19.21	32.17	38.60
Pubjab	57.03	63.56	60.30	17.29	31.92	37.50
	18,75,755	24,39,633	27,72,502	3,24,275	7,78,613	10,39,683
	(100.00)	(130.06)	(147.81)	(100.00)	(240.10)	(320.62)

Source: *Statistical Abstract of Punjab* for Various Years.

This phenomenon of increasing proportion of agricultural labourer in total agricultural workers appear to be mainly the result of two major factors. First, large number of tenant cultivators were evicted from land in the wake of land reforms, prescribing maximum ceiling on land-holdings, enacted in the erstwhile Punjab in 1953 and in PEPSU in 1955. For example, according to a Planning Commission report in March 1955, the number of tenants recorded in the revenue records was 5,83,400 whereas their number was only 80,520 in 1964.[2] The report also brings out that till 1964 in the Punjab areas, the number of tenants who were given proprietary rights was 13,533 which means around 5,69,867 of 5,83,400 tenants who were holding land at the commencement of the Act were either ejected from the holdings they held earlier or at least their names were removed from revenue records. Even if we assume that many of them were not actually ejected from their holdings and their contracts were simply turned into oral leases even then a substantial proportion of them must have been actually ejected who would have joined the ranks of wage earners. This contention is also borne out by the NSS data. For example, NSS data show that area under tenant cultivation in 1953-54 in Punjab was nearly 40 per cent of the total cultivated area which came down to 35 per cent in 1961-62 and was only 25.84 per cent by 1971-72.[3]

TABLE 2.6: Rural Male Workers in Haryana: 1961-81

District/State	Agricultural workers as percentage of total workers			Agricultural labour as percentage of total agricultural workers		
	1961	1971	1981	1961	1971	1981
1. Hissar	74.14	71.16	68.70	9.92	23.53	25.39
2. Sirsa	—	75.90	71.10	—	27.51	31.67
3. Bhiwani	—	70.64	67.79	—	15.36	13.77
4. Gurgaon	64.07	57.04	52.54	7.15	17.35	22.73
5. Jind	73.39	74.80	73.42	11.77	22.30	22.51
6. Mohin-dergarh	89.17	66.91	61.97	18.26	15.56	13.91
7. Ambala	44.27	50.22	47.20	16.26	32.40	35.87
8. Karnal	66.76	64.30	59.65	15.49	33.46	36.35
9. Kuruk-shetra	—	73.87	70.20	—	28.69	33.05
10. Rohtak	63.49	63.71	57.60	12.94	21.37	21.05
11. Sonepat	—	63.71	56.85	—	28.12	27.82
12. Faridabad	—	—	42.12	—	—	20.36
Haryana	66.57	65.40	60.48	12.50	24.13	26.28
	14,10,975	16,62,186	19,94,845	1,76,388	4,01,132	5,24,200
	(100.00)	(117.80)	(141.38)	(100.00)	(227.41)	(297.18)

Source: For 1961 and 1971, *Census of India*, Series 6, Haryana, Part ii-B. For 1981, *Statistical Abstract of Haryana*, 1980-81.

Secondly, in Punjab at least the total number of operational holdings has gone down from 13,75,392 in 1970-71 to 10,27,127 in 1980-81 (see Table 2.7). Out of a total decrease of 3,48,265 in the number of operational holding in Punjab during this period, 3,20,245 has occurred in the category of marginal farmers alone, i.e., with holding up to one hectare and below. If we also include in it the category of small farmers, i.e., those cultivating between one and two hectares, then the total decrease in their number is of the order of 3,80,960 which is more than the total decrease in the number of holdings in Punjab between 1970-71 and 1980-81. A large proportion of these small and marginal cultivators who have gone out of cultivation must have joined the ranks of agricultural labourers thereby swelling their number.

TABLE 2.7: Distribution of Land Holdings in Pubjab and Haryana

Size class (in hectares)	Pubjab		Haryana	
	1970-71	1980-81	1970-71	1980-81
Below 0.5	3,10,049 (22.54)	81,569 (7.94)	1,32,049 (14.46)	1,87,966 (18.58)
0.5-1.00	2,07,519 (15.09)	1,15,754 11.27)	1,17,990 (12.92)	1,37,554 (13.60)
1.00-2.00	2,60,083 (18.91)	1,99,368 (19.41)	1,72,679 (18.90)	1,94,079 (19.19)
2.00-3.00	1,69,826 (12.35)	1,76,427 (17.18)	1,19,846 (13.12)	1,23,478 (12.21)
3,00-400	1,11,277 (8.09)	1,10,996 (10.81)	85,320 (9.34)	87.387 (8.64)
4.00-5.00	79,021 (5.75)	1,04,932 (10.22)	62,986 (6.90)	67,131 (6.64)
5.00-10.00	1,68,734 (12.27)	1,64,140 (15.98)	1,48,342 (16.24)	1,49,031 (14.73)
10.00-20.00	58,498 (4.25)	61,680 (6.00)	61,592 (6.74)	53,467 (5.29)
20.00-30.00	7,631 (0.55)	9,098 (0.88)	9,287 (1.02)	7,711 (0.76)
30.00-40.00	1801 (0.13)	1,826 (0.18)	2,201 (0.24)	2,075 (0.21)
40.00-50.00	652 (0.05)	749 (0.07)	758 (0.08)	741 (0.07)
50.00 and above	301 (0.02)	588 (0.06)	420 (0.05)	939 (0.09)
Total	13,75,392 (100.00)	10,27,127 (100.00)	9,13,470 (100.00)	10,11,564 (100.00)

Note: Figures in the brackets are percentages.
Source: Statistical Abstracts of Pubjab and Haryana for Various Years. Figures for 1980-81 are based on 10 per cent sample survey.

Growth of Sectoral Incomes

Tables 2.8 and 2.9 contain net State domestic product of Punjab and Haryana, respectively, at factor cost by industrial origin for various years from 1960-61 onwards. A number of points emerge from these tables very clearly. First, both Punjab and Haryana have been able to register very impressive growth rate in their Net States Domestic Products (NSDP). The Punjab economy grew at a rate of 6.22 per cent per annum compound during 1960-61 to 1982-83. Haryana's net State domestic product registered a rate of growth of 5.99 per cent per annum compound during the same period. In comparison to other States both the States have performed very well.

Secondly, in both the States growth has not been contributed by any particular sector, all sectors of both the economies have been growing at an impressive rate. In Punjab, during 1960-61 to 1982-83 primary sector registered a growth rate of 5.90, secondary sector 6.53 and tertiary sector 6.52 per cent per annum. Similarly in Haryana during the same period, primary sector registered a growth rate of 4.87, secondary sector 6.77 and tertiary sector 7.96 per cent per annum. Within the secondary sector in both the States 'registered manufacturing' and 'electricity, gas and water supply' registered a very fast growth rate during this period. Similarly, in tertiary sector, in both the economies, 'Transport and Communication', 'Trade, Storage, Hotels and Restaurants,' and 'Banking and Insurance' registered very impressive growth. However, in both the States growth has been much faster after mid-1960s as compared to 1960-61 to 1965-66 period. In fact, Haryana had a negative growth of -0.46 per cent in the primary sector during 1960-61 to 1965-66.

Thirdly, as a consequence of the very impressive growth rates in their NSDP, both Punjab and Haryana registered a fairly impressive growth in their per capita real income during this period. Punjab's per capita real income grew at a rate of 4.04 per cent per annum and Haryana's at a rate of 3.22 per cent per annum.

Fourthly, despite the fact that both the economies continue to be predominantly agrarian, yet both Punjab and Haryana have attained some sectoral diversification during this period. For example, the share of primary sector in the total net State domestic product in Punjab declined from 54.01 per cent in 1960-61 to 50.65 per cent in 1982-83. On the other hand, the share of the secondary sector increased from 15.62 to 16.92 per cent and that of the tertiary sector from 30.36 to

TABLE 2.8: Net State Domestic Product of Punjab at Factor Cost

(at 1960-61 prices in Rs. Crores)

Sector	1960-61	1965-66	1970-71	1975-76	1982-83	Annual growth rate (Compound)				
						1965-66 over 1960-61	1970-71 over 1965-66	1970-71 over 1960-61	1982-83 over 1970-71	1982-83 over 1960-61
(1)	(2)	(3)	(4)	(5)	(6)	(7)	(8)	(9)	(10)	(11)
Primary	218.07	245.18	345.56	392.16	769.16	2.38	7.10	4.71	6.90	5.90
	(54.01)	(50.81)	(51.90)	(48.10)	(50.65)					
Agriculture	188.52	198.35	276.73	303.60	555.45	1.02	6.89	3.91	5.96	5.03
	(46.68)	(41.11)	(41.57)	(37.24)	(36.58)					
Livestock	28.16	45.66	66.89	86.17	209.28	10.14	7.92	9.03	9.97	9.54
	(6.97)	(9.46)	(10.05)	(10.57)	(13.78)					
Secondary	63.89	84.44	110.70	152.48	(256.93)	5.83	5.55	5.65	7.26	6.53
	(15.82)	17.50)	(16.62)	(18.70)	(16.92)					
Regd. Manufacturing	18.46	28.90	36.52	53.22	86.65	9.39	4.79	7.06	7.46	6.12
	(4.57)	(5.99)	(5.49)	(6.53)	(5.71)					
Unregd. Manufacturing	22.39	26.59	36.72	49.11	79.14	3.50	6.67	5.07	6.61	5.21
	(5.55)	(5.51)	(5.52)	(6.02)	(5.21)					
Construction	19.39	24.08	29.90	39.30	72.23	4.42	4.42	4.43	7.63	6.16
	(4.80)	(4.99)	(4.50)	(4.82)	(4.76)					
Electricity, Gas and Water Supply	2.85	4.87	7.56	10.85	18.89	11.31	9.20	10.25	7.93	8.98
	(0.71)	(1.01)	(1.14)	(1.33)	(1.24)					

Contd.

TABLE 2.8 — *Contd.*

(1)	(2)	(3)	(4)	(5)	(6)	(7)	(8)	(9)	(10)	(11)
Tertiary	122.61	152.69	209.57	270.53	492.39	4.49	6.54	5.50	7.38	6.52
	(30.36)	(31.64)	(31.47)	(33.19)	(32.43)					
Transport, Communication and Storage	17.19	18.05	26.92	35.45	62.63	0.98	8.33	4.60	7.29	6.05
	(4.26)	(3.74)	(4.05)	(4.35)	(4.12)					
Trade, Hotels and Restaurants	59.98	76.36	107.90	141.75	247.39	4.95	7.17	6.05	7.16	6.65
	(14.85)	(15.82)	(16.21)	(17.39)	(16.29)					
Banking and Insurance	5.38	7.22	9.90	12.32	40.16	6.06	6.52	6.29	12.38	9.57
	(1.33)	(1.50)	(1.49)	(1.51)	(2.64)					
Real Estate and Ownership of Dwellings	10.00	10.35	10.71	11.09	20.30	0.70	0.68	0.69	5.47	3.32
	(2.48)	(2.14)	(1.60)	(1.36)	(1.34)					
Public Administration	9.61	14.33	22.26	27.25	53.41	8.33	9.21	8.76	7.57	8.11
	(2.38)	(2.97)	(3.34)	(3.34)	(3.52)					
Other Services	20.45	26.60	31.88	42.69	68.49	5.40	3.69	4.54	6.58	5.65
	(5.06)	(5.51)	(4.79)	(5.24)	(4.51)					
Total N.S.D.P.	403.77	482.53	665.73	815.17	1518.49	3.64	6.65	5.13	7.11	6.22
	(100.00)	(100.00)	(100.00)	(100.00)	(100.00)					
Per Capita Income (Rs.)	366	396	496	551	874	1.58	4.60	3.08	4.83	4.04

Note: Figures in the parentheses are percentages to total Net State Domestic Product (N.S.D.P.)

Source: Statistical Abstract of Punjab for Various Years.

TABLE 2.9: Net State Domestic Product of Haryana at Factor Cost

(at 1960-61 prices in Rs. Crores)

Sector	1960-61	1965-66	1970-71	1975-76	1982-83	Annual growth rate (Compound)				
						1965-66 over 1960-61	1970-71 over 1965-66	1970-71 over 1960-61	1982-83 over 1970-71	1982-83 over 1960-61
(1)	(2)	(3)	(4)	(5)	(6)	(7)	(8)	(9)	(10)	(11)
Primary	154.23	150.97	293.58	322.54	438.86	-0.46	14.23	6.65	3.40	4.87
	(62.94)	(54.84)	(64.76)	(58.38)	(49.77)					
Agriculture and Animal Husbandry	152.95	150.19	292.05	320.53	434.84	-0.34	14.23	6.68	3.37	4.87
	(62.42)	(54.56)	(64.42)	(58.01)	(49.31)					
Other including Forestry, Fishery, Mining and Quarrying	1.28	0.78	1.53	2.01	4.02	-10.40	14.42	1.80	8.38	5.38
	(0.52)	(0.28)	(0.34)	(0.36)	(0.46)					
Secondary	39.50	58.94	69.00	94.15	167.03	8.35	3.20	5.74	7.64	6.77
	(16.12)	(21.41)	(15.22)	(17.04)	(18.94)					
Regd. Manufacturing	9.24	23.33	30.49	44.82	85.40	20.35	2.49	12.68	8.96	10.65
	(3.77)	(8.47)	(6.72)	(8.11)	(9.68)					
Unregd. Manufacturing	18.30	20.71	14.30	19.67	33.21	2.50	-7.72	-2.50	7.27	2.83
	(7.47)	(7.52)	(3.15)	(3.56)	(3.76)					
Construction	10.21	11.63	18.99	21.05	31.90	2.64	10.30	6.40	4.42	5.32
	(4.16)	(4.22)	(4.19)	(3.81)	(3.62)					
Electricity, Gas, Water Supply and Sanitary	1.75	3.27	5.21	8.61	16.50	13.31	9.77	11.52	10.08	10.73
	(0.71)	(1.19)	(1.15)	(1.56)	(1.87)					

Contd.

TABLE 2.9 — *Contd.*

(1)	(2)	(3)	(4)	(5)	(6)	(7)	(8)	(9)	(10)	(11)
Tertiary	51.30	65.36	90.71	135.83	275.87	4.96	6.77	5.86	9.71	7.96
	(20.94)	(23.74)	(20.01)	(24.58)	(31.29)					
Transport and Communication	7.69	10.10	15.16	22.19	42.39	5.60	8.46	7.02	8.95	8.07
	(3.14)	(3.67)	(3.34)	(4.02)	(4.81)					
Trade, Storage, Hotels and Restaurants	18.54	19.27	33.16	57.20	131.31	0.78	11.47	5.99	12.15	9.35
	(7.56)	(7.00)	(7.32)	(10.35)	(14.89)					
Banking and Insurance	1.47	1.86	4.87	7.11	19.85	4.81	21.22	12.72	12.42	12.55
	(0.60)	(0.67)	(1.07)	(1.28)	(2.25)					
Real Estate and Ownership of Dwellings	3.91	4.59	7.86	9.36	17.45	3.25	11.36	7.23	6.87	7.03
	(1.59)	(1.66)	(1.73)	(1.69)	(1.98)					
Public Administration	5.50	10.49	10.18	16.26	28.75	13.79	-0.62	6.35	9.04	7.82
	(2.24)	(3.81)	(2.24)	(2.94)	(3.26)					
Other Services	14.19	19.05	19.48	23.71	36.12	6.06	0.44	3.23	5.25	4.33
	(5.79)	(6.92)	(4.30)	(4.29)	(4.09)					
Total N.S.D.P.	245.03	275.27	453.30	552.53	881.77	2.36	10.49	6.35	5.70	5.99
	(100.00)	(100.00)	(100.00)	(100.00)	(100.00)					
Per Capita Income	327.00	341.94	457.55	489.90	657.15	0.90	6.00	3.42	3.06	3.22

Note: Figures in the parentheses are percentages to Total Net State Domestic Product (N.S.D.P.).
Source: Statistical Abstract of Haryana for Various Years.

32.43 per cent respectively. Similarly, in Haryana the share of primary sector in NSDP dropped from 62.94 per cent in 1960-61 to 49.77 per cent in 1982-83 and of the secondary sector rose to 18.94 from 16.12 per cent and that of tertiary sector to 31.29 from 20.94 per cent. Thus, in Punjab and Haryana, secondary and tertiary sectors' relative share in total net State domestic product rose by about three and 13 per cent, respectively, during this period.

Within the primary sector, crop, husbandry and livestock and dairying almost sum, up to the primary sector as a whole. Forestry and Logging, Fishing and Mining and quarrying together account for less than one per cent of total State domestic product in both the States. For Haryana, break-up of the primary sector between agriculture and animal husbandry is not available but break-up for Punjab is: The expansion of the livestock income has been very impressive. Between 1960-61 and 1982-83 it increased by more than seven times. In 1960-61, the proportion of income generated in the livestock sector to that of crop husbandry was as little as 15 per cent. In 1982-83, it was as high as 37.67 per cent. However, in spite of this phenomenal increase the share of livestock and dairying in total State domestic product is still 13.78 per cent and it has increased only marginally since 1970-71. This is an area of great promise and further effort should be made towards this direction.

II

Infrastructure for Agricultural Development

From the very inception of planned development, strategy of Punjab (including Haryana) had been to develop agriculture and small-scale consumer and agro-based industries. It was perhaps the right choice because due to lack of mineral resources and its proximity to a rather sensitive international border, the state could not have attracted large-scale private capital for heavy industrialisation. Therefore, modern industry never found priority in Punjab's planned economic development. Some modern industry did come up with the active support of State in centres, like, Faridabad, on the outskirts of Delhi far away from the international border. But more than the incentives by the State, it was its proximity to Delhi metropolitan centre which helped Faridabad to come up as an important industrial centre. Wars with Pakistan further reinforced the tendency for larger capital of the area to concentrate around Delhi. This is partly reflected in the relatively larger share of registered manufacturing sector in the net State domestic product of Haryana as compared to Punjab. But broadly speaking both states followed the agriculture-based development strategy as the area, as a whole, has many favourable factors for such a development strategy to succeed. Large parts of the two States consist of plain alluvial fertile soil. Coupled with this, an abundant supply of agricultural raw materials, a fairly well-developed canal irrigation system, availability of sub-soil water, adequate financial support by co-operative societies and nationalised banks and a hard working peasantry were all favourable factors. Thus, when the opportunity came in the form of new high yielding varieties of certain crops grown in the area in mid-1960s, backed by a favourable support price offered by the government, the two States just grabbed it and made it a resounding success. This section discusses the growth of infrastructural facilities and other important inputs since 1960-61 which helped the two States achieve remarkable success in agricultural production.

Land-use Pattern

Tables 2.10 and 2.11 provide some of the broad features of land-use patterns in Punjab and Haryana, respectively, since 1960-61. During this period net area sown as well as area sown more than once has been increasing in both the States but the expansion in net area sown has been much slower as compared to area sown more than once. Net area sown registered an increase of 12.32 per cent in Punjab and 5.76 per cent in Haryana during this period giving an annual compound rate of 0.49 per cent for Punjab and only 0.25 per cent for Haryana. On the other hand, area sown more than once grew at a compound rate of 4.66 per cent per annum in Punjab and 1.69 per cent per annum in Haryana. By 1983-84 as much as 65.64 per cent of net area sown in Punjab and 47.55 per cent of Haryana was double cropped thereby giving a cropping intensity of 1.66 and 1.47 per cent for Punjab and Haryana, respectively. As a result during 1960-61 and 1983-84 Gross Cropped Area (CGA) registered a growth rate of 1.71 per cent in Punjab and 0.67 per cent in Haryana.

Thus, it is clear from the above discussion that under the prevailing circumstances in both the States there does not seem to be much scope for expansion in the net sown area. In 1983-84 the proportion of net area sown in total area was as high as 83.63 per cent in Punjab.

Similarly during 1982-83 it was 81.83 per cent in Haryana. On the other hand, there is possibility of net area sown actually declining under the pressure of rural housing, infrastructural and other developmental activities including the penetration of industrial activities into rural areas. Therefore, it is absolutely certain that the cushion of 'extending margin of cultivation' in the Ricardian sense is lost to Punjab and Haryana agriculture for all times to come. All future growth of agricultural production in these two States has to come by way of increased productivity and increase in cropping intensity. This requires extension in the coverage and intensity of irrigation and an ever increasing use of modern inputs and improved farm practices. In what follows we shall discuss the expansion in irrigation and use of other modern inputs.

TABLE 2.10: Land Utilization in Punjab

(Thousand Hectares)

Sl. No.	Classification	1960-61	1965-66	1970-71	1975-76	1983-84
1.	Total Area	5,021 (100.00)	5,026 (100.00)	5,031 (100.00)	5,033 (100.00)	5,036 (100.00)
2.	Area under forests	35 (0.70)	87 (1.73)	123 (2.44)	209 (4.15)	222 (4.41)
3.	Land not available for cultivation	674 (13.42)	648 (12.89)	624 (12.40)	531 (10.55)	524 (10.41)
4.	Other uncultivated land	251 (5.00)	181 (3.60)	93 (1.85)	68 (1.35)	42 (0.95)
5.	Current Fallow	311 (6.19)	314 (6.25)	138 (2.74)	67 (1.33)	33 (0.83)
6.	Net Area Sown	3,750 (74.69)	3,796 (75.53)	4,053 (80.56)	4,158 (82.61)	4,212 (83.63)
7.	Area Sown more than once	973	1,082	1,625	2,097	2,765
8.	Area Sown more than once as percentage of NSA	25.95	28.50	40.09	50.43	65.64
9.	Gross Cropped Area	4,723	4,878	5,678	6,255	6,977
10.	Intensity of Cropping	1.26	1.29	1.40	1.50	1.66

Note: Figures in the parentheses are percentage to total area for land utilization purposes.

Source: Statistical Abstract of Punjab for Various Years.

Irrigation Expansion

Irrigation is necessary for almost any kind of agricultural development but it is a prerequisite for the success of modern technology in agriculture. Punjab and Haryana have been fortunate in this respect. Planned investments in the past had already created a fairly wide spread irrigation network. This is one of the major reasons why new agricultural technology which is a package of new high yielding varieties of seeds and other modern inputs, like, chemical fertilisers, etc., could be adopted more successfully in these two States than anywhere else in the country. A look at the Tables 2.12 and 2.13 will show that even as far back as 1960-61, 55.59 per cent of Gross Cropped Area of Punjab and 26.29 per cent of Haryana were irrigated as compared to an all-India figure of 18.26 per cent. In 1966-67, i.e., on the eve of the introduction of new high yielding varieties of major food crops 65.09 per cent of GCA of Punjab and 37.75 per cent of Haryana were under irrigation. In Punjab, during 1960-61 and 1983-84 net sown area irrigated grew at a compound rate of 2.56 per cent per annum and gross area irrigated at a still faster rate of 3.84 per cent. In Haryana, during 1960-61 and 1982-83 net sown area irrigated and gross area irrigated increased at the rate of 3.94 and 5.04 per cent per annum respectively. By 1983-84, 86 per cent of net area sown and 89.91 per cent of gross cropped area in Punjab were under irrigation. Similarly, in Haryana by 1982-83, 61.30 per cent of net area sown and 65.11 per cent of gross cropped area were under irrigation. These are very impressive achievements when compared to the all-India figure of net area sown irrigated constituting only 27 per cent of NAS during 1979-80.

Apart from the very impressive expansion in area under irrigation in Punjab and Haryana, the structure of irrigation in both the States has also been changing in favour of tube-wells. In Punjab, during 1960-61, of the total net sown area irrigated, 58.49 per cent was covered by canals and 40.81 per cent by wells and tube-wells. By 1983-84 the position had reversed and 40.95 per cent was irrigated by canals and 58.82 per cent by tube-wells. In Haryana in 1960-61, 81.82 per cent of total net sown area irrigated was served by canals and only 16.48 per cent by wells and tube-wells. By 1982-83, the proportion of area irrigated was roughly 54 per cent and 46 per cent, respectively. Thus, while in pre-Green Revolution period canal irrigation created through huge public investments was the main source of irrigation, in the post-

1966-67 period private investments in tube-wells have made significant contribution to irrigation expansion. A look at Table 2.14 will prove this point. Number of tube-wells during 1966-67 and 1983-84 increased by nearly twelve fold in Punjab and fifteen fold in Haryana.

Increasing proportion of area irrigated coming under assured irrigation made the application of modern inputs, like, chemical fertilizers, possible. In what follows the progress of fertilizer use after the introduction of new technology in mid-1960s would be discussed in detail.

Fertilizer Consumption

Tables 2.15 and 2.16 give nutrient-wise yearly break-up of fertilizer consumption in Punjab and Haryana, respectively. It is clear that in both the States, the growth in fertilizers consumption has been phenomenal by almost any standards. Between 1967-68, i.e., the first

TABLE 2.11: Land Utilization in Haryana

(Thousand Hectares)

Sl. No.	Classification	1960-61	1965-66	1970-71	1975-76	1982-83
1.	Total Area	4,389	4,399	4,402	4,404	4,394
		(100.00)	(100.00)	(100.00)	(100.00)	(100.00)
2.	Area under forests	64	86	110	104	136
		(1.46)	(1.95)	(2.50)	(2.36)	(3.09)
3.	Land not available for cultivation	516	486	480	473	417
		(11.75)	(11.04)	(10.90)	(10.74)	(9.49)
4.	Other uncultivated land	222	145	86	78	75
		(5.06)	(3.30)	(1.95)	(1.77)	(1.70)
5.	Current Fallow	187	337	159	125	170
		(4.26)	(7.66)	(3.61)	(2.84)	(3.87)
6.	Net Area Sown	3,400	3,345	3,567	3,624	3,596
		(77.47)	(76.04)	(81.03)	(82.29)	(81.84)
7.	Area Sown more than once	1,183	731	1,481	1,827	1,710
8.	Area Sown more than once as percentage of NSA	34.79	21.85	41.52	50.41	51.64
9.	Gross Cropped Area	4,583	4,076	5,048	5,451	5,306
10.	Intensity of Cropping	1.35	1.22	1.42	1.50	1.47

Note: Figures in the parentheses are percentage to total area for land utilization purposes.

Source: Statistical Abstract of Haryana for Various Years.

TABLE 2.12: Irrigation Expansion in Punjab

Years	Index of net sown area irrigated	NSAI as percentage of net sown area	Percentage of NSAI by		Index of Gross Area Irrigated	GAI as Percentage of GCA
			Canals	Wells & Tubewells		
1960-61	100.00	54	58.49	40.81	100.00	55.59
1965-66	112.08	59	57.22	39.19	118.43	64.12
1966-67	112.72	59	55.88	43.14	127.16	65.09
1967-68	113.37	57	56.48	43.20	130.86	63.66
1968-69	131.35	67	48.79	50.98	144.42	72.29
1969-70	140.41	70	46.06	53.75	154.13	74.19
1970-71	143.04	71	44.73	55.09	160.29	74.72
1971-72	146.35	72	46.32	52.58	—	—
1972-73	145.61	72	43.53	56.19	—	—
1973-74	147.39	72	43.31	56.45	174.49	76.51
1974-75	157.65	78	44.29	55.48	180.20	80.79
1975-76	154.48	75	43.92	55.85	185.28	83.51
1976-77	158.19	77	43.39	56.41	191.91	78.83
1977-78	162.75	79	42.42	56.57	196.26	81.29
1978-79	161.56	78	42.55	56.46	208.00	83.04
1979-80	174.49	84	43.00	56.68	215.30	87.20
1980-81	167.50	81	42.19	57.33	218.43	85.49
1981-82	168.78	81	38.82	60.82	225.39	86.09
1982-83	175.82	84	41.18	58.59	232.30	88.91
1983-84	178.74	86	40.95	58.82	237.02	89.91
Growth Rate (Compound) 1980-81 over 1960-61	(2.46)				(3.84)	

Source: Statistical Abstracts of Punjab, Various Years.

year of introduction of new high yielding varieties in Punjab, and 1983-84 the consumption of nitrogen increased more than eight-fold, that of phosphorous more than 20-fold and that of potash more than 13-fold. Total consumption of NPK increased 10-fold during this period. In Haryana during the same period consumption of nitrogen increased more than eight-fold and that of phosphorous and potash more than 30 and 25-fold, respectively. Total consumption of NPK during this period increased by more than 10-fold in Haryana. This is perhaps a unique achievement compared with the general historical experience anywhere in the world. For example, the use of fertilizer in US agriculture increased a little over four-fold in 25 years since 1940, and that too, because of nearly halving of fertilizer prices relative to both farm product and other inputs.[4] This progress of Punjab and Haryana looks still more impressive if it is seen in the context that fertilizer prices were revised upwards on a number of occasions most notably during 1974-75. As a result of this massive upward revision during 1974-75 the consumption of fertilizer came down sharply. The fall in total NPK consumption compared to the previous year was of the order of 20 per cent in Punjab and 34 per cent in Haryana. However, it picked up next year and by 1976-77 the total consumption of fertilizers had crossed the previous highest level in both the States. By 1983-84 the consumption of fertilizer per hectare of cropped area was 142.04 kg in Punjab but 49.61 kg per hectare in Haryana.

TABLE 2.13: Irrigation Expansion in Haryana

Years	Index of net sown area irrigated	NSAI as percentage of net sown area	Percentage of NSAI by		Index of gross area irrigated	GAI as percentage of GCA
			Canals	Wells & Tubewells		
1960-61	100.00	29.6	81.82	16.48	100.00	26.29
1965-66	121.64	36.6	78.28	17.32	123.07	36.38
1966-67	128.40	37.8	76.64	22.35	144.07	37.75
1967-68	112.41	32.2	78.53	20.05	147.72	34.56
1968-69	130.29	40.1	69.13	29.34	154.69	45.99
1969-70	139.82	39.7	67.47	31.03	179.09	43.67
1970-71	152.14	43.0	62.14	37.46	185.06	44.99
1971-72	155.41	43.9	61.66	37.95	192.95	46.06
1972-73	162.06	45.9	58.39	41.76	205.56	47.74
1973-74	172.39	48.7	58.29	41.41	214.44	50.17
1974-75	176.66	50.6	57.95	41.76	215.44	53.61
1975-76	174.18	48.4	59.06	40.64	226.72	50.12
1976-77	178.55	48.3	58.78	40.82	223.90	51.08
1977-78	186.00	51.4	58.51	41.16	230.37	51.08
1978-79	190.37	52.5	58.26	41.47	247.22	53.95
1979-80	215.89	61.1	55.19	44.57	259.83	64.40
1980-81	211.91	59.2	54.40	45.31	274.60	60.58
1981-82	223.23	58.4	52.62	46.93	286.71	56.79
1982-83	233.95	61.3	53.56	46.26	295.34	65.11
Growth Rate (Compound) 1980-81 over 1960-61	(3.94)				(5.04)	

Source: Statistical Abstract of Haryana, Various Years.

TABLE 2.14: Growth in the Number of Tube-wells and Pumping Sets in Punjab and Haryana

Year	Punjab	Haryana
1966-67	30,894 (1.00)	23,311 (1.00)
1967-68	44,491 (1.44)	38,461 (1.52)
1968-69	62,863 (2.03)	58,047 (2.29)
1969-70	87,562 (2.83)	84,199 (3.33)
1970-71	98,569 (3.19)	1,04,358 (4.12)
1971-72	—	1,19,529 (4.72)
1972-73	1,80,480 (5.84)	1,49,160 (5.89)
1973-74	1,88,255 (6.09)	1,68,659 (6.66)
1974-75	2,04,166 (6.61)	1,91,074 (7.55)
1975-76	2,08,765 (6.75)	2,04,736 (8.08)
1976-77	2,26,522 (7.33)	2,21,592 (8.75)
1977-78	2,47,872 (8.02)	2,38,857 (9.43)
1978-79	2,58,755 (8.37)	2,58,689 (10.22)
1979-80	2,69,430 (8.72)	3,05,520 (12.07)
1980-81	2,80,000 (9.06)	3,32,027 (13.12)
1981-82	3,00,000 (9.71)	3,43,467 (13.56)
1982-83	3,33,000 (10.78)	3,61,650 (14.28)
1983-84	3,80,000 (12.30)	3,88,201 (15.33)

Note: Figures in parentheses are index numbers.
Source: Statistical Abstracts of Punjab and Haryana for Various Years.

Co-operative Credit

The phenomenal growth in the consumption of chemical fertilizers in Punjab and Haryana was made possible largely because of liberal provision of co-operative credit advanced to the cultivators through primary agricultural credit societies. These societies extend short-term credit facilities mainly for the purchase of fertilizers. Tables 2.17 and 2.18 show the expansion in membership of primary agricultural credit societies and the loans disbursed by these societies in Punjab and Haryana, respectively. A look at these tables would show that there was no attempt to multiply the number of societies as such. On the other hand, efforts have been made from time to time to make these societies financially viable. The deposits and working capital of these societies have been increasing at a very fast rate during this period. Amount of loans issued during this period increased more than nine-fold in Punjab and about 15-fold in Haryana. In Punjab, loan disbursed per hectare of cropped area was Rs. 60.56 in 1967-68. It rose to Rs. 426.03 per hectare by 1983-84. In Haryana it rose from merely Rs. 21.34 to Rs. 310.69 during roughly the same period. Although Haryana is still quite far behind Punjab in this respect but it is catching up fast. Both the States are at a very privileged position when compared to the all-India figure of Rs. 80.43 per cropped hectare during 1978-79.

Besides loans from these primary agricultural co-operative societies, State Land Mortgage Bank, commercial banks and other financial institutions have been extending substantial amounts as medium and long-term loans for installation of tube-wells and purchase of tractors and other agricultural implements and land improvement activities. Easy availability of institutional credit at reasonable rates has played a very important role in making all categories of cultivators participate in the new production technology.

Tractorisation

New agricultural technology is not only a package of hybrid seeds and other modern inputs, like, fertilizers, pesticides, herbicides and controlled water supply, but it also incorporates new agricultural practices. Given the short maturing period of new varieties and the possibility of multiple cropping, the new technology follows a rather rigid crop calendar. Timeliness of sowing and proper preparation of seed bed are very important factors for achieving good results from new technology. This has made the use of mechanical power necessary for some operations. The trend towards mechanisation has also been reinforced by scarcity of labour and relatively high wage rates particularly during the peak seasons. It has also been facilitated by ready availability of cheap institutional credit for this purpose and large remittances from abroad, particularly in Punjab. Table 2.19 shows growth of tractors since 1966 in Punjab and Haryana. Between 1966 and 1981 the number of tractors in Punjab increased more than 11-fold. It increased nearly 12-fold in Haryana. Whereas in 1966 on an average a tractor was serving 357 hectares of net area sown in Punjab, by 1981 a tractor was available for every 34 hectares. Similarly, in

TABLE 2.15: Fertilizer Consumption in Punjab (Tonnes)

Year	N	P	K	Total NPK	Per hectare (in kg)
1967-68	83,000 (100)	12,000 (100)	4,000 (100)	99,000 (100)	12.19
1968-69	1,35,000 (162)	27,000 (225)	10,000 (250)	1,72,000 (174)	32.52
1969-70	1,46,800 (176)	20,960 (174)	6,600 (165)	1,74,360 (176)	31.70
1970-71	1,74,800 (210)	31,360 (261)	7,200 (180)	2,13,360 (216)	37.57
1971-72	2,40,000 (270)	52,800 (440)	12,000 (300)	2,89,200 (292)	50.52
1972-73	2,40,000 (289)	65,600 (546)	18,600 (465)	3,24,200 (327)	54.66
1973-74	2,18,000 (262)	68,480 (570)	21,000 (525)	3,07,480 (310)	50.93
1974-75	1,88,800 (227)	42,080 (350)	13,200 (330)	2,44,080 (246)	41.34
1975-76	2,33,000 (280)	52,800 (440)	9,600 (240)	2,95,400 (298)	47.22
1976-77	2,59,000 (312)	93,000 (775)	21,000 (525)	3,73,000 (377)	59.35
1977-78	3,31,000 (398)	1,05,000 (875)	29,000 (725)	4,65,000 (470)	72.77
1978-79	4,19,000 (504)	1,55,000 (1,291)	29,000 (725)	6,03,000 (609)	90.95
1979-80	4,77,000 (574)	1,79,000 (1,491)	30,000 (750)	6,86,000 (693)	104.97
1980-81	5,26,000 (633)	2,07,000 (1,725)	29,000 (725)	7,62,000 (770)	112.67
1981-82	5,62,000 (677)	2,17,000 (1,808)	34,000 (850)	8,13,000 (812)	117.33
1982-83	6,26,000 (754)	2,30,000 (1,917)	36,000 (900)	8,92,000 (901)	128.99
1983-84	7,06,000 (850)	2,53,000 (2,108)	32,000 (800)	9,91,000 (1,001)	142.04

Note: Figures in paraentheses are index numbers.
Source: Statistical Abstract of Punjab for Various Years.

Haryana the net area sown per tractor came down from 713 hectares in 1966 to 62 hectares in 1981. Thus, the pace of mechanisation in the post-1966 era in Punjab and Haryana has been extremely fast. Mechanisation of this magnitude is bound to have significant impact on labour employment also. While it replaces labour in certain operations, to the extent it increases productivity of land through timeliness and better preparation of seed bed, etc., it is also likely to increase demand for labour. The net impact, of course, would depend upon the relative strength of these two opposing tendencies.

TABLE 2.16: Fertilizer Consumption in Haryana (Tonnes)

Year	N	P	K	Total NPK	Per hectare (in kg)
1967-68	30,227	1,726	521	32,474	6.30
	(100)	(100)	(100)	(100)	
1968-69	40,325	5,513	1,186	47,024	11.60
	(133.4)	(319.4)	(227)	(145)	
1969-70	47,000	5,120	1,800	53,920	10.91
	(155.5)	(296.6)	(345)	(166)	
1970-71	60,972	6,860	2,228	70,060	13.88
	(201.7)	(397.4)	(427)	(216)	
1971-72	73,432	6,305	2,397	82,134	16.27
	(242.9)	(365.3)	(460)	(253)	
1972-73	83,106	8,175	2,611	93,892	18.09
	(274.9)	(473.6)	(501)	(289)	
1973-74	94,060	16,473	4,464	1,14,997	22.33
	(311.2)	(954.4)	(857)	(354)	
1974-75	66,081	7,117	2,279	75,477	15.58
	(218.6)	(412.3)	(437)	(232)	
1975-76	86,308	8,322	2,285	96,915	17.78
	(285.5)	(482.1)	(438)	(298)	
1976-77	1,15,503	15,661	5,981	1,37,145	23.96
	(382.1)	(907.3)	(1,148)	(422)	
1977-78	1,50,195	28,654	9,262	1,88,111	34.61
	(496.9)	(1660.1)	(1,778)	(579)	
1978-79	1,61,933	31,833	10,301	2,04,067	36.95
	(535.7)	(1,844.3)	(1,977)	(628)	
1979-80	1,74,539	30,242	10,657	2,15,438	44.31
	(577.43)	(1,752.14)	(2,045)	(663)	
1980-81	1,87,385	31,340	12,098	2,30,823	42.26
	(619.59)	(1,815.76)	(2,322)	(711)	
1981-82	2,08,726	32,047	10,801	2,51,574	43.18
	(690.53)	(1,856.72)	(2,073.13)	(774.69)	
1982-83	2,16,175	37,337	9,717	2,63,229	49.61
	(715.17)	(2,163.21)	(1,865.07)	(810.58)	
1983-84	2,59,543	53,028	13,669	3,26,250	
	(858.65)	(3,072.31)	(2,623.61)	(1,004.65)	

Note: Figures in parentheses are index numbers.
Source: Statistical Abstract of Haryana for Various Years.

TABLE 2.17: Expansion of Primary Agricultural Credit Societies in Pubjab

Year	Total No. of societies	Membership (000s)	Deposits (Rs. Lakhs)	Working capital (Rs. Lakhs)	Loans issued (Rs. Lakhs)	Loans disbursed per hectare of cropped area (Rs.)
1967-68	11,954	1,349	1,111.30	4,404.18	3,294.86	60.56
	(100.00)**	(100.00)	(100.00)	(100.00)	(100.00)	
1970-71	10,274	1,438	1,774.09	7,643.21	5,726.59	100.86
	(85.94)	(106.59)	(159.64)	(173.54)	(173.80)	
1974-75	10,938	1,596	2,244.23	10,348.37	6,534.66	110.68
	(91.50)	(118.31)	(201.95)	(234.96)	(198.33)	
1979-80	4,271*	1,755	2,463.30	18,715.71	19,811.63	300.16
	(35.72)	(130.09)	(221.66)	(424.95)	(601.29)	
1983-84	4,270	1,825	2,926.14	37,894.14	29,724.14	426.03
	(35.72)	(135.28)	(263.31)	(860.41)	(902.13)	

* In order to make agricultural credit societies financially viable, relatively weak societies were amalgamated with other societies in the adjoining villages. Hence there is a steep fall in the number of societies between 1974-75 to 1979-80.

** The number in parentheses are index numbers.

Source: Statistical Abstract of Punjab for Various Years.

TABLE 2.18: Expansion of Primary Agricultural Credit Societies in Haryana

Year	Total No. of societies	Membership (000s)	Deposits (Rs. Lakhs)	Working capital (Rs. Lakhs)	Loans issued (Rs. Lakhs)	Loans disbursed per hectare of cropped area (Rs.)
1967-68	6,648	553	81.20	1,347.04	1099.23	21.34
	(100.00)**	(100.00)	(100.00)	(100.00)	(100.00)	
1970-71	6,582	629	80.23	2,252.75	1850.64	37.33
	(99.00)	(113.74)	(98.80)	(167.24)	(168.36)	
1974-75	6,565	789	97.32	4,616.36	3459.86	71.46
	(98.75)	(142.67)	(119.85)	(342.70)	(314.75)	
1979-80	2,390*	1,095	214.64	12,666.29	10160.58	208.98
	(35.95)	(198.01)	(264.33)	(940.30)	(924.33)	
1982-83	2,574	1,296	350.39	16,570.08	16485.50	310.69
	(38.72)	(234.36)	(431.51)	(1230.11)	(1499.73)	

* In order to make agricultural credit societies financially viable, relatively weak societies were amalgamated with other societies in the adjoining villages. Hence there is a steep fall in the number of societies between 1974-75 to 1979-80.

** The numbers in parentheses are index numbers.

Source: Statistical Abstract of Haryana for Various Years.

Progress of HYV Programme

Perhaps the most important input which resulted in the break-through in agricultural production in Punjab and Haryana in mid-1960s was the use of new high yielding varieties (HYV) of wheat, rice, maize and *bajra*. These new varieties of seeds, coupled with high and regulated application of irrigation, chemical fertilizers and pesticides and herbicides to control weeds, pests and diseases, ushered in the era of Green Revolution in Punjab and Haryana. Tables 2.20 and 2.21 describe the growth of area under high yielding varieties of seeds of wheat, rice, maize and bajra since 1967-68 in Punjab and Haryana, respectively. Most important of these four crops in undoubtedly wheat in both the States. The second most important crop for Punjab in the early phase of Green Revolution was maize, but since mid-1970s it has been replaced by rice. In Haryana the second most important crop continues to be *bajra* though since mid-'70s rice has also started picking up very fast. It is surprising to note that nearly 35 per cent of total area under wheat in Punjab came under new seed varieties during 1967-68 itself, the very first year when new seed varieties were thrown open for general use. Since then each year witnessed a phenomenal expansion. By 1983-84 almost entire wheat area in Punjab has been covered under HYVs. Initially, Haryana was slow in adoption of new varieties. By 1972-73, however, it overtook Punjab when nearly 78 per cent of its total wheat area was under new varieties. By 1983-84, about 92 per cent of total wheat area in Haryana was covered under HYVs. Because of very high productivity and profitability not only that almost the entire area under wheat in both the States has been covered by new HYVs but the area under wheat has increased by about 57 per cent in Punjab and 76 per cent in Haryana during this period.

The HYV programme for rice also witnessed an equally fast expansion in both the States, particularly in Punjab. For example, in Punjab, to start with, a mere 5.41 per cent of total rice area was under HYVs in 1967-68, by 1983-84 nearly 95 per cent of total rice area was under HYVs, while the area under rice increased nearly four-fold during this period. By 1976-77 rice emerged as the second most important crop in Punjab and was fast replacing maize. In Haryana in 1967-68, less than two per cent of total rice area was under HYVs, by 1982-83 the State expanded this to more than 87 per cent, while the area under rice more than doubled during this period. Punjab and Haryana, which were traditionally wheat producing States, have also emerged as major rice producing States since late 1970s. The HYV programme for maize and bajra has not made much headway in either of the States and area under these has been shrinking.

To sum-up, the very impressive agricultural growth achieved by the two States particularly since the mid-1960s is the net result of a configuration of a number of favourable factors. Even before the advent of the Green Revolution the two States had a high proportion of area under irrigation. Consolidation of land holdings had already taken place. A predominantly owner-operated land tenure system and a relatively high land-man ratio, apart from better soil conditions and availability of sub-soil water, were all favourable factors. Minimum required infrastructure for agricultural growth was already existing. When the opportunity came in the form of new high yielding varieties, it was made use of by a hard working peasantry. Their efforts were ably supported by easy availability of cheap institutional credit through co-operative societies and land mortgage banks. A realistic agricultural price support policy adopted by the government also played its part. The net result of all this was a remarkable success in agricultural production achieved by the two States.

TABLE 2.19: Number of Tractors in Punjab and Haryana

Year	Punjab		Haryana	
	Number of tractors	Net sown area per tractor (in hectares)	Number of tractors	Net sown area per tractor (in hectares)
1966	10,636 (100.00)*	357	4,803 (100.00)	713
1972	41,185 (387.22)	99	19,414 (404.21)	183
1978	98,345 (924.64)	42	37,965 (790.44)	96
1981	120,000 (1128.24)	34	58,435 (1216.63)	62

* Figures in brackets are index numbers.

Source: (1) Statistical Abstract of Punjab and Haryana for Various Years.
(2) For 1981 figures for Punjab see A.S. Kahlon; *Modernisation of Punjab Agriculture*, Allied Publishers, New Delhi, 1984, p. 30.

TABLE 2.20: Progress of HYV Programme in Punjab

(000 hectares)

Year	Rice			Maize			Bajra			Wheat		
	Area under HYV	Total Area	HYV as percent-age of total	Area under HYV	Total Area	HYV as percent-age of total	Area under HYV	Total Area	HYV as percent-age of total	Area under HYV	Total Area	HYV as percent-age of total
(1)	(2)	(3)	(4)	(5)	(6)	(7)	(8)	(9)	(10)	(11)	(12)	(13)
1967-68	17	314	5.41	29	476	6.09	51	209	24.40	621	1790	34.69
1968-69	26	345	7.54	49	490	10.00	82	193	42.48	1194	2063	57.88
1969-70	72	359	20.05	52	534	9.74	100	213	46.95	1502	2166	69.34
1970-71	130	390	33.33	49	555	8.83	126	207	60.87	1589	2299	69.12
1971-72	311	450	69.11	40	548	7.30	69	145	47.59	1695	2336	72.56
1972-73	362	476	76.05	29	562	5.16	9	129	6.98	1890	2404	78.62
1973-74	416	499	83.37	25	567	4.41	6	147	4.08	1970	2338	84.26
1974-75	481	569	84.53	88	522	16.86	33	135	24.44	1956	2207	88.62
1975-76	517	568	91.02	100	580	17.24	40	182	21.97	2195	2449	89.63
1976-77	601	680	88.38	108	580	18.62	40	182	21.97	2376	2630	90.34
1977-78	768	858	89.51	91	444	20.49	43	106	40.56	2447	2617	93.50
1978-79	1,001	1,052	95.15	65	424	15.33	34	87	39.08	2634	2739	96.17
1979-80	1,076	1,172	91.81	71	393	18.07	21	46	45.65	2775	2813	98.65
1980-81	1,109	1,182	93.82	127	382	33.25	33	69	47.83	2755	2811	98.00
1981-82	1,204	1,269	94.87	122	340	35.88	38	60	63.33	2885	2914	99.00
1982-83	1,263	1,322	95.53	126	307	41.04	31	41	75.61	3033	3052	99.37
1983-84	1,414	1,481	95.48	127	294	43.19	30	45	67.67	3107	3124	99.45

Source: Statistical Abstract of Punjab for Various Years.

TABLE 2.21: Progress of HYV Programme in Haryana

(000 hectares)

Year	Rice			Maize			Bajra			Wheat		
	Area under HYV	Total Area	HYV as percentage of total	Area under HYV	Total Area	HYV as percentage of total	Area under HYV	Total Area	HYV as percentage of total	Area under HYV	Total Area	HYV as percentage of total
(1)	(2)	(3)	(4)	(5)	(6)	(7)	(8)	(9)	(10)	(11)	(12)	(13)
1967-68	4	217	1.84	3	115	2.61	34	885	3.84	100	841	11.89
1968-69	10	229	4.37	8	88	9.09	51	874	5.83	256	898	28.51
1969-70	20	241	8.30	11	111	9.91	131	931	14.07	440	1017	43.26
1970-71	30	269	11.15	14	114	12.28	240	879	27.30	630	1129	55.80
1971-72	70	291	24.05	14	114	12.28	214	882	24.26	796	1177	67.63
1972-73	92	291	31.62	14	112	12.50	219	904	24.23	1,000	1271	78.68
1973-74	125	292	42.81	13	119	10.92	240	956	25.10	1,018	1177	86.41
1974-75	145	275	52.73	14	124	11.29	300	919	32.64	990	1177	84.62
1975-76	169	304	55.59	17	139	12.23	250	1006	24.86	1,087	1226	88.66
1976-77	190	330	57.58	20	123	16.26	250	947	26.39	1,200	1349	88.95
1977-78	252	371	67.92	20	96	20.83	250	886	28.21	1,224	1360	90.00
1978-79	330	459	71.90	25	89	28.08	300	872	34.40	1,340	1482	90.41
1979-80	416	509	81.73	25	77	32.47	322	815	39.51	1,346	1477	91.13
1980-81	414	484	85.54	28	71	39.43	335	870	38.50	1,357	1479	91.75
1981-82	441	504	87.50	25	70	35.71	485	851	56.99	1,437	1561	92.05
1982-83	430	489	87.93	20	56	35.71	515	778	66.20	1,585	1723	91.99

Source: Statistical Abstract of Haryana for Various Years.

III

Production Performance of Agriculture

Punjab was re-organised in 1966 and Haryana came into being. Because of the appearance of new high yielding varieties of some major food crops, that year also represents an important dividing line in the growth profile of agriculture in these two States. Even before the mid-1960s, erstwhile Punjab had recorded an impressive growth of output since the beginning of the planning era.[5] But increase in output during this period was largely contributed by increases in cropped area. For example, between 1951-54 and 1958-61, the contribution of area to total output expansion was 70 per cent, of changes in cropping pattern was about 22 per cent and that of crop yield was only eight per cent.[6] Although Punjab was leading other States in terms of growth of total agricultural production, yet it was trailing behind Gujarat, Madras, Mysore, etc., as far as growth of overall productivity is concerned; Gujarat, Madras, Andhra Pradesh and Kerala as regards growth of foodgrains productivity, and Mysore, Maharashtra and Andhra Pradesh as regards the growth of non-food productivity.[7] Thus it is clear that the States did not enjoy any all-round edge over other States till about the mid-1960s.

Growth of Agricultural Output

Tables 2.22 and 2.23 give index number of agricultural production for aggregate agricultural output and output of important crops in Punjab and Haryana, respectively, since 1960-61. Between 1960-61 and 1983-84, total crop production in Punjab grew at a rate of 5.11 per cent per annum. Similarly, in Haryana it registered a growth rate of 4.13 per cent during 1960-61 and 1982-83. This period, however, can be conveniently divided into two phases, i.e., pre-Green Revolution phase of 1960-61 to 1966-67 and post-1966-67 period which can be termed as Green Revolution period.[8] It is interesting to note that growth in post-1966-67 period is much higher as compared to pre-Green Revolution period. For example, Punjab recorded an impressive growth rate of 5.90 per cent per annum in all crops production during 1966-67 to 1983-84 as compared to only 3.50 per cent during 1960-61 to 1966-67. Haryana had virtually no growth in agricultural production during 1960-61 and 1966-67, whereas in the post-1966-67 period it

TABLE 2.22: Index Number of Agricultural Production in Punjab

(Base 1960-61 = 100)

Crop	1960-61	1966-67	1970-71	1975-76	1980-81	1983-84	Annual growth rate (Compound)		
							1966-67 over 1960-61	1983-84 over 1966-67	1983-84 over 1960-61
(1)	(2)	(3)	(4)	(5)	(6)	(7)	(8)	(9)	(10)
Rice	100	147.6	299.8	630.5	1,406.6	1,980.8	6.69	17.51	13.86
Bajra	100	258.6	418.9	325.9	141.7	94.8	20.93	- 6.01	- 0.23
Maize	100	165.5	232.1	228.1	169.9	145.3	8.73	- 0.73	1.64
Jowar	100	165.0	217.4	240.9	43.4	240.0	8.71	2.33	3.88
Wheat	100	140.7	295.4	332.3	440.6	540.9	5.86	8.24	7.62
Barley	100	169.3	109.6	292.4	203.0	180.8	9.18	0.38	2.61
Total Cereals	100	147.0	288.4	342.6	474.9	592.9	8.01	8.55	8.05
Gram & Pulses	100	74.4	42.4	55.5	24.6	19.2	- 3.01	- 8.31	- 7.46
Total Foodgrains	100	128.9	227.3	271.3	363.1	450.4	5.22	7.64	6.76
Oilseeds	100	203.1	180.5	234.3	161.1	98.5	12.54	- 4.35	- 0.06
Cotton	100	109.4	122.8	177.3	170.4	99.7	1.80	- 0.55	- 0.09
Sugarcane	100	89.7	108.4	126.1	80.7	113.8	- 2.20	1.41	0.56
Total Non-Foodgrains	100	103.1	117.5	153.2	123.6	106.9	0.62	0.21	0.29
All Crops	100	118.7	183.9	224.6	268.3	314.5	3.50	5.90	5.11

Source: Statistical Abstract of Punjab for Various Years.

TABLE 2.23: Index Number of Agricultural Production in Haryana

(*Base 1960-61 = 100*)

Crop	1960-61	1966-67	1970-71	1975-76	1980-81	1982-83	Annual growth rate (Compound)		
							1966-67 over 1960-61	1982-83 over 1966-67	1982-83 over 1960-61
(1)	(2)	(3)	(4)	(5)	(6)	(7)	(8)	(9)	(10)
Rice	100	127.4	262.9	357.2	719.5	729.3	4.11	11.52	9.45
Bajra	100	158.7	351.5	258.8	201.8	214.5	8.01	1.90	3.56
Maize	100	94.5	142.9	188.0	89.1	61.6	- 0.95	- 2.72	- 2.24
Jowar	100	94.2	142.2	87.2	119.6	69.8	- 1.00	- 1.90	- 1.65
Wheat	100	130.1	287.7	298.0	428.3	533.5	4.52	9.22	7.94
Barley	100	284.5	147.6	263.1	215.5	146.4	19.05	- 4.25	2.10
Total Cereals	100	136.7	275.8	283.5	386.4	450.5	5.35	7.74	7.08
Gram & Pulses	100	43.5	63.2	72.9	38.5	24.1	- 14.88	- 3.76	- 6.79
Total Foodgrains	100	89.7	170.4	178.8	213.4	238.5	- 1.98	6.30	4.04
Oilseeds	100	108.2	118.3	93.8	221.5	139.3	1.33	1.59	1.52
Cotton	100	236.5	283.2	349.0	482.6	630.4	15.44	6.32	8.81
Sugarcane	100	98.3	136.2	132.4	88.6	106.0	- 0.22	0.47	0.28
Total Non-Foodgrains	100	131.5	170.6	187.4	217.1	254.5	4.67	4.20	4.33
All Crops	100	100.7	170.5	181.1	214.4	242.3	0.10	5.64	4.13

Source: Statistical Abstract of Haryana for Various Years.

achieved a remarkable growth of 5.64 per cent per annum compound. It should, however, be kept in mind that Punjab registered this growth rate on a much higher base as compared to Haryana. Another point worth noting is that whereas in Punjab the upward trend in total agricultural production since 1966-67 has been steady without any sharp fluctuations, in Haryana the higher growth has also been accompanied by wider fluctuations.

In Punjab for the entire period of 1960-61 to 1983-84 as a whole foodgrains grew at a much faster rate of 6.76 per cent per annum as compared to non-foodgrains rate of growth of 0.29 per cent only. This difference becomes still sharper during the post-1966-67 period. During this period while foodgrains registered a growth of 7.64 per cent, non-foodgrains grew at an annual rate of 0.21 per cent only. In Haryana, while for the entire period since 1960-61 both foodgrains as well as non-foodgrains grew at a more or less the same rate, in the post-1966-67 period foodgrains registered a higher growth rate of 6.30 per cent as compared to non-foodgrains growth rate of 4.20 per cent per annum. Thus, since 1966-67 agricultural economies of both the States are becoming heavily foodgrains-oriented. Within foodgrains it is the cereals which have registered a very high rate of growth of 8.55 per cent per annum in Punjab and 7.74 per cent per annum in Haryana in the post-1966-67 period. On the other hand, there was an absolute decline in the output of gram and pulses in both Punjab and Haryana since 1960-61. On the whole, however, this decline was sharper in Punjab as compared to Haryana.

A very high growth in the output of cereals in both the States has been contributed by phenomenal growth in the output of rice and wheat. For the period as a whole, rice and wheat, respectively, registered an annual growth rate of 13.86 and 7.62 per cent in Punjab and 9.45 and 7.94 per cent in Haryana. In the post-1966-67 period, the growth in the output of two crops has been absolutely fantastic being 17.51 and 8.24 per cent per annum in Punjab and 11.52 and 9.22 per cent per annum in Haryana. In the pre-Green Revolution period, bajra, maize, jowar and barley in Punjab and bajra and barley in Haryana had higher growth rate than either wheat or rice in both the States. After the advent of new high yielding varieties of wheat and rice, these crops started losing very heavily to wheat and rice. Output of bajra and maize in Punjab and maize, jowar and barley in Haryana registered a sharp decline during the post-1966-67 period. Thus, in both Punjab and Haryana, within foodgrains, trend is towards a wheat-rice combination.

Within non-foodgrains, cotton has had a high positive growth in output throughout the period in Haryana. Oilseeds have a positive growth in Haryana for the entire period since 1960-61. However, in Punjab the growth in oilseeds had taken place only in the pre-1966-67 period. In the post-1966-67 period oilseeds registered a negative growth rate of 4.35 per cent per annum in Punjab. Output of sugarcane has increased marginally in both Punjab and Haryana for the period as a whole.

To sum-up, both the States have taken very impressive strides towards growth of agricultural output particularly since 1966-67. The trend in both the States is towards foodgrains and within foodgrains towards wheat and rice because wheat-rice combination gives better returns than perhaps any other crop combination.

Table 2.24 presents the growth in production, area and yield of rice and wheat, the two major crops which contributed most towards the overall growth in agricultural production in Punjab and Haryana during the past two decades. Taking a three-year average during 1960-63 to 1980-83 wheat output grew at a very impressive rate of 8.05 per cent per annum in Punjab and 8.15 per cent per annum in Haryana. However, the growth in wheat output was much faster during '60s as compared to '70s in both the States. During '60s it recorded a phenomenal growth rate of nearly 13 per cent per annum in Punjab and about 12 per cent per annum in Haryana. During '70s it registered nearly the same rate of growth of 4.15 and 4.81 per cent per annum in Punjab and Haryana, respectively. This phenomenal growth in the output of wheat has been contributed both by the growth in area and yield per unit of area. During '60s as a result of introduction of new high yielding varieties of wheat its yield registered a very impressive rate of growth of 7.36 per cent per annum in Punjab and 5.52 per cent per annum in Haryana. During 1970s however, yield increases in wheat slowed down considerably in both the States, being merely 1.84 and 1.50 per cent per annum in Punjab and Haryana respectively. The reasons for this slowing down are not far to seek. By 1971-72 more resourceful areas and more resourceful farmers had already been covered under the new high yielding varieties programme. During 1970s when the less resourceful areas cultivated by less resourceful farmers were also brought under the new HYVs of wheat, it inevitably brought down the average wheat yields. Yet, for the period as a whole, a growth rate in the yield of wheat of 4.32 and 3.30 per cent per annum in Punjab and Haryana respectively is respectable by almost any standards.

In the case of rice, the output and yield increases have been still more impressive in both the States. In Punjab, rice output recorded a spectacular growth rate of 12.86 per cent per annum during '60s and 16.26 per cent per annum during '70s. In Haryana, it recorded a growth rate of about 11 per cent per annum during '60s and about 10 per cent during '70s. As in the case of wheat, in the case of rice, also, this spectacular growth in output in both the States has been partly due to very impressive increase in yields. For example, during '60s rice yield registered a growth rate of 6.24 per cent per annum in Punjab and 4.92 per cent per annum in Haryana. It slowed down marginally in both the States during '70s but this decrease in growth rate of yield of rice was not as marked as in the case of wheat. Even during '70s, rice yields registered an impressive growth of 5.08 per cent per annum in Punjab and 3.83 per cent per annum in Haryana. During 1960-1963 to 1980-1983, for the period as a whole, rice yield recorded a very impressive growth of 5.60 per cent per annum in Punjab and 4.80 per cent per annum in Haryana. Thus, in the wake of such impressive increase in the yields of wheat and rice it is only natural that there has been a strong tendency towards a wheat-rice combination in Punjab and Haryana agriculture.

TABLE 2.24: Growth of Output, Area and Yield of Major Crops in Punjab and Haryana

	Punjab		Haryana	
	Wheat	Rice	Wheat	Rice
1969-72 over 1960-63				
Output	12.82	12.86	11.98	11.06
Area	5.09	6.13	6.14	5.78
Yield	7.36	6.24	5.52	4.92
1980-83 over 1969-72				
Output	4.15	16.26	4.81	9.70
Area	2.35	10.99	3.33	5.73
Yield	1.84	5.08	1.50	3.83
1980-83 over 1960-63				
Output	8.05	14.73	8.15	10.58
Area	3.58	8.80	5.39	5.75
Yield	4.32	5.60	3.30	4.80

NOTES

1. G.S. Bhalla and G.K. Chadha (1980). "Structure of Institutional Set-up of Rural Punjab in the year 2000" FAO Rome (Mimeo), p. 138.
2. Planning Commission (1966). 'Implementation of Land Reforms', New Delhi, p. 116.
3. See for example G.K. Chadha (1981). *Dynamics of Rural Transformation: A study of Punjab 1950-80* (Mimeo), J.N.U. New Delhi, p. 201; also see S.K. Sanyal (1972). "Has there been a decline in Agricultural Tenancy", *Economic and Political Weekly*, 7, May 6.
4. Zvi Griliches (1968). "Productivity and Technology" in *International Encyclopaedia of Social Sciences*, Macmillan, New York, p. 243.
5. See Government of India, Ministry of Food and Community Development; "Regional Differences in Crop Output Growth in Punjab 1952-53 to 1964-65".
6. B.S. Minhas and A. Vaidyanathan (1965). "Growth of Crop Output in India 1951-54 to 1958-61: An analysis by Component Elements", *Journal of the Indian Society of Agricultural Statistics*, December.
7. K.N. Raj (1972), "Some Questions Concerning Growth, Transformation and Planning of Agriculture in Developing Countries" in *Comparative Experience*, Indian Society of Agricultural Economics, Table 4, p. 251.
8. Some researchers take 1965-66 as the cut off point. See, for example, G.K. Chadha (1983). *Dynamics of Rural Transformation — A Study of Punjab 1950-80*, New Delhi, (Mimeo). We believe that it is more appropriate to take 1966-67 as the dividing point first because 1965-66 was a bad agricultural year not only for Punjab and Haryana but for the country as a whole. Therefore, taking 1965-66 period as the base gives unduly inflated growth rates for the post-1965-66 period. On the contrary, 1966-67 was a normal year. Secondly, although new seed varieties for wheat were tested and became available in 1966-67 but these were thrown open for general use in 1967-68 only. Therefore, 1966-67 can be considered as the last year before Green Revolution as far as Punjab and Haryana are concerned.

3

DATABASE, CONCEPTS AND METHODOLOGY

THIS CHAPTER contains a brief account of the database of the study, the concepts employed and the methodology followed.

Database

The present study is based on an analysis of a part of data collected through a primary survey conducted in 1975-76 of a cross-section of cultivating, wage labour and other non-cultivating households spread over all the districts of Punjab and Haryana. The survey was designed for an ICSSR project entitled "The Structure of Income Distribution: A Study of the Impact of Green Revolution in Punjab and Haryana", directed by Prof. G.S. Bhalla, and was conducted by the Economic and Statistical Organisations of the two States along with the 30th round of the NSS. The survey covered 1,663 cultivating, 1,029 wage labour and 330 other non-cultivating households of Punjab spread over 333 villages which were covered by the 30th round of NSS. Similarly, the survey covered 3,412 cultivating, 484 wage labour and 485 other non-cultivating household from 329 villages of Haryana. Whereas the data regarding cultivators were fully analysed by the director and the report submitted to the ICSSR[1] the data on wage labour and other non-cultivating households were left unanalysed. The availability of this extensive and rich source of data on non-cultivating households provided an opportunity to undertake the present study.[2]

The methodology of the survey was basically the same as adopted by the NSS. In this context it may be pointed out that, for selection of villages, the NSS first divided the country into a number of basic strata in such a way that it does not cut across district boundaries. Each district with less than 1.5 million rural population according to 1971 Census formed one basic stratum by itself. Districts with more than 1.5 million rural population (1971 Census) were divided into more than one basic stratum, depending on the rural population, by grouping contiguous tahsils. While grouping tahsils to form a stratum as far as possible, care was taken that tahsils which were more or less homogeneous in terms of population density and cropping pattern were clubbed together. But in the case of Punjab and Haryana, since none of the districts had a population of more than 1.5 million according to 1971 Census, therefore, the problem of dividing district into more than one basic stratum did not arise. As a result both in Punjab and Haryana basic strata of NSS 30th round were co-terminous with the administrative boundaries of each district. From each rural basic stratum, sample villages were selected randomly, their number being proportionate to the rural population of that stratum in the State. Sample villages with large population (generally having more than 200 households) were further sub-divided into hamlets and one of these hamlets in the sample village was selected at random.[3]

Besides the designated number of cultivating households, on an average three households were selected from the category of wage labourers and one from the category of other non-cultivating households from each sample village of Punjab. In Haryana, however, altogether three households belonging to the non-cultivating sections were selected at random from each sample village. About half of them belong to the category of wage labourers and the rest to other non-cultivating households. A household whose main source of income is wage labour has been defined as wage labour household. On the other hand, a household whose main source of income is neither wage labour nor cultivation, but some other activity, has been defined as belonging to the category of other non-cultivating households. Thus, whereas our wage labour category is a homogeneous group, our category of other non-cultivating households is an amorphous grouping. It includes all sorts of people in the village other than wage labourers and cultivating households, such as artisans, carpenters, blacksmiths, goldsmiths, milkmen, village retailers, weavers, potters, masons, plumbers, cobblers, barbers and village temple priests, etc. Since the number of such households in the village is rather small as compared to wage labourers, therefore, the number of households selected in our sample, from this category, does not, strictly speaking, represent their proportion to the total non-cultivating population in the village. Therefore, throughout our study 'wage labourers' and 'other non-cultivating households' have been treated as two separate categories. For the wage labour households, the representation of each district in the sample is proportionate to its share in rural population of the State. Thus, for the category of wage labour, the results obtained on the basis of sample data at the district or State level will be true representative of that category for that district or State. However, because of reasons stated earlier this cannot be said about the category of other non-cultivating households. The district-wise and region-wise break-up of the number of villages and the number of households of each category covered in sample from Punjab and Haryana are given in Tables 3.1 and 3.2.

TABLE 3.1: District-wise and Region-wise Distribution of Sample Villages and Households (Punjab)

Sl. No.	District Region/State	No. of villages	Wage labour households	Other non-cultivating households
1.	Amritsar	42	122	43
2.	Bhatinda	36	100	35
3.	Faridkot	27	83	27
4.	Ferozepur	20	65	22
5.	Gurdaspur	35	113	25
6.	Hoshiarpur	29	97	27
7.	Jalandhar	32	91	43
8.	Kapurthala	9	37	14
9.	Ludhiana	32	103	28
10.	Patiala	25	81	24
11.	Ropar	16	45	14
12.	Sangrur	30	92	28
	Region - I	140	434	152
	Region - II	113	340	112
	Region - III	80	255	66
	Punjab	333	1,029	330

Unlike industry, agriculture is a seasonal activity and every one who is involved in agriculture or is dependent on it is bound to be effected by its seasonal variations. This is particularly true for wage labourer and other non-cultivating sections of rural population. In the case of wage labourers their work availability, wage rates and consequently incomes vary from season to season. Although not to the same extent as wage labourers, but to a large extent, even the employment prospects and the income of other non-cultivating households also vary seasonally. To take care of the seasonal variations the survey was conducted in four sub-rounds consisting of three months each, i.e., from July 1975 to September 1975; October 1975 to December 1975; January 1976 to March 1976 and April 1976 to June 1976. The sub-round-wise distribution of sample villages and the number of households covered in each category for Punjab and Haryana are given in Table 3.3. A look at this table reveals that the sample households of wage labour and other non-cultivating households for both the States are more or less equally spread over the four sub-rounds.

TABLE 3.2: District-wise and Region-wise Distribution of Sample Village and Households (Haryana)

Sl. No.	District Region/State	No. of villages	Wage labour households	Other non-cultivating households
1.	Ambala	32	49	48
2.	Bhiwani	24	20	28
3.	Gurgaon	44	51	54
4.	Hissar	54	96	57
5.	Jind	24	48	43
6.	Karnal	33	64	56
7.	Kurukshetra	29	51	58
8.	Mohindergarh	26	17	40
9.	Rohtak	36	41	52
10.	Sonepat	27	47	49
	Region - I	121	211	211
	Region - II	114	185	152
	Region - III	94	88	122
	Haryana	329	484	485

The information collected from the sample households includes particulars of family members, their relation to the head of the family, sex, marital status, age, education standard, status as earner and usual occupation. If the household owns and/or cultivates any land, information regarding annual rent of land leased out or net agricultural income, if he cultivates himself, is also included. Information regarding income from 'other sources', such as rents (other than land), interest, pension and remittances, etc., received during the period of 30 days preceding the date of survey, was also collected. Similarly, receipts and disbursements of the household from rearing and maintenance of livestock and poultry for 30 days preceding the date of enquiry were also recorded. Also recorded was the information regarding receipts and disbursements of household enterprises, if any, (other than farming, rearing and maintenance of livestock and poultry) during 30 days preceding the date of enquiry. For those members of the household who were working on regular basis in agriculture or non-agriculture, information regarding their income from wage employment in the form of cash, kind and perquisites received during 365 days preceding the date of enquiry was recorded. For casual workers the day-wise information regarding type of work done, operation in which worked (if employed in agriculture) and income from wage employment in terms of cash, kind and perquisites for seven days preceding the date of enquiry was collected. The wage received in kind was valued at whole-sale price prevailing in the village. Perquisites usually consisting of meals and tea given to wage labourers by the employer were given imputed value in consultation with the workers. Finally, this survey also included detailed information on consumption expenditure of the household and its break-up in cash and kind or home grown during 30 days preceding the date of enquiry. The items of consumption on which information was collected in the survey included expenditure on wheat and wheat products, rice, other cereals (including maize and bajra), gram, pulses, milk and milk products, edible oils (including *ghee*, mustard oil, etc.), meat, eggs and fish, vegetables; fruits and nuts, sugar and gur, salt and spices, beverages and refreshments, *paan*, tobacco and intoxicants, fuel and light, clothing, footwear, rents, taxes, durable goods, miscellaneous goods and services. It may, however, be pointed out that the number of households with positive response in the case of certain items, like, beverages and refreshments, fruits and nuts, rents, taxes and durable goods, is relatively small in our sample. Therefore, while analysing the consumption pattern of wage labour and other non-cultivating households some of these items were clubbed with other items, such as fruits and nuts with vegetables, *paan*, tobacco and intoxicants with beverages and refreshments, and rents with taxes.

Similarly, cereals and cereal products of all types were considered as one category.

TABLE 3.3: Sub-round-wise Distribution of Sample Villages and Households

States	Sub-round	No. of villages	Wage labour household	Other non-cultivating households
Punjab	I	80	250	78
	II	81	255	79
	III	84	256	79
	IV	88	268	94
	Total	333	1029	330
Haryana	I	73	126	132
	II	83	124	122
	III	89	122	116
	IV	84	112	115
	Total	329	484	485

Concepts and Definitions

In the following pages a brief description of the concepts and terms used in the present study is given.

Non-Cultivating Households

In this study we are concerned with the non-cultivating sections of rural population of Punjab and Haryana. We define a household as a non-cultivating household if the major proportion of its income comes from sources other than cultivation. That, however, does not mean that none of these households own any land or undertake cultivation but their major source of income is not rent from land or income from cultivation. Thus, the criterion for differentiating a non-cultivating household from a cultivating household is income of the household and not the profession of the head of the household.

These non-cultivating households are further divided into two categories, i.e., 'wage labour households' and 'other non-cultivating households'. Once again the criterion is income. If the major part of household income comes from wage labour then the household is defined as belonging to the wage labour category irrespective of the profession of the head of the family. If, however, the major source of income of the household is neither wage labour nor cultivation but some other activity or household enterprise, then the household is defined as belonging to the category of other non-cultivating households. Thus, the category of other non-cultivating households, as already mentioned, includes people, such as village artisans, carpenters, smiths, weavers, potters, tailors, masons, plumbers, cobblers, barbers, milkmen, village retailers and village temple priests, etc. Unlike wage labourers most of these non-cultivating households are not directly involved in agriculture but any large-scale change in agrarian economy of the area is bound to effect, apart from wage labourer, the employment pattern and consequently the income prospects of these non-cultivating households also. But the impact of technological change in agriculture may not be similar on both these categories of non-cultivating households.

Household

A household is a unit in which all members of the family take meals from a common kitchen. Sometimes some working members of wage labour households are provided meals by the employer but that does not mean that they are not members of the household. The imputed value of the meals of such members, which they take outside, has also been included in the income and consumption expenditure of the household.

Rate of Participation

Rate of participation refers to the ratio of persons in the labour force to the total population expressed as per cent. Labour force includes all such persons who are economically active. It includes all persons who actually work for production of goods and/or services for exchange (i.e., employed) and those who, although not working, want to do so or seek an opportunity to do so (i.e., unemployed). Thus, the labour force is the inventory of persons who constitute the economically active population, i.e., who are working, who are seeking work and those who are available for work, and no attempt has been made to differentiate them in terms of the intensity with which they work or would like to work.

Working Age Group

All persons who have completed 15 years of age, but have not yet attained the age of 60 years, have been defined as being in the 'working age group'. Although no specific upper age limit is relevant in the case of rural wage labourers because they continue to participate in work to augment the meagre earnings of their family so long as they are able to work and are able to get work, yet we have used this category of working age group also to make our results comparable with other empirical studies in India which use this category. Incidentally most of the empirical studies in India, including those based on NSS data, use the category of working age group 15-59.

Unemployment

Unemployment is a situation in which men though willing to work at the current wage rate are unable to get it. Thus when we use the term unemployment we mean involuntary unemployment only. Out of various criteria which have been suggested in the existing literature for measuring unemployment, we have chosen time criterion for measuring unemployment. Since in our study we are dealing with that section of population which works as wage labour, therefore, we feel the question of their being productively employed is automatically taken care of in a way, because a wage labourer will be employed by the employer only when he feels that the labourer's contribution to production is not only positive but it, at least, covers the wage paid to the labourer. Otherwise, it would not be rational on the part of the employer to employ a wage labourer. Similarly, income criterion was also not considered relevant for the purpose of our study because we feel that so long as a labourer works for a wage, strictly speaking, he is employed. Whether the wage paid to him is sufficient to meet the minimum needs of his family or not is another question. Even otherwise, despite the fact that income criterion catches an important dimension of the problem of unemployment, yet the estimates of unemployment obtained by using income criterion have been criticised as being hotch-potch of unemployed, under-employed and the poor. It is argued that going by the income criterion some people, otherwise fully employed, would also be counted as unemployed because in India it is possible to be employed and be poor at the same time. Considering all these points and keeping in view the section of population with which we are dealing, we decided to use time criterion for measuring unemployment. Within the time criterion, day has been used as a unit of time since generally wages are paid in rural areas in terms of number of days worked and not according to the number of hours worked. For the purpose of calculating rate of unemployment half days have been converted into their full days' equivalent. Thus, by unemployment we mean difference between labour supply (L^s) and labour demand (L^d), both measured in terms of time. Unemployment rate (U) is defined as the difference between labour supply and labour demand divided by the labour supply. Symbolically:

$$U = (L^s - L^d)/ L^s$$

Where

U = Rate of unemployment
L^s = Labour Supply; and
L^d = Labour demand

Under-employment

We define all those workers as under-employed who though willing to work or were available for work for more days actually got work for less than six days during the reference week. Those who are under-employed, according to the abovementioned criterion, are further sub-divided into two categories: (a) moderately under-employed and (b) severely under-employed. Those employed for five or four days in the reference week are included in the category of moderately under-employed. Those who got work for less than four days but have worked for at least some time in the reference week are included in the category of severely under-employed. Thus, our definition of moderately under-employed and severely under-employed roughly corresponds to that of Raj Krishna (1976) where he defines a person with less than 28 hours of work in the reference week as severely under-employed and a person with between 28 and 42 hours of work in the reference week as moderately under-employed.[4]

Weekly Status Unemployment

A person who did not get any work during the reference week but was willing to work or was available for work has been defined as unemployed according to weekly status. Thus, weekly status unemployment is a ratio of those persons who did not get any work during the reference week (i.e., unemployed) to total persons in the labour force during the reference week (i.e., employed plus unemployed). Because it is calculated by taking into account the total stock of persons at a particular point of time, it is clearly a stock concept of unemployment.

Person-days Unemployment Rate

The basic problem with weekly status unemployment is that, in its calculations, a person's status over the week has to be frozen in one and only one activity. A person under the weekly status is either employed or unemployed provided he is in the labour force during the reference week. Therefore, it does not take into account the day to day changing status of a person and hence does not reflect the true magnitude of unemployment. The extent of under-employment cannot be taken care of within weekly status unemployment terms and it also does not tally with our understanding of unemployment as defined above. To take care of this problem we have used the concept of person-days rate of unemployment (PDUR). It is defined as the ratio of unemployment days per week (seeking or available for work) to the total labour supply by that person during the reference week. Thus, it is clearly a flow concept where not only the labour is being measured in time but it is also being measured as a flow per unit of time such as so many hours offered/demanded per day or so many person-days offered/demanded per week. In the calculation of PDUR, half days are converted into their full days' equivalent.

Income Concept

In our study income means actual income of non-cultivating households from various sources such as income from wages and salaries which we call 'wage component' and income from non-wage sources which we call 'non-wage component' of income. The wage component of household income includes wages and salaries of all the earning members of the household, i.e., men, women and children, from both agricultural and non-agricultural employment. The non-wage component of the household income includes net income from household enterprises and income from dairying, poultry and rearing of livestock. Net income from land, if any, and income from rent, interest, pension and remittances, etc. are also included in it.

But our concept of income does not include the benefits, if any, received by households from government expenditure on education, health and other social and economic services for the simple reason that it is extremely difficult to correctly allocate the differential benefits of such expenditure to households in a study of this type. Thus, to the extent these households receive benefits from government expenditure on social services and other benefits for the weaker sections, our estimates of household income are under-estimated.

Income Recipient Unit

While calculating income we have taken household as a recipient unit and not a family. This wider definition has been preferred partly because we do not have comprehensive information on inner family units and also because so long as more than one family units are part of the same household and take meals from the same kitchen, it becomes easier to calculate their total expenditure. Since household size differ across districts, therefore, while analysing the impact of agricultural development on the incomes of wage labour and other non-cultivating sections, apart from household income, we have also used the concept of per capita income.

Consumption Expenditure

Total consumption expenditure includes expenditure on food as well as on non-food items in both cash and kind. The kind part may be home grown but more often it consists of wages received in kind for certain operations, like, wheat harvesting, etc. The items of consumption included in total expenditure are wheat and wheat products; rice; other cereals (including maize and bajra), gram and pulses; milk and milk products; edible oils (including *ghee* and mustard oil, etc.); meat, eggs and fish; vegetables; fruits and nuts; sugar and *gur*; salt and spices; beverages and refreshments; *paan*, tobacco and intoxicants; fuel and light; clothing; footwear, durable items, like, transistors, sewing machines, bicycles, domestic utensils; furniture and ornaments, etc. and miscellaneous goods and services (such as expenditure on medicines and health care, education, conveyance, laundry and toiletry, etc.). The value of consumption items which are home grown or received in kind have been valued at village prices. Similarly, items, such as free collection of firewood and twigs collected from the fields, etc., to be used as fuel for cooking food, have been given some notional value. But incidental charges, such as expenditure on litigation, etc., have not been included in the total expenditure.

The expenditure on items discussed above is the actual monthly expenditure on these items reported by the household. But most of the attached labourers and many of the casual workers are also given tea and meals by their employer, with whom they work. The estimated value of this food was recorded in the questionnaire as 'perquisites'. Thus the recorded monthly expenditure of the household does not include this part of consumption which the working members of the household had consumed outside during the period they were working. If, however, these family members had in fact taken food from the family kitchen during this period, the family expenditure would have gone up to that extent. Thus, perquisites, if any, by the working members were brought at their monthly equivalent and have been included in the consumption expenditure of the household. Since these perquisites consist of food only its recorded value has been distributed on food items in the same proportion in which the rest of the family members' total expenditure on food is distributed. We are aware of the fact that strictly speaking perquisites received by the working members are not consumption expenditure of the entire household and instead represent consumption of the particular person or persons but we decided to add it to the household expenditure because ignoring it would result in a bigger error than adding it to the household expenditure.

Poverty Line

There are two broad concepts of poverty, i.e., the relative poverty and absolute poverty. While relative poverty is measured in terms of inequality in the distribution of income or wealth, absolute poverty is reckoned in terms of some kind of notion of subsistence considered necessary, keeping in view the socio-cultural and climatic circumstances of the area concerned. In India the discussion of poverty among academics has tended to concentrate on absolute poverty.

Defined in the absolute sense of deprivation, a poor person is one who does not have command over or access to the basic needs of life, both material as well as non-material. On the material plane, basic needs are fundamental physical needs, like, adequate food, clothings and shelter, etc. The non-material needs include basic social services, like, education and health, etc. Almost all Indian studies on poverty have taken into account poverty in terms of material needs only. The usual procedure has been to translate certain minimum nutritional requirements into a specific food basket, such as cereals, pulses, sugar, milk, vegetables and edible oils, and by valuing this food basket at rural and urban rates separately a figure is arrived at for each area which represent per capita expenditure within which the minimum normative diet could be accommodated. Different authorities, such as FAO, the Indian Council of Medical Research (ICMR) and the Second Pay Commission for Central Government Employees (1957-59), have suggested different yardsticks for minimum nutritional requirements. Roughly speaking these have varied between 2,100 and 2,400 calories per person per day.

In 1962, a distinguished working group appointed by the Government of India recommended the minimum per capita expenditure of Rs. 20 per month in rural India and Rs. 25 per month in urban areas at 1960-61 prices. This figure, however, does not include expenditure on health and education both of which were expected to be provided by State according to the Constitution and in the light of its other commitments. Incidentally this estimate is also not related to any nutritional norm and by using various and equally plausible nutritional norms different authors arrived at a fairly wide range of estimates for where the line should be drawn and where it is actually drawn makes a great deal of difference to the estimates of the number of 'poor' whose consumption falls below the chosen limit.[5]

In the present study, following Bardhan (1970), we have taken consumer expenditure of Rs. 15 per person for 30 days at all-India 1960-61 rural prices as our poverty line.[6] According to Bardhan the expenditure level of Rs. 15 in 1960-61 at all-India rural prices correspond to Rs. 20 per person at all-India 1960-61 prices which is the minimum level originally adopted by the Planning Commission in 1962 and subsequently became a nationally accepted poverty line. Since commodity prices vary significantly across States so that the same real consumption level requires different levels of nominal consumption, Bardhan estimated rural poverty line for each State in 1960-61 prices corresponding to all-India rural poverty line of Rs. 15. It works out to Rs. 15.90 for rural Punjab (including Haryana). Thus, we take Rs. 15.90 per person for 30 days as our poverty line. Dandekar and Rath (1971) had also adopted this line for measuring rural poverty on the ground that it corresponded to expenditure level at which consumption, on an average, provided the norm of 2,250 calories per day.[7] However, we shall not try to justify it in terms of some independently measurable real living standard nor shall we try to interpret this line as corresponding to any nutritional minimum. Suffice it to say that this level of expenditure represents an extremely low level of living and the one that has been most commonly used in Indian studies.

The next problem is that of selecting an appropriate price deflater to arrive at the poverty line figure for the year of the present study. Different researchers have made different choices. Dandekar and Rath (1971)[8] and Minhas (1970)[9] have used the National Income deflater. Bardhan (1970), however, argues that prices of coarse cereals usually consumed by the poor have gone up in this period at a higher rate and, therefore, he uses Consumer Price Index for Agricultural Labourer (CPIAL). Since we are dealing with wage labour and other non-cultivating rural households, therefore, we have also used (CPIAL) to arrive at the poverty line corresponding to the year of our study, i.e., 1975-76. The CPIAL for Punjab (including Haryana) during July 1975 and June 1976 stood at 308.[10] By multiplying our poverty figure with a factor of 3.08 we obtained a poverty line figure of Rs. 48.97 per capita at current prices for 1975-76. Thus, all households having per capita monthly expenditure below Rs. 48.97 have been defined as poor.

Level of Agricultural Development

To see the impact of agricultural development of the region on variables, like, rates of work participation of both male and female, unemployment prevailing among wage labourers, their work availability, the attached-casual composition, wage rates, consumption pattern and levels of living, etc., level of output per acre during 1975-76 has been used as an index of the level of agricultural development of the region. Twelve major crops that together account for more than 85 per cent of the total gross cropped area in Punjab and Haryana have been taken to calculate the productivity per acre. To convert the output of each crop during 1975-76 into rupees, the post-harvest prices of these crops during 1975-76 as reported in the Statistical Abstracts of Punjab and Haryana have been used. Apart from output per acre at certain places we have also used the concept of productivity per male agricultural worker. For this purpose total output of the district or State has been divided by total number of male agricultural workers in that district or State taken from 1971 Census.

Division of Punjab and Haryana into Regions

Generally the analysis has been carried on at the district level but to have an idea at somewhat more aggregative level each of the two States have been divided into three, more or less, homogeneous agricultural regions. At certain places the analysis has been carried on at the region level instead of at the district level particularly where more number of observations are required than are available at the district level, as in the case of estimation on Engel elasticities for different commodities in Chapter 6. A number of methods of regionalisation have been suggested by regional scientists. However, the objective of the specific study should determine the basis for forming homogeneous agricultural regions. For the present purpose we have used the work of some scholars who have built regions on the basis of cropping pattern, per acre productivity, percentage of area irrigated and area under HYV's.[11] On this basis five districts of central Punjab, i.e., Amritsar, Kapurthala, Jalandhar, Ludhiana and Patiala, constitute the first region. The second region consists of four southern districts of Punjab, i.e., Sangrur, Bhatinda, Faridkot and Ferozepur. Sub-mountainous areas of Punjab, consisting of Gurdaspur, Hoshiarpur and Ropar districts, constitute region - III. Similarly, in Haryana the relatively more developed eastern districts of Ambala, Karnal, Kurukshetra and Sonepat form region - I. Region - II includes districts of Rohtak, Jind and Hissar which are at a slightly lower level of agricultural development as compared to the districts included in the first region. The southern dry districts of Bhiwani, Gurgaon and Mohindargarh constitute region - III.

Methodology

To analyse the impact of agricultural development of the region on rates of work participation of males and females, on employment/unemployment, on work availability and attached-casual composition of wage labourers, their income levels, wage rates and extent of poverty prevailing among wage labour and other non-cultivating households we take a cross-section of 22 districts of Punjab and Haryana and see the association between these variables and the level of agricultural development of the districts defined as productivity per acre. This has been done in the first step by using simple correlation coefficients. To see whether the association between the two series is statistically significant or not we apply T-test. Wherever the association has been found to be statistically significant, we pursue it further by using the method of regression analysis. There we not only try to quantify the role of agricultural development of the region in explaining the inter-district variation in dependent variable but also take into account the other possible variables which one can theoretically think of having impact on the dependent variable. In all such cases, multiple regression analysis has been used. The equations have been estimated by using the method of ordinary Least Squares (OLS).

To study the determinant of variation in wages a wage determination model has been evolved in terms of supply and demand factors which determine the market clearing wage. Barring the complications arising out of the pressure of trade unionism representing the relative bargaining strength of workers and segmentation in the labour market, it is hypothesised that the actual wage rate will be positively correlated with the market clearing wage. The greater the difference between the market clearing rate and the actual wage rate, for whatever reasons, the higher will be the unemployment among wage labourers. The market clearing wage is likely to be negatively related to demographic pressure on land. It should be positively related to factors which increase productivity of land, like, extent of irrigation, use of fertilizers and proportion of area under high yielding varieties. Since most of these variables are likely to be highly correlated to each other, putting them separately as explanatory variables is likely to give rise to the problem of multi-collinearity. Hence we use productivity per acre as a surrogate variable for these various productivity augmenting factors. Segmentation in the labour market is likely to depress the average wage rate. However, the impact of inequality in land-holding distribution on wage rate is unpredictable and it will depend upon the relative strength of its supply increasing and demand boosting effects. The following model has been employed:

Let

U = Unemployment prevailing among wage labourer.
W = Actual wage rate
$\overline{W}$ = Market clearing wage rate
S_t = Total supply of labour
S_w = Supply of wage labour
D_w = Demand for wage labour
O = Output per acre
P_{Nsc} = Proportion of non-scheduled castes labour in total wage labourers representing segmentation in the labour market.
I = Index of inequality in the distribution of land holdings.
E = Index of relative numerical strength of wage labour in total agricultural labourers.

Then we hypothesise that[12]

$$W = f_1(W, P_{Nsc}, E, U) \quad (3.1)$$
$$\overline{W} = f_2(S_w, D_w) \quad (3.2)$$
$$S_w = f_3(S_t, I, W) \quad (3.3)$$
$$D_w = f_4(S_t, I, O, W) \quad (3.4)$$

Substituting (3.3) and (3.4) into (3.2) we get

$$\overline{W} = f_5(S_t, I, O, W) \quad (3.5)$$

Substituting (3.5) into (3.1) and expressing the function wholly in terms of exogenous variable we get

$$W = f_1 (S_t, I, O, P_{Nsc}, E, U) \quad (3.6)$$

Taking log of both sides

$$Log\ W = a - b_1 \text{ Log } S_t + b_2 \text{Log } I + b_3 \text{ Log } O$$
$$- b_4 \text{Log } P_{Nsc} - b_5 \text{Log } E - b_6 \text{Log } U$$

Thus, we except wage rate to be negatively associated with S_t, U, P_{Nsc} and E and positively with O. However, the effect of I on wage rate is indeterminate and it can be either way depending upon the relative strength of its supply increasing and demand boosting effects. Our hypothesis is that the higher the extent of segmentation in the labour market the less the chances of workers joining hands for their common cause and hence the lower the wages. It is because of this reason that we expect a negative relationship between wage rate and index of segmentation in the labour market (P_{Nsc}).

The model has been tested with district level data since most of the explanatory variables can be had at the district level. The results obtained are discussed in Section II of Chapter 5.

To analyse the consumption pattern of wage labour and other non-cultivating households of Punjab and Haryana, expenditure elasticities of different items of consumption expenditure have been calculated. All the currently existing theories on the subject postulate consumption as a function of income, other things remaining the same. The basic concern of an empirical analysis of family budgets is to isolate the influence of economic determinants, like, income and prices, etc., on the consumption of a particular commodity holding constant the effect of other possibly relevant but less important variables, like, age, family composition, location of residence; social classes and their habits and various other psychological factors. We assume that the numerous non-economic determinants are unimportant and individually give rise to an error term conforming to some probability distribution with zero mean and constant variance. Then the demand of the jth household for the ith commodity can be expressed as :

$$Dij = f_1 (y_j; P_1 \quad \ldots_n; \ E_{ij})$$

Where

Y_j is the income of jth household
$P_1 \ldots P_n$ are the prices of the n commodities.
E_{ij} is a random variable.

If prices are assumed constant and only income is allowed to vary among households, we get the following relationship:

$$Q = f_1(Y_1), Q_2 = f_2(Y_2) \ldots Q_n = F_n(Y_n)$$

Where

Q is the quantity consumed, f denotes the functional relationship and Y is the income.

The above function assumes different values depending on the value of Y and it is possible to trace a curve in n-dimensional quantity space ($Q_1, Q_2 \ldots Q_n$). This curve is known as the Engel Curve, named after Ernest Engel.

The analysis of consumption pattern using Engel Curve technique turns around the criteria for an algebraic formulation of Engel Curve and the actual form or forms investigated. Broadly speaking three considerations seem to guide the specification of the form of the Engel function. These are :

(i) Economic plausibility so that it fulfils the theoretical requirements of the existing consumption theory.
(ii) Statistical acceptability and
(iii) Pragmaticality.

As far as the economic plausibility is concerned generally two properties are incorporated into the formulation. These are :

(i) That there is an initial income level below which a commodity is not purchased; and
(ii) that there is a satiety level or a maximum beyond which the quantity of the commodity consumed does not exceed, however high is the income.

It is clear that all commodities will not have Engel Curves with these properties. The notion of a saturation is only applicable to items of expenditure for which there is no greater shift to higher qualities as income rises. Except for some staple food items for most other commodities such shift takes place sooner or later with the result that if expenditure on the commodity is measured on the vertical axis, rather than quantity, the satiety level will have upward slope. In addition to this there is a third point which should be considered in the algebraic formulation of an Engel Curve. This is the constraint imposed on the parameters of the curve so that sum of all expenditures is equal to income at all income levels. The consequence of this adding-up criterion is that Engel Curve for all commodities cannot have asymptotic values for, then, there would be some income level at which the whole of the income would not be spent. This criterion leads to the conclusion that if there are some commodities which have a satiety level there are others which do not. Therefore, a better representation of the consumer behaviour may be obtained by postulating different forms of Engel Curves for different types of commodities.

Apart from economic considerations discussed above, certain statistical considerations also have to be kept in mind. One of these is that the selected function should show a satisfactory fit. It is in this context that usually a number of alternative forms of Engel functions chosen on the basis of economic plausibility are fitted to the same data and the one giving the best fit out of these is considered to be the best approximation to the true but unknown Engel Curve for a particular expenditure item. The criterion for the overall goodness of fit is the coefficient of determination, i.e., R^2. In considering the alternative algebraic forms of the Engel Curve the case of numerical estimation of its parameters should also be considered.

Among the pragmatic considerations governing the choice of the Engel functions are their satisfactory estimation. Simplicity both in terms of computation and interpretation of the parameters and comparative prevalence in economic literature are other consideration. Perhaps this explains why log-linear form of the Engel Curve is used so commonly.

The following eight forms of the Engel Curves have been suggested in the literature on the family budget studies:

1. $Y = a + bx$ (Linear)
2. $Y = a + bx + Cx^2$ (Quadratic)
3. $Y = a - b/x$ (Hyperbolic)
4. $Y = a + b \log x$ (Semi-log)
5. $\log Y = a - b.1/x$ (Log-inverse)
6. $\log Y = a + b \log x - c.1/x$ (Log-log-inverse)
7. $\log Y = a + b \log x$ (Log linear)
8. $\log Y = a + b \log x - C (\log x)^2$ (Log-quadratic)

Where

Y is the expenditure on a particular commodity;
x is the total expenditure both in per capita terms;
a is the intercept term
b and *c* are the regression parameters.

The examination of alternative, regression forms can be regarded as testing between alternative hypothesis about the income elasticity or the marginal propensity to consume. From this point of view, forms (1) linear and (7) log-linear are equivalent to the hypothesis that the marginal propensity to consume is constant. Forms (3) hyperbolic and (5) the log-inverse are equivalent, respectively, to the hypothesis that marginal propensity to consume varies inversely with income and that its logarithm varics inversely with income. Form (4) semi-log implies that income elasticity is proportional to the logarithms of total income and that changes in it are expected to be gradual. Similarly, form (6) log-log inverse implies that it varies with log of income and is inversely proportional to income. Forms (2) Quadratic and (8) log-quadratic, on the other hand, are equivalent to the hypothesis that the marginal propensity to consume varies following a parabolic path with respect to income.

It is difficult to choose between the above hypotheses on *a priori* grounds. Almost all of them have some advantages as well as disadvantages. For example, linear hypothesis implies that income elasticity of all goods tend to unity as income increases, and this may be unreasonable. The double-log, log-inverse and log-quadratic have the disadvantage that these pass through the origin and thus do not give an initial income. Log forms also lead to difficulties in the treatment of households that do not have expenditure on the commodity. Semi-log form has also been extensively used but it neither agrees with the theory nor has it any provision for saturation. However, it has the positive income below which the commodity is not consumed. The hyperbolic form allows the investigation of a saturation level in its simplest form while the log-inverse has a sigmoid shape and passes through the origin. The only difference between log and log-quadratic is that the addition of second term modifies the slope of the curve.

Keeping these points in view we have experimented with all the eight forms discussed above and rejected all those functions whose coefficient of determination (R^2) was not significant at one per cent level of significance. For this purpose, F-test has been used. All the functions which satisfy F-test have been tested for linearity of the fit by calculating $D - W$ statistics. Out of the functional forms which satisfy both these tests the one which gives the highest R^2 and higher t-values for the parameters have been preferred. Economic plausibility and comparative prevalence of the selected function in economic literature have been our other considerations.

In our family budget data we have only expenditure data on various commodities and groups of commodities. Therefore, monthly per capita expenditure on each commodity has been used as dependent variable. Even otherwise, since we have considered some composite commodities and groups, taking expenditure rather than quantity has a distinct advantage. As regards the determining variable, total expenditure is used and not income.. Since the income of wage labour and other non-cultivating households from wages has been arrived at by blowing up weekly income from wage labour and this component is quite large in their total incomes, therefore, recorded income in our case is likely to include transistory and unexpected elements which are not very relevant for spending decisions. Even otherwise this stand is justified on the ground that while total expenditure may depend in a complicated way on income — past, present and expected, etc. — the allocation of expenditure among the various commodities depend on the level of total expenditure.

Effects of variation in household size are taken care of by assuming that the homogeneity hypothesis holds good that consumption per person depends only on the level of expenditure per person. This is done by taking both the figures for total expenditure and that for expenditure on particular commodity in per capita terms. To take care of the poor positive response for certain items, the households, in our sample for each region and State, have been divided into 15 expenditure classes on the basis of per capita expenditure. Altogether 14 commodities and commodity groups have been studied. The results obtained by using plausible Engel functions for each commodity are discussed in Section II of Chapter 6.

To explore the question of unemployment-poverty nexus, i.e., to see whether poverty of wage labourers is largely because of unemployment, we take the percentage of wage labour households below the poverty line for a cross section of 22 districts of Punjab and Haryana and try to relate it with person-days rate of unemployment prevailing among wage labour households of various districts. To see the association between the two series we have used the method of correlation as discussed earlier. In the second exercise, instead of proportion of households below the poverty line we take per capita monthly expenditure of wage labour households for different districts and try to relate with unemployment prevailing among different districts of Punjab and Haryana. Since in neither of the cases the relationship turns out to be significant, in the third exercise we try to explore the determinant of poverty prevailing among wage labour households of Punjab and Haryana by using regression analysis. The results obtained are discussed in the Chapter 7.

NOTES

1. Since published in the form of a book, see, G.S. Bhalla and G.K. Chadha (1983). '*Green Revolution and the Small Peasant*, Concept Publishing Company, New Delhi.
2. I am thankful to Prof. G.S. Bhalla for allowing me to use this data for the purpose of the present study.
3. For details of the methodology followed by NSS in the selection of villages in 30th round see, Government of India (1979), *Sarvekshana*, II, 4, April, pp. 135-39.
4. Raj Krishna (1976): "Rural Unemployment — A Survey of Concept and Estimates for India", *World Bank Staff Working Paper No. 234*, April, Table 7, p. 28.
5. A detailed review of Indian studies on poverty is given in Chapter 6, Section III of our study.
6. Pranab K. Bardhan (1970): "On the Minimum Level of Living and the Rural Poor", *Indian Economic Review*, 5, (New Series), April, pp. 126-36.
7. V.M. Dandekar and Nilkantha Rath (1971): "Poverty in India" *Economic and Political Weekly*, Bombay, 6, 1 and 2, January 2 and 9.
8. *Ibid.*

9. B.S. Minhas (1970): "Rural Poverty, Land Redistribution and Development Strategy: Facts and Policy", *Indian Economic Review*, V, (New Series), April, p. 128.
10. See *RBI Bulletin*, July 1977, p. 5415.
11. See for example H.S. Sidhu (1980): "Technological Change in Agriculture and Income Distribution — A Regional Analysis of Haryana" M.Phil Dissertation of School of Social Science, J.N.U., New Delhi, pp. 62-74.
12. A detailed discussion of the model is given in Chapter 5, Section II.

4

EMPLOYMENT/UNEMPLOYMENT AND AGRICULTURAL GROWTH

IN THIS chapter, we propose to study the rates of work participation of male and female wage labourers and the extent of unemployment and under-employment prevailing among them in Punjab and Haryana. We shall try to analyse the impact of new agricultural technology as reflected in agricultural productivity per acre on rates of participation, particularly female participation, attached-casual composition of labour, the availability of work to wage labourers and the extent of unemployment and under-employment prevailing among wage labourers. Throughout the chapter the analysis has been carried out at the district level. For this purpose, 22 districts of Punjab and Haryana have been used as number of observations.

This chapter is divided into three section. In Section I, concepts of unemployment, under-employment and disguised unemployment as used in the existing literature have been clarified and different criteria of measuring them are discussed. Various estimates of the magnitude of unemployment, under-employment and surplus labour prevailing in rural India are also presented here. Some important studies on other allied topics, like, factors effecting rates of participation, particularly female participation, are also briefly reviewed in this section. In Section II we briefly discuss how we have measured unemployment in the present study and present our results. In Section III, an attempt has been made to identify the factors which explain the inter-district variations in the rate of unemployment prevailing among wage labour households of Punjab and Haryana.

I

Unemployment and Under-employment: Concepts and Measurement — A Review

It is generally believed that there prevails a widespread unemployment and under-employment in over-populated under-developed countries, but there is no concensus on the question of magnitude of this problem. Partly, this confusion has arisen because of differences over the meaning of the concept of unemployment. Generally speaking the term unemployment denotes a condition of joblessness at the current wage rate. Where this joblessness is caused by the incapacity of the economic system it is called involuntary unemployment. Thus, in the field of economic analysis as the term unemployment is generally understood, it means involuntary unemployment only. Therefore, unemployment is usually defined as a situation in which men though willing to work at a certain minimum subsistence real wage fail to get it.

Two main sources of nation-wide data on unemployment in India are the Decennial Censuses and the National Sample Surveys. According to 1961 Census some regular work of more than one hour a day is required throughout the greater part of the working season for seasonal occupations to qualify as employed, and an employment for "15 days precedings the day you visit the household" for qualifying to be employed in non-seasonal occupations.[1] The NSS qualifies a person as employed if he or she had worked on any one day in the reference week.[2] The census included only those seeking work in the labour force while the NSS required either seeking or available for work. Thus the census and particularly NSS's basic approach is a labour force approach which combines time, income and willingness criteria and takes note of the recognition aspect. It requires two conditions to be fulfilled for qualifying a person to be treated as unemployed, viz., (a) the person must be in need of employment which he overtly or covertly recognises, i.e., he must seek a job or he must be available for one; and (b) the person must be without employment involuntarily.

The figures of unemployment yielded by Census and NSS surveys, however, are very low, which seemed to be in contrast to the widely held belief of abundant labour. It was 0.5 per cent for rural males and 0.1 per cent for rural females, according to 1961 Census. Because of slightly broader definition of unemployment adopted by NSS, its estimates of unemployment for 16th (1960-61) and 17th (1961-62) rounds are slightly higher than that of Census, being 2.59 and 3.74 per cent, respectively, for rural males and 6.49 and 8.53 per cent for rural females.[3] There was so much criticism of the estimates of unemployment yielded by these agencies that by late 1960s the authorities responsible for collecting data on unemployment decided to withdraw temporarily. The Census opted out of counting the unemployment in its 1971 enumeration and NSS discontinued its rural labour survey from the 17th round on the grounds that the concept of unemployment, as the concept is generally understood, was not applicable to rural areas. It was thought that the whole matter should go before a body of experts for more light. Thus, the 'Committee of Experts on Unemployment Estimates' was appointed under the Chairmanship of Prof. M.L. Dantwala.

Dantwala Committee was critical of the existing data on unemployment and the methodology used for obtaining it. It questioned the validity of the concept of labour force in the Indian socio-economic situation pointing out that even a distinction between 'job seeking' and availability for work, introduced by the NSS, did not overcome the basic difficulties which lie in sizable proportion of labour being involved in self-employed household activity. The Committee felt that the practice of estimating growth in the labour force and employment, generated in the Plans and under-employment, in one dimensional magnitudes should be given up as they are neither meaningful nor useful. Its recommendation, therefore, was "estimation of different segments of the labour force taking into account such important characteristics as region (State), sex, age, rural/urban residence, status of class of workers and educational attainment."[4]

The Committee also objected to the definition being used by NSS to identify a person as unemployed. According to the NSS definition, as noted earlier, in rural areas only those who are unable to get work even on a single day, during the reference week, are classified as unemployed. On the other hand, the definition of NSS for urban areas was that such person should not only be unable to get work in the reference period but also be seeking work. The Committee noted that the NSS "criteria for distinguishing between 'employed' and 'unemployed' would have a tendency to under-estimate the degree of unemployment actually prevailing."[5] To overcome this problem to some extent the Committee recommended that the respondent's activity on each day of the reference week be recorded whether he is employed during the week or not at all. This, the Committee felt, should result in the measurement in terms of the number of days the respondents are unemployed, expressed as a proportion of the number of days on which the respondents report themselves to be in the labour force.[6]

However, in a subsequent study based on the preliminary data from the 25th round of the NSS, Dantwala himself remarked that the data suggest that *prima facie* "the problem of unemployment in rural areas is not serious; perhaps we are yet unable to fathom the situation."[7] This statement of Dantwala is significant because some important changes in the procedure in line with the Dantwala Committee's recommendations were incorporated in the 25th round of NSS.

Raj Krishna (1973) in an illuminating article identifies four major criteria by which a person may be identified as employed or unemployed. A person may be called as unemployed or under-employed if either

(i) he is gainfully occupied during the year for a number of hours (or days) less than some normal or optimal hours (or days) defined as full employment hours (or days); or
(ii) he earns an income per year less than some desirable minimum; or
(iii) he is willing to do more work than he is doing at present. He may either be actively searching for more work or he is available for more work if it is offered on terms to which he is accustomed; or
(iv) he is removable from his present employment in the sense that his contribution to output is less than some normal productivity and, therefore, his removal would not reduce output if the productivity of the remaining workers is normalised with minor change in technique and/or organisation.[8]

He points out that most of the controversies about definitions of unemployment has arisen because of a strange desire to seek, defend or use a single criterion which may be useful for all purposes. He, however, argues that there is absolutely no need to have single measure and that we can have three or four estimates of unemployment for the same population because each one of these estimates will have its own utility in that each answers an important but different policy question. If, however, we are forced to choose a single category which approximates most closely to the state of unemployment, he recommends to choose the category of those who are idle and willing to work more.[9] Thus, in Raj Krishna's view the basic NSS approach of labour force survey, which is a combination of time and willingness criterion, is the correct approach.

Some studies have also used income alone as criterion of measuring unemployment. For example, Dandekar and Rath (1971) have abandoned the time criterion altogether. They have not only taken poverty as a consequence of unemployment but, in fact, rejected the distinction between poverty considered as a level of consumption below a certain minimum and unemployment considered as an involuntary failure to get income yielding work for the normal number of working days in a year. Their contention is that an adequate level of employment must be defined in terms of its capacity to provide minimum living to the population.[10] They observe that the poverty of at least 30 per cent of the rural population must be attributed to lack of adequate employment for its working members and they move on to convert it into its rupee equivalent and find that "if this is to be done by providing additional employment, Rs. 822.4 crores becomes the measure of the rural unemployment or under-employment prevailing at the beginning of the Fourth Plan."[11] This estimate excludes the poorest 10 per cent of the rural population on the ground that their poverty "may have to be relieved by means of special assistance rather than by providing additional employment".[12]

On the other hand, Raj Krishna (1973) on the basis of data relating to 487 male-workers from four villages of Rajasthan calculates all the seven possible estimates based on one or more of the three criteria, i.e., time, income and willingness. By taking workers who are gainfully occupied for less than 30 hours in the week as idle and those earning an income of less than Rs. 60 per month in January 1972 as 'poor', Raj Krishna maintains that "the poor (33%) are clearly more numerous than the idle (28%) and the idle more numerous than the willing (14%)" and that "only a fraction of the idle are willing to work more". Thus, he observes, "the elimination of poverty is a much more gigantic undertaking than the elimination of the idleness of those who are available for additional work. Any attempt to identify the two by definition cannot help the policy-makers".[13]

Sen (1973), however, argues that we cannot do without an income concept in the study of unemployment even if we reject the definition of an unemployed person in the Dandekar and Rath sense, i.e., unemployed as a person who earns an income per year less than some desirable minimum.[14] He feels, "poverty may be an odd measure of unemployment but to catch one important dimension of the problem of unemployment we do need some income criterion, in addition to the criteria based on time, willingness and productivity".[15]

Bhatty (1973) takes Sen's argument of taking income as an important aspect of measuring unemployment/under-employment still further and argues that in situations of the kind we have in rural economy where two-thirds of the rural workers are self-employed and function primarily as an integrated part of the household to which they belong, a more useful and appropriate approach towards understanding the nature of employment and extent of under-employment would be an emphasis upon what he calls the "effectiveness of employment of the household".[16] He argues that the household operates as a unified productive enterprise having command over certain resources of which family labour is perhaps the most important and that it would be meaningless to conceive of employment or unemployment without reckoning with integrated entity of the household. The household labour is thus committed labour and the effectiveness of its use depends far more on the other resources of the household with which it combines in self-employed activity than on the total number of days or hours it is physically engaged in work. Thus, Bhatty argues, "one should treat household as a composite unit representing a combination of resources at any time, where a proper measure of the effectiveness with which the household (or household labour) is employed ought, obviously, to be derived from, what is produced by the household or, more precisely, from the value added by it. An immediate advantage of such a measure", he argues, "will be that it will directly link employment (not unemployment) with poverty which is the basic problem and not with unemployment, for, in India, it is possible to be employed and be poor".[17]

Perhaps the best attempt to estimate the sectoral employment by using effectiveness of employment as criterion and separating effective employment from employment which does not provide a minimum level of living at the all-India level is by Alagh (1979).[18] He defines effective employment as the one "which permits the worker (or workers of household as the case may be) to earn an income or maintain an expenditure level above poverty level," where, "poverty level expenditure is defined as Rs. 18 per month per capita for the rural population in 1960-61 price and Rs. 22.5 per month per capita in 1960-61 price for the urban population". Using this definition of poverty line, Alagh estimates that only 15 per cent of agricultural labour and small farmers (those operating holdings less than two hectares) are effectively employed.[19]

S.K. Rao (1973), however, feels that while this income criterion undoubtedly has the merit of getting around the problem of disproving with that component of labour time which in survey appears as gainfully spent but which is in fact production unemployment (we shall discuss this point a little later) but feels that it contains an opposite error, namely, it might include the class of people who are employed for very long hours but nevertheless earn very little income because the wage rates are low.[20] For example, using the same data of 487 male-workers in Rajasthan villages, as used by Raj Krishna (1973), Rao estimates that nearly one-fourth of the workers, who were working for more than 36 hours a week, nevertheless managed to earn less than two rupees a day. Assuming that each one of these male-workers had a family of five and that the wife earned half the male-worker's earnings, their monthly per capita income will be below Rs. 18 in January 1972, which falls below the poverty line of Rs. 15 at 1960-61 prices. Consequently, Dandekar and Rath method would have included these people in the estimated unemployed despite the fact that their income was low not because they were unemployed or under-employed but because the wage rates were low and employment was not self-created but was offered in the market. Similar results are also suggested by the 15th and the 16th rounds of the NSS.[21] Therefore, Rao concludes,

> "the Dandekar-Rath method yields an estimate which is a hotch-potch of the unemployed, under-employed and the poor and it has no clear meaning in the context of employment policy. Properly speaking, it is an estimate of the poor and on the basis of it one cannot go to say how much additional employment needs to be created at the going wage rate to relieve poverty, for some of the poor were poor not because they were under-employed but because

the wage rates were not high enough."[22]

There is, however, near unanimity that the concept of employment has to be related to some notion of the value of work. This is the production aspect of employment or the productivity criterion, to use Raj Krishna's terminology. According to this criterion a person may be called unemployed or under-employed if he is removable from his present employment and his removal would not reduce the total output. Consideration of this criterion also leads us to the whole question of disguised unemployment, that is, a person may seem to be working or is in fact working but his net contribution to total output is zero. The term disguised unemployment was coined by Joan Robinson in 1936 to describe a situation in the context of developed countries where workers accepted inferior occupations as a result of being laid off from industries due to the lack of effective demand.[23] Obviously, she was referring to workers having low rather than zero marginal product of labour. However, the latter debate on disguised unemployment have entirely centred around its existence in peasant economies where the wage system is weak and self-employed and family labour are common.

Studies by Buck (1930)[24], Warriner (1939)[25] and Rosenstein-Rodan (1943)[26] in the 1930s and 1940s for China and Eastern and South-Eastern Europe suggested that a large percentage of agricultural labour was idle for substantial part of the year in these areas. It was estimated that between 20 and 27 per cent of active rural workers in Greece, Yugoslavia, Poland, Hungary, Rumania and Bulgaria were redundant. This view also found expression in a United Nations report by a group of experts which points out,

> "It seems safe to assume that for many regions of India, Pakistan and for certain parts of Philippines and Indonesia, the surplus (rural population) cannot be less than the pre-war average for the Eastern European region".[27]

Nurkse (1953) was perhaps the first person to concretise the notion of surplus labour into a theory of development. He pointed out

> "Underdeveloped countries suffer from large-scale disguised unemployment in the sense that even with unchanged technique of

agriculture a large part of the population engaged in agriculture could be removed without reducing agricultural output."[28]

He argued that "in technical terms the marginal productivity of labour over a wide range is zero". This could explain why a reduction in the use of labour would not affect output. The idea that there was an excess of labour supply in agriculture and that it could be removed without any loss in output has also been discussed by Lewis (1954),[29] Rosenstein-Rodan (1957)[30] and Leibenstein (1959).[31]

But the question arises if marginal productivity of labour is zero over a wide range, as Nurkse puts it, then why the labour is being applied at all over this wide range? There would seem to be something unnatural in such behaviour. Sen (1960) argues that the answer to this question lies in the distinction between labour time and the number of labourers. It is not that too much labour is being spent in the production process but that too many labourers are spending it.[32] For example if a household with six workers is producing output *X* in 30 hours, each labour working for five hours a day, now if a labour is withdrawn, the other things remaining the same, 30 hours of work must continue to be done in order to produce *X* output. To do this it would be necessary for the remaining five workers to work for six hours a day. Per worker labour input as well as output would increase, though there would be a decrease in the number of workers.

If for some reason the remaining workers were not prepared to work for the additional hour the output would fall. This would mean that marginal product of labour was not zero. Surplus labour theory, therefore, postulated some organisational changes in the production system. Rosenstein-Rodan (1957), however, argued that the organisational changes must be minimal in character so that it is compatible with static assumptions. Thus, change was regarded as a sort of adjustment. However, considerable difficulties arose when he applied the minimum change notion to an empirical measure of surplus labour because the permissible minimum change could not be defined. Ultimately he simply resorted to a purely subjective judgement that the self-employed who worked for less than 50 days in a year were really surplus. But he gave no justification for this nor did he think it was necessary. Clearly the problem was that labour, when measured in man-hours, did not have zero marginal product but it was assumed that the work of *X* number of workers could be done by fewer number of workers and, therefore, some workers could be withdrawn from this sector for work in other sectors. Therefore, in the later discussion of surplus labour the assumption of *cetris paribus* was dropped and the reduction of labour meant *mutatis-mutandis* withdrawal.

Warriner and Schultz in the meantime, however, reversed their earlier position and attacked the concept of disguised unemployment. Warriner who, in her earlier study on land and poverty in the Middle East,[33] had shown that 50 per cent of the Egyptian rural population was surplus now took the position that she had "omitted the labour requirement for capital maintenance in agriculture".[34] Schultz cited examples from Latin American countries where the removal of agricultural labour resulted in a decline in agricultural output and argued that on a broader scale "I know of no evidence for any poor country anywhere that would even suggest that a transfer of some small fraction, say five per cent of the existing labour force out of agriculture with other things equal, could be made without reducing its (agricultural) production."[35]

Similarly, Viner (1957) argued that marginal product of labour in agriculture can hardly fall to zero.[36] The existence of a positive wage everywhere in these countries also seemed to challenge the theory of zero marginal productivity. The wage rate according to classical theory should be equal to the marginal product. If the marginal product is zero, the wage should also be zero. Lewis argued that though the marginal product was zero, the average product was not and it was this that determined wage in traditional societies and made the worker to work. Similarly, Nurkse asserted that in traditional societies wages were institutionally determined and not by market forces. Explanations of certain other questions, like, why workers should continue to work if they are not producing anything? What is the incentive for remaining workers to work harder after some workers are withdrawn so that the total amount of work done does not decrease? And how, after removal of some workers from the disguised unemployment sector, total production not only would not fall but might even increase, were put forward by many others, like, Eckaus (1955),[37] Leibenstein (1957),[38] Mellor and Stevens (1956),[39] Sen (1960),[40] Wonnacott (1962),[41] Georgescu-Roegen (1963),[42] Myint (1964),[43] Prasad (1970)[44] and Sen (1975)[45] but doubts about zero marginal product of labour continued to be raised.

Meanwhile, there have been a vigorous debate on the detailed empirical evidence in favour of or against the thesis of disguised unemployment. Some researchers, like, Mellor and Stevens (1956),[46] Sarkar (1957),[47] Mehra (1966),[48] Sanghavi (1966),[49] Rudra (1973)[50] and Kanta Ahuja (1975),[51] have found evidence of its existence in varying degrees depending upon the assumptions made etc., while others, like, Oshima (1958),[52] Schultz (1964),[53] Hansen (1966)[54] and Jorgenson (1976)[55] have presented evidence to the contrary.

Broadly speaking, two methods are available to measure the disguised unemployment. First method is to estimate directly the marginal productivity of labour through production function technique. Most of the studies using this technique have, however, found marginal productivity of labour to be not only positive but usually higher than the wage rate for hired labour. Studies, like, Rao (1965),[56] Saini (1969)[57] and Bardhan (1973),[58] fall in this category. The labour input in these studies was defined as actual labour time used. As Raj Krishna (1973) pointed out,

> "if this is done the marginal productivity must turn out to be positive. It is only when the labour input is defined as the entire labour force dependent on agriculture that there is some chance of its marginal productivity turning up as zero in a production function. Most of the production function analyses have shown little awareness of the difference between these two definitions of the labour input although it is critical for testing the hypothesis of zero marginal productivity".[59]

The second method is an indirect one in the sense that the difference between the labour time required and the labour time actually available from the active agrarian population with some normative standards of working time per person is calculated and the surplus time is converted into number of surplus workers using the same norm as initially used to calculate the total labour supply. Most of the studies of disguised unemployment belong to this category. Among the earlier Indian studies in this category, mention may be made to Tarlok Singh (1945),[60] Sovani (1959),[61] Majumdar (1961),[62] Bhattacharjee (1961),[63] and Quayum (1962).[64] These studies concluded that a substantial proportion of rural working force was disguisedly unemployed.

A lively controversy about the existence of surplus labour in India was further revived by the famous study of Theodore Schultz (1964) who examined the relationship between agricultural output (measured by taking acreage as a proxy) and the change in agricultural labour force as a result of the influenza epidemic of 1918-19 when about five per cent of the total population of Indian sub-continent died.[65] Schultz estimated the existence of disguised employment by comparing the reduction in acreage sown with the reduction in the labour force. Such a comparison assumes that if disguised unemployment exists, the acreage sown will be reduced as a result of a sudden reduction in the labour force. The estimate of reduction in the labour force differs but Schultz accepted a figure of 8.3 per cent reduction in the labour force for the provinces he studied. Taking a labour coefficient of 0.4, he argued, if there was no surplus labour force in agriculture, reduction of this magnitude of labour force would lead to 3.3 per cent reduction in the area sown. From his data he observed "the area sown in 1919-20 was, however, 10 million acres below, or 3.8 per cent less, than that of the base year 1916-17. In general, the provinces of India that had the highest death rate due to epidemic also had the largest percentage decline in acreage sown to crops". He, therefore, concluded "it would be hard to find any support in these data for the doctrine that a part of the labour force in agriculture in India at the time of the epidemic had a marginal product of zero".[66]

Several objections were raised on Schultz's study, most notable amongst them being by Mehra (1966)[67] and Sen (1967).[68] Despite its shortcomings, Schultz's study set the ball of controversy, about the existence of disguised unemployment, rolling once again. A number of studies appeared in late 1960s and 1970s on the subject most well known amongst them being Mehra (1966),[69] Rudra (1973)[70] and Ahuja (1978).[71] Mehra's approach is based on the idea that in family farms the shortage of productive work is shared by all and takes the form of a smaller amount of work per head. She treats output as function of all factors of production including labour time and considers withdrawal of labour keeping all factors, including labour time, constant. Her estimates are based on farm management data for the year 1956-57. Farm management data show that there are considerable variations in the amount of work done per person by different size classes of farms. Mehra assumed that the largest farms would be having the highest amount of work time per cultivator and would have no surplus at all. Taking work done per person in the largest category as the norm,

Mehra calculated the number of people in other farms who would be released if the cultivators there could work for the same amount of time per head as the cultivators in the non-surplus category. On this basis, she estimated 29.1 per cent of the work force in Indian agriculture as surplus in the reference year. This she called uncorrected maximal estimate. Since people are indivisible and a fraction of a person being surplus on a farm does not allow anyone to be withdrawn, in her second estimate she added one person per farm to the 'required' work force in all such cases and arrived at a surplus figure of 6.4 per cent. This she calls the 'minimal estimate' of surplus labour. The actual surplus will, of course, be larger than the minimal estimate and will be somewhere between these minimal estimates and the uncorrected maximal estimates. Thus, she arrived at the mean figure of 17 per cent for the country as a whole, which is indeed a high ratio compared to the NSS and Census estimates of unemployment.

In Mehra's methodology the estimate of surplus labour depends on the extent to which large farms have a higher intensity of effort per person employed. If, however, in some States this assumption does not hold and the highest effort per person is not in the largest size group but in some other category then the estimate of surplus labour for these States, in Mehra's calculations, will be an underestimate. Sen (1975) points out that this is, in fact, the case for States of Maharashtra, Andhra Pradesh, Gujarat, Madhya Pradesh and Kerala and for this reason the first three States, in fact, end up yielding negative volumes or surplus labour in Mehra's calculations, which she treats as zero on the ground that the available labour force is, in fact, producing the existing output. Sen calculates that if one chooses the activity norm not from the largest holding size class, but from the size group which in fact, happens to have the highest intensity of activity then the surplus labour figure has to be revised upward for these five States and for India as a whole this would add another 4.6 per cent of the work force to the total size of surplus labour thereby taking the uncorrected percentage of disguised unemployment to a staggering 33.7 per cent of the rural labour force.[72]

Rudra's study to estimate surplus labour is based on the sample survey of 148 farms in the Hooghly district of West Bengal and relates to the year 1970-71. Rudra calculates the amount of labour put in by 265 adult males of these farms and finds that only 108 male adults would be required to do that, if all of them worked for 2,400 hours a year. Therefore, 157 males or 59 per cent of the total number can be counted as surplus workers. But in order to cope with 15,360 hours of peak season work within 10 days, 192 males would be needed. Therefore, even after providing for the peak season work load, 73 male workers or 27.5 per cent of the total number could be released. It should be noted that, like, Mehra, Rudra also keeps the labour time required and hence the technology and organisation of production unchanged. However, Rudra's definition of work is more stringent. Rudra defines farm work as "manual labour on actual farming operations (preparatory tillage, sowing, interculature and harvesting) thus leaving out all supervisory work, all work connected with business aspects of farming (sale and purchase of crops and raw materials, obtaining and managing financial resources, procuring of crops after the harvest stage, transportation of crops and raw materials, etc.)[73] To the extent time on these things, left out by Rudra, is necessary for maintaining present level of output, his estimate of surplus labour is biased upward.

In Ahuja's calculations of surplus labour in the agriculture of Rajasthan surplus labour time is calculated instead of the number of surplus workers. For calculating available labour time, Ahuja takes a norm of 300 days of eight hours' work for male workers and 225 days of eight hours' work for female workers. The required labour time is calculated on the basis of person-days per hectare and per animal estimated from Farm Management Studies with suitable adjustments. On these assumptions, Ahuja concludes that surplus labour time as a proportion of available time would be only 3.2 per cent in Rajasthan as a whole in 1970-71. Fourteen out of 26 districts had a surplus labour ratio of 11.4 per cent and 12 districts had a labour deficit of 8.2 per cent. Season-wise break down of the labour surplus reveals that in kharif season the deficit was 26 per cent and in the rabi season the surplus was 33 per cent. One would note a striking difference between Mehra's estimates of surplus labour for Rajasthan and that of Ahuja's estimates. Whereas in Mehra's study even the minimal estimate for Rajasthan was 20.5 per cent (the uncorrected maximal being 50.9 per cent), according to Ahuja's calculations it is only 3.2 per cent. One possible reason is that in Mehra's study the labour requirement per acre is determined by the actual labour used by the biggest size farm, but it is a more or less established fact that the intensity of farming in the small farms is higher than the intensity on the large farms, therefore, Mehra's methodology would result in a relatively higher estimate of the surplus. But the more important difference seems to lie in the very definition of work itself. Whereas Mehra's study is based on Farm Management Data which excludes the labour utilisation in the upkeep and maintenance of cattle as well as labour required for allied field-work, Ahuja's detailed analysis of labour time disposition of farm households show that agricultural work, including allied activity and supervision but excluding livestock maintenance, does not account for more than 60 per cent of work actually performed. It is not surprising, therefore, that Mehra and Ahuja's estimates of surplus labour in rural Rajasthan differ so widely.[74]

Apart from the studies on unemployment/under-employment and surplus labour discussed above, certain allied topics, like, factors effecting the participation rates, particularly female participation rates; labour force projections, impact of likely population growth on the size of the labour force; and its implications in terms of investment in various sectors to create employment opportunities at a rate adequate to absorb net additions to the labour force, have also attracted attention of some scholars. Most of the studies on participation rates are based on Census data though some are also based on NSS data. For example, Khan (1963)[75] tried to reconcile the participation rates calculated from various Censuses. Sinha (1964) observed that the trend in India, excluding the three States of Andhra Pradesh, Madras and Mysore, was more stable and did not indicate any significant rise in the participation rates between 1951 and 1961.[76] Visaria (1965), however, pointed out that the younger age distribution of the 1961 population would have resulted in a lower participation rate even for males and, therefore, even the stable participation rate in India suggests some undercount of workers in 1951.[77] Ambannavar (1969) examined the historical census data and suggested that wide fluctuations in the ratio of workers to adults reflect varying coverage of workers in different censuses.

However, inter-district or inter-State difference in the participation rates for any Census or Inter-Census changes are more pronounced in the case of females than in the case of males. This is because of the fact that in almost all societies a very large majority of able-bodied men in the working age group participate in economic activity. The female work participation rate, on the other hand, is influenced by a large number of complex factors, such as age composition of the population, its educational attainments, marital status, number of young children needing attention from mothers, social arrangements and, above all, the demand for labour and the opportunities for combining participation in economic activity with other roles to perform. Naturally, therefore, larger number of studies on participation rates are directed towards explaining the factors affecting the female work participation rates.

Namboodri (1956),[78] Sinha (1965),[79] Chandra (1967)[80] and Visaria (1970)[81] have tried to examine the causes behind variations in female work participation rates. Namboodri attempted to examine the inter-district differences in participation rates in terms of their association with the extent of urbanization, the sex ratio, the literacy rate and density of population. Sinha (1965), on the basis of percentage of earners to population and annual per family income reported for various States in the First Agricultural Labour Inquiry 1951, found an inverse association between income and labour force participation rates of women. However, data from 9th round of the NSS (August-November 1955) suggest a U-shaped relationship between the labour force participation rate of rural females and per capita expenditure which can be taken as proxy of income. An inverse relationship can be inferred if the highest per capita expenditure group of persons is excluded from consideration on the ground that the number of persons in the sample in the relevant group was exceedingly small. Among rural males, however, the work participation rates and per capita expenditure show a positive relationship. Visaria (1970) found wide variations in female work participation rates of different States and that within each State the rate is generally higher for scheduled tribes than for scheduled castes and both of them being significantly higher than the rates for the non-Scheduled females. Chandra (1967) tried to go into the reasons behind variations in female participation rates and pointed out that very low female participation rates in the Gangetic and Trans-Gangetic plains in Northern India are due to cultural factors associated partly with the influence of religion and the impact of invasions which have restricted the freedom and mobility of females. However, many students view the census data on the subject with scepticism and it is argued that the female work participation rates reported by the census even for neighbouring villages with similar cropping patterns vary substantially.

Some scholars have also tried to project the likely growth in labour force over time and financial implications of creating employment opportunities in various sectors under alternative assumptions. The main conclusions of these exercises has been to highlight the difficulty of accelerating the growth of non-agricultural employment opportunities at a rate adequate to absorb the net additions to the labour force in the non-agricultural sector in order to bring about a significant reduction in the proportion of workers engaged in agriculture.[82]

II

In this section we shall discuss our results obtained from primary data regarding rate of participation, attached casual composition of labour and extent of unemployment and under-employment prevailing among wage labourers of different districts of Punjab and Haryana. We shall try to analyse impact of new agricultural technology as reflected in productivity per acre on these variables to see how agricultural development of the region has effected them. Specifically, we shall be testing the following hypotheses :

(i) The rate of male participation is positively related to the level of agricultural development of the region whereas the relationship is inverse in the case of female labourer.
(ii) The proportion of tied labour in total wage labourers is positively related with the level of agricultural development of the region.
(iii) The rate of unemployment and under-employment prevailing among wage labourers is inversely related with the level of agricultural development of the region.

Before presenting our results, however, we shall briefly discuss the criterion used in the present study to measure unemployment. Since we have used both the stock and flow concept of unemployment to avoid any confusion, we shall also clearly define these two concepts here.

Concept of Unemployment

Our discussion of the concept of unemployment in the preceding section, as used by various scholars, reveals that time, income willingness and productivity or a combination of two or more of these criteria have been used to measure unemployment. As argued in

Chapter 3, we have used time criterion to measure unemployment in the present study.

Stock and Flow Concept

In measuring the rate of unemployment by time criterion what we essentially do is that we measure the demand for and supply of labour and then divide the difference between supply and demand by the labour supplied. When labour is measured as a flow of labour, for instance, like so many hours of labour offered/demanded per day or so many days of labour offered/demanded per week, etc., it is essential to remember that not only labour is being measured in terms of labour time but it is also being measured as flow per unit of time. Alternatively, we can measure labour not as a flow of labour time but as stock of persons at a particular point of time. Therefore, when we say that one out of 10 workers did not find any work at all during the reference week and, therefore, the weekly status unemployment rate is 10 per cent, what we are essentially referring to is the stock rate of unemployment during the reference week. But when we say that all the 10 labourers who worked during the reference week, worked for a total of 45 man-days in the reference week whereas they were willing to work or were available for work (i.e., total labour supply) for 60 man-days and hence the person-days rate of unemployment during the reference week is 25 per cent, the concept we are using is the flow concept of employment. We have used both these concepts in our study. Our unemployment estimates during the reference week or what we call as weekly status unemployment rate is a stock concept whereas our person-days rate of unemployment is a flow concept. This difference should be kept in mind while interpreting the results.

Rate of Participation

Rate of participation refers to the ratio of persons in the labour force to the total population expressed as per cent. Labour force here is defined to include all such persons which are economically active. It includes all persons who actually work for production of good and/or services for exchange (i.e., the employed) and those who although not working want to do so or seek an opportunity to do so (i.e., the unemployed). Thus, the labour force in our study is the inventory of persons who constitute the economically active population, i.e., who seek work or are available for work and no attempt has been made to differentiate them in terms of the intensity with which they work or would want to work.

We have calculated two types of rate of participation for male, female and all persons. First set of rate of participation takes into account all adults, – male or female. All persons who have attained the age of 15 years have been defined as adults. The second set of participation rate relates to the working age group only. The age group of 15 to 59, i.e., all those who have completed 15 years of age but have not yet attained the age of 60 years, has been defined as working age group. The first set of all adults has been used because no specific upper age limit is relevant in the case of rural wage labourers. Unlike urban industrial workers they do not cease to participate in work just because they have attained a specific age. However, most of the empirical studies in India, including those based on NSS data, use the category of working age group of 15-59. Therefore, to make our results comparable with other studies we have also calculated rates of work participation for this specific age group separately.

Tables 4.1 and 4.2 give rates of participation for males, females and all persons for different districts of Punjab and Haryana for all adults and for working age group separately. As is expected, the rate of participation, both for males and females, is usually higher by about three to five per cent in the working age group of 15-59 as compared to all adults. Whether we consider the set of all adults or working age group only, a very high proportion of adult male participate in work. About 86 per cent of all adult male and 89.24 per cent of those in the working age group in Punjab participate in work. The figures for Haryana are slightly lower, being 85.09 per cent for all adults and 88 per cent for the working age group. The inter-district variations in the case of male participation are not very large. Barring Amritsar district, which has unusually high rate of work participation in all other districts of Punjab and Haryana, the rate of work participation for all adult males varies between 80 and 90 per cent.

There appears to be no systematic relationship between the level of agricultural development of the district and the rate of work participation in the case of male labourers. For example, in Punjab, Amritsar has the highest rate of work participation but in terms of level of agricultural development its productivity per acre is marginally below the State average (Productivity per acre for different districts of Punjab and Haryana is given in columns 5 of Tables 4.5 and 4.6, respectively). Similarly, Faridkot, Hoshiarpur and Ropar have below average productivity but above average rate of work participation. On the other hand, Jalandhar and Kapurthala are high productivity districts but have below average rate of work participation. But then we also have Ferozepur, Ludhiana, Patiala and Sangrur which are high productivity districts and also have above average rate of work participation whereas Bhatinda is a low productivity district and has low rate of work participation for male labourers.

TABLE 4.1: Rates of Work Participation in Punjab

Districts/ State	All adults			Working age group of 15-59		
	Males	Females	All persons	Male	Female	All persons
Amritsar	95.12	27.59	60.35	99.34	28.57	62.30
Bhatinda	80.72	2.01	43.49	89.66	2.17	47.00
Faridkot	91.06	11.11	53.68	94.69	8.91	54.21
Ferozepur	89.79	13.41	55.00	92.13	14.10	55.69
Gurdaspur	80.20	11.18	47.79	81.76	12.16	49.37
Hoshiarpur	86.31	4.20	48.55	87.23	4.88	48.86
Jalandhar	81.25	7.86	47.00	84.78	7.38	48.46
Kapurthala	80.65	8.20	44.72	90.20	9.09	48.11
Ludhina	86.54	7.41	46.23	90.91	8.16	48.96
Patiala	87.07	12.50	52.36	90.30	13.22	53.73
Ropar	86.36	13.85	50.38	87.93	14.75	50.42
Sangrur	86.16	3.37	46.25	84.87	3.55	45.73
Punjab	85.85	10.72	49.83	89.24	11.26	51.38

A more or less similar picture emerges from Haryana. There are low productivity, low rate of participation districts, like, Bhiwani and Gurgaon, and also high productivity, high rate of participation districts, like, Sonepat. But then we also have Ambala, Karnal and Kurukshetra which are high productivity districts but have below average rate of work participation. On the other hand, Jind, Hissar, Mohindergarh and Rohtak are below average productivity districts but have above average rate of work participation. Thus, on the whole there appears to be no systematic relationship between the rate of work participation by male adults and the level of agricultural development of the area. This conclusion is also borne out when we calculate correlation between the rate of work participation by all adult males and productivity per acre of the district for a cross section of 22 districts of Punjab and Haryana. The correlation coefficient works out to be 0.047 only, which is statistically insignificant. Thus, we find there is no relationship between the rate of work participation of male adults and the level of agricultural development of the area.

TABLE 4.2: Rates of Work Participation in Haryana

Districts State	All adults			Working age group of 15-59		
	Males	Females	All persons	Male	Female	All persons
Ambala	83.54	14.70	51.70	87.50	15.38	53.28
Bhiwani	81.82	73.91	78.57	83.87	73.91	79.63
Gurgaon	80.90	28.76	57.41	84.15	30.43	59.60
Hissar	85.91	44.63	67.41	87.50	45.38	68.44
Jind	88.51	8.22	51.87	88.09	8.45	51.61
Karnal	83.33	21.79	55.75	90.69	23.61	60.13
Khruksheta	85.06	12.20	49.70	86.08	12.66	49.38
Mohindergarh	87.09	42.86	66.10	90.00	42.86	67.24
Rohtak	85.33	36.50	63.04	91.18	37.29	66.14
Sonepat	88.61	41.09	65.79	90.54	42.25	66.90
Haryana	85.09	29.18	59.45	88.00	30.18	61.02

Unlike male adults, in the case of female labourers, however, there are wide variations in the rate of work participation between the two States as well as across districts within each State. For example, in Punjab, the rate of work participation in the case of female labourers is 10.72 per cent for all adult category and 11.26 per cent for the working age group of 15-59 whereas in the case of Haryana the rate of work participation by female labourers is roughly three times higher as compared to Punjab. Within each State there are large inter-district variations in female work participation rate.

Unlike males, in the case of females there appears to be a negative relationship between their work participation and level of agricultural development of the district. For example, within the two States generally the low productivity districts are showing high rate of female work participation although there are exceptions too. In Punjab, districts, like, Amritsar, Faridkot and Ropar, which have high rate of females work participation happen to be low productivity districts whereas most of the high productivity districts are having below average rate of work participation. In Haryana, the relationship appears to be even more clear. For example, the three high productivity districts of Ambala, Karnal and Kurukshetra are having below average rates of female work participation. On the other hand, all low productivity districts, like, Bhiwani, Hissar, Mohindergarh and Rohtak with the exception of Gurgaon, are having rates of female work participation well above the State average. Even the figure for Gurgaon is only marginally below the State average. When we take a cross section of all 22 districts of Punjab and Haryana there emerges a clear cut negative relationship between the rate of female work participation and level of agricultural productivity of the district. The correlation between the two works out to be -0.707 which has significance at one per cent level. Thus, we find that while there is no relationship between the rate of work participation of male labourers and the level of agricultural development of the region, there is a negative relationship between the rate of female participation and the level of agricultural development of the area as hypothesised by us.

Attached-casual Composition

Columns 2 and 3 of Tables 4.3 and 4.4 give district-wise break-up of total male workers in terms of their attached-casual composition for Punjab and Haryana, respectively. A look at these tables would reveal that about two-fifths of all male wage labourers in both Punjab and Haryana States are working as attached labourers. The rest three-fifths are working as casual labourers. Within each State, however, there are large inter-district variations in the proportion of tied labourer in total wage labourers. For example, in Punjab this proportion varies between as low as 10.49 per cent in Hoshiarpur to as high as 58.21 per cent in Sangrur. Similarly, in Haryana it varies between 11.11 per cent in Bhiwani to 52.70 per cent in Kurukshetra.

Generally, one would expect a positive relationship between the proportion of attached labour and level of agricultural development. The rationale behind this expectation is that improved agricultural technology particularly that using HYV seeds, chemical fertilizers and controlled irrigation is likely to change the duration and periodicity of agricultural crop cycle in such a way that it will increase the timeliness of each operation requiring labour at a short notice. This may raise the recruitment costs and sharpen wage peaks in the busy season. Under these circumstances, it would be preferable for employer to have relatively more attached labour to have some kind of assured labour supply during busy seasons and to avoid higher costs of casual labour during peaks. Some recent studies in the context of new agricultural technology support this hypothesis. For example, Bhalla (1976) shows

TABLE 4.3: Unemployment/Under-employment in Punjab (All Male Workers)

District/ State	Total worker	Attac-hed wo-rker	Casual worker	Fully employed	Moderat-ely under employed	Severely under employed	Unempl-oyed
	(1)	(2)	(3)	(4)	(5)	(6)	(7)
Amritsar	154	55	99	127	16	6	5
	(100.00)	(35.72)	(64.28)	(82.47)	(10.39)	(3.89)	(3.25)
Bhatinda	130	71	59	103	10	8	9
	(100.00)	(54.62)	(45.38)	(79.23)	(7.69)	(6.15)	(6.92)
Faridkot	109	51	58	83	9	10	7
	(100.00)	(46.79)	(53.21)	(76.15)	(8.26)	(9.17)	(6.42)
Ferozepur	87	46	41	65	11	5	6
	(100.00)	(52.87)	(47.13)	(74.71)	(12.64)	(5.75)	(6.90)
Gurdaspur	154	54	100	107	12	9	26
	(100.00)	(35.06)	(64.96)	(69.48)	(7.79)	(5.84)	(16.88)
Hoshiarpur	143	15	128	82	18	8	35
	(100.00)	(10.49)	(89.51)	(57.34)	(12.59)	(5.59)	(24.48)
Jalandhar	127	29	98	71	20	24	12
	(100.00)	(22.83)	(77.17)	(55.91)	(15.75)	(18.90)	(9.44)
Kapurthala	49	6	43	27	9	5	8
	(100.00)	(12.24)	(87.76)	(55.10)	(18.37)	(10.20)	(16.33)
Ludhiana	131	55	76	99	16	11	5
	(100.00)	(41.98)	(58.02)	(75.57)	(12.21)	(8.40)	(3.82)
Patiala	125	49	76	75	9	18	23
	(100.00)	(39.20)	(60.80)	(60.00)	(7.20)	(14.40)	(18.40)
Ropar	55	26	29	37	8	3	7
	(100.00)	(47.27)	(52.73)	(67.27)	(14.55)	(5.45)	(12.73)
Sangrur	134	78	56	97	16	9	12
	(100.00)	(58.21)	(41.79)	(72.39)	(11.94)	(6.72)	(8.95)
Punjab	1,398	535	863	973	154	116	155
	(100.00)	(38.27)	(61.73)	(69.60)	(11.01)	(8.30)	(11.09)

TABLE 4.4: Unemployment/Under-employment in Haryana (All Male Workers)

District/ State	Total worker	Attac- hed wo- rker	Casual worker	Fully employed	Moderat- ely under employed	Severely under employed	Unempl- oyed
	(1)	(2)	(3)	(4)	(5)	(6)	(7)
Ambala	65	44	21	54	5	1	5
	(100.00)	(67.69)	(32.31)	(83.08)	(7.69)	(1.54)	(7.69)
Bhiwani	27	3	24	16	6	0	5
	(100.00)	(11.11)	(88.89)	(59.26)	(22.22)	(0.00)	(18.52)
Gurgaon	71	21	50	55	5	5	6
	(100.00)	(29.58)	(70.42)	(77.46)	(7.04)	(7.04)	(8.45)
Hissar	128	54	74	110	12	1	5
	(100.00)	(42.19)	(57.81)	(85.94)	(9.37)	(0.78)	(3.91)
Jind	76	40	36	60	5	0	11
	(100.00)	(52.63)	(47.37)	(78.95)	(6.58)	(0.00)	(14.47)
Karnal	80	42	38	59	17	2	2
	(100.00)	(52.50)	(47.50)	(73.75)	(21.25)	(2.50)	(2.50)
Kurukshetra	74	39	35	47	14	6	7
	(100.00)	(52.70)	(47.30)	(63.51)	(18.92)	(8.11)	(9.46)
Mohindergarh	27	8	19	20	3	1	3
	(100.00)	(29.63)	(70.37)	(74.07)	(11.11)	(3.70)	(11.11)
Rohtak	64	14	50	55	3	0	6
	(100.00)	(21.87)	(78.13)	(85.94)	(4.69)	(0.00)	(9.37)
Sonepat	70	20	50	33	15	5	17
	(100.00)	(28.57)	(71.43)	(47.14)	(21.43)	(7.14)	(24.29)
Haryana	682	285	397	509	85	21	67
	(100.00)	(41.79)	(58.21)	(74.63)	(12.46)	(3.08)	(9.82)

in her study of Karnal region, the prime Green Revolution area of the State of Haryana, that compared with other less-developed regions of the same State or with the same region earlier, a much higher proportion of agricultural labourers are employed on rather long term contracts.[83] Similarly, Bardhan and Rudra (1981) in their study of West Bengal sample villages find that the proportion of tied-labour families to total farm families was almost twice as large in agriculturally more advanced villages as compared to backward villages.[84]

In our study, however, the relationship between the proportion of attached labourers and level of agricultural development of the district defined as productivity per acre (given in column number 4 of Tables 4.5 and 4.6) is not very clear. For example, in Punjab, on the one hand, we have Ferozepur, Ludhiana, Patiala and Sangrur, four high productivity districts having above average proportion of attached labour, and Amritsar and Hoshiarpur, low productivity districts having below average proportion of attached labourers, which is consistent with our hypothesis. But, on the other hand, we also have Jalandhar, Kapurthala and Gurdaspur which are high productivity districts but where proportion of attached labourer is much below average and Bhatinda, Faridkot and Ropar, low productivity districts, having above average proportion of attached labourers. In the case of Haryana, however, the relationship appears to be positive. For example, the three high productivity districts of Ambala, Karnal and Kurukshetra are having much higher proportion of attached labourers as compared to the State average. On the other hand, Bhiwani, Gurgaon, Mohindergarh and Rohtak are agriculturally backward districts and in these districts the proportion of attached labourers is also far below the State average. This appears consistent with our hypothesis of positive relationship between proportion of attached labourers and the level of agricultural development of the area. But there are exceptions here too. We have calculated correlation between the proportion of attached labourer in total wage labourers and the level of agricultural development of the district, defined as productivity per acre, for a cross-section of 22 districts of Punjab and Haryana to see if there is any relationship between the two. The correlation works out to be 0.234 but it is statistically insignificant within the acceptable confidence limits.

If we were expecting a higher proportion of attached labourers in agriculturally advanced districts because generally more the demand pressure in the labour market relative to supply (i.e., tighter labour market condition), the larger the proportional importance of tied labour, then we should expect a negative relationship between the proportion of attached labourer and extent of unemployment because where there is higher demand pressure in the labour market relative to supply there the unemployment rate is likely to be lower. In our study to test this relationship when we compare percentages of attached labourer (given in columns 2 of Tables 4.3 and 4.4) with the weekly status unemployment rate (given in columns 7 of the same Tables) we find that there, in fact, appears to be a negative relationship between the proportion of attached labourers and the rate of unemployment of the district. For example, in Punjab, with the exception of Patiala, in all the other districts where unemployment rate is high, the proportion of attached labourer is low as compared to other districts and the State average. On the other hand, in most of the districts with low rate of unemployment, like, Bhatinda, Faridkot, Ferozepur, Ludhiana and Sangrur, etc., the proportion of attached labourers is higher as compared to the State average. Similarly, in Haryana, with the exception of Jind, in all other districts, like, Bhiwani, Mohindergarh and Sonepat, where the unemployment is high there the proportion of attached labourer is low. On the other hand, in districts, like, Ambala, Hissar, Karnal and Kurukshetra, where the unemployment is comparatively low there the proportion of attached labourer is higher compared to the State average. The correlation between the proportion of attached labourer in total wage labour and the level of weekly status unemployment for a cross-section of 22 districts of Punjab and Haryana works out to be -0.631 which is significant at one per cent level of significance. Thus, contrary to the common pre-supposition that it is the need for unemployment insurance for workers in areas of larger unemployment which primarily determines the incidence of tied-labour contracts, it appears that it is the tighter labour market conditions which lead to more tied-labourer contracts.

Weekly Status Unemployment

Tables 4.3 and 4.4 also give district-wise break-up of the male workers in terms of their status as fully employed, moderately under-employed, severely under-employed and unemployed for Punjab and Haryana, respectively. All those workers who are employed for seven or six days in the reference week have been defined as fully employed. Those employed for five or four days in the reference week are included in the category of moderately under-employed. Those who get work for less than four days but have worked for at least some time in the reference week are included in the category of severely under-employed. Those who did not get any work during the reference week but were available for work have been included in the category of unemployed. Thus, the unemployment here refers to weekly status unemployment rate corresponding to the stock concept of unemployment. A look at these tables reveal that about 70 per cent of all wage labourers in Punjab are fully employed during the reference week. Another 11 per cent are moderately under-empoyed. Yet another 8.30 per cent are severely under-employed. About 11 per cent have not got any work during the reference week and are, therefore, unemployed. In Haryana, the proportion of fully employed and moderately under-employed is slightly higher as compared to Punjab. The percentage of fully employed and moderately under-employed in Haryana is 74.63 per cent and 12.46 per cent respectively. Consequently the percentage of labourers who are severely under-employed and unemployed during the reference week is lower in Haryana as compared to Punjab. In Haryana the percentage of severely under-employed is only 3.08 per cent as compared to 8.30 per cent in Punjab. Similarly, the percentage of weekly status unemployment among Haryana labourers is 9.82 per cent compared to 11.09 per cent in Punjab.

In both the States, however, there are wide inter-district variations in the weekly status unemployment rates. For example, in Punjab it varies between as low as 3.25 per cent in Amritsar and as high as 24.48 per cent in Hoshiarpur. Similarly, in Haryana it varies between only 2.50 per cent in Karnal and as high as 24.49 per cent in Sonepat. There appears to be no relationship between the weekly status unemployment rate and the level of agricultural development of the districts. For example, in Punjab, in three of the low productivity districts of Amritsar, Bhatinda and Faridkot unemployment rates are lower than the State average. But in two other low productivity districts of Hoshiarpur and Ropar unemployment rate is well above the State average. Similarly, among the high productivity districts Ferozepur, Jalandhar, Ludhiana and Sangrur are having below average unemployment rates whereas in three other districts, i.e., Gurdaspur, Kapurthala and Patiala it is well above the State average. A similar picture emerges from Haryana, where out of four high productivity districts, three, i.e., Ambala, Karnal and Kurukshetra, have below average weekly status unemployment rate whereas the fourth, i.e., Sonepat, has the highest rate of unemployment in the State. Similarly, from amongst the six low productivity districts, Gurgaon, Hissar and Rohtak are having low unemployment whereas Bhiwani, Jind and Mohindergarh are having above average rates of unemployment. The correlation between the weekly status unemployment and the agricultural productivity of the districts for a cross-section of 22 districts works out to be -0.069 which is statistically insignificant.

Person-days Rate of Unemployment

But the weekly status unemployment rate as discussed above is only a rough measure of the proportion of worker remaining unemployed and it does not fully reflect the magnitude of unemployment. The basic problem with weekly status unemployment is that in its calculations a person's status over the week has to be frozen in one and only one activity. A person under the weekly status is either employed or unemployed provided he is in the labour force. Therefore, it does not take into account the day-to-day changing status of a person and hence does not reflect the true magnitude of unemployment. As discussed earlier, the cxtent of under-employment cannot be taken care of by using weekly status rates of unemployment. This problem can be solved by using person-days rate of unemployment (PDUR) where the change of status is possible not only from day-to-day but from half-day to half-day. It is the ratio of unemployment days per week (seeking or available for work) to the total labour supply (i.e., working plus seeking and/or available days). Thus, it is clearly a flow concept where not only the labour is being measured in time units but it is also being measured as a flow per unit of time. In the calculation of days the half-days are converted into their full days equivalent. Because the person-day rate of unemployment takes into account the full magnitude of the problem of unemployment (i.e., unemployment and under-employment), except in exceptional cases, it is bound to be higher than the weekly status unemployment rate.

TABLE 4.5: Person-Days Unemployment Rate (PDUR) in Punjab (All Male Workers)

District/ State	PDUR		Normative unemploy-ment with 300 days as full employment norm	Work availability (No. of days)	Produc-tivity per Acre (in Rs.)
	Assumption-I	Assumption-II			
(0)	(1)	(2)	(3)	(4)	(5)
Amritsar	8.63	5.84	-11.16	333.50	1,849
Bhatinda	14.07	10.53	-4.54	313.64	1,336
Faridkot	16.13	12.33	-2.04	306.12	1,721
Ferozepur	14.95	11.31	-3.47	310.43	1,900
Gurdaspur	23.29	19.64	6.67	279.99	2,050
Hoshiarpur	33.27	28.48	18.81	243.56	1,647
Jalandhar	28.13	22.17	12.56	262.32	2,243
Kapurthala	30.33	24.37	15.23	254.29	2,122
Ludhiana	15.49	10.92	-2.82	308.46	2,166
Patiala	30.98	26.53	16.02	251.92	2,016
Ropar	22.08	17.36	5.20	284.40	1,856
Sangrur	17.38	13.89	-0.55	301.65	1,869
Punjab	20.81	16.58	3.65	289.04	1,864

TABLE 4.6: Person-Days Unemployment Rate (PDUR) in Haryana (All Male Workers)

District/ State	PDUR		Normative unemploy- ment with 300 days as full employment norm	Work availability (No. of days)	Produc- tivity per acre (in Rs.)
	Assumption-I	Assumption-II			
1	2	3	4	5	6
Ambala	10.11	7.89	-9.36	328.09	1,860
Bhiwani	29.11	23.87	13.75	258.74	732
Gurgaon	15.50	12.69	-2.80	308.42	1,094
Hissar	7.82	5.71	-12.15	336.45	1,101
Jind	18.61	14.26	0.97	297.07	1,261
Karnal	11.61	7.83	-7.54	322.62	1,922
Kurukshetra	22.21	17.42	5.35	283.93	1,932
Mohindergarh	16.41	13.19	-1.70	305.10	785
Rohtak	12.50	9.26	-3.24	309.37	1,175
Sonepat	39.80	34.74	26.75	219.73	1,673
Haryana	16.95	13.32	-1.04	303.13	1,270

Tables 4.5 and 4.6 contain person-days rate of unemployment (PDUR) for male workers for different districts of Punjab and Haryana, respectively. We, in fact, have calculated two sets of PDUR under two different assumptions. The difference between the two sets lies in the assumptions made while calculating the denominator, i.e., total labour supply. While calculating PDUR under Assumption-I we are assuming that all those persons who are in the labour force in the reference week (i.e., who are seeking work or are available for work) are available for all the seven days in the week which means, we are simply multiplying the number of persons in the labour force during the reference week by seven to arrive at the total supply of labour. But that is only a theoretical possibility and it is quite likely that all the persons in the labour force during the reference week are not seeking work or are available for work for all the seven days in the week. After all they are also human beings and would like to take a day off once in a while to take rest, to attend social ceremonies and on account of illness, etc. Therefore, under the second assumption we presume that all those who are in fact working for the seven days in the reference week were obviously seeking work for all the seven days but all others

who are working for six or fewer days in the week or have not got any work during the week are seeking and/or available for work for six days during the reference week. This reduces the total supply of labour or the denominator in the calculations of person-days rate of unemployment. That explains why the PDUR under Assumption-II given in column 2 of Tables 4.5 and 4.6 are lower than PUDR under assumption-I given in column 1. However, as expected, both these rates are much higher than the weekly status unemployment rates for respective districts and the two States. Apart from PDUR under two different assumptions as discussed we have also calculated a normative rate of unemployment with 300 days as full employment norm. This 300-day norm appears to be reasonable and it has been used by some other studies on rural India on this subject.[85] The normative unemployment rate for all male workers for different districts of Punjab and Haryana and the two States are given in columns 3 of Tables 4.5 and 4.6, respectively.

A look at the same Tables reveals that as in the case of weekly status unemployment, in the case of PDUR, also, unemployment rate among wage labourers is slightly higher in Punjab as compared to Haryana. Person-days unemployment rate under assumption-I is 20.18 per cent in Punjab and 16.95 per cent in Haryana. If, however, we go by the PDUR under assumption-II the unemployment rate in Punjab is 16.58 per cent and in Haryana 13.32 per cent. Thus, our assumption-II has the effect of bringing down total labour supply by about 5.09 per cent in Punjab and 4.23 per cent in Haryana.[86] Our assumption-II appears to be reasonable and wholly justified when we compare the decrease in total labour supply as a result of this assumption with NSS data. For example, Raj Krishna (1976) while calculating person-days rate of unemployment with the 27th round data for 19 States and/or Territories put the all-India average figures of person-days "not in the labour force" at 4.24 per cent.[87] Sinha (1978) working with 25th round data put the loss of days on account of illness, festivals, etc., at six per cent.[88] Therefore, our figures of decrease in the total labour supply of 5.09 per cent for Punjab and 4.23 per cent for Haryana under assumption-II appears reasonable. Thus, for our subsequent discussion we will take the person-days unemployment rate under assumption-II as the actual unemployment rate. The normative rate of unemployment with 300 days as norm is, however, only 3.65 per cent in Punjab and -1.04 per cent in Haryana.

As in the case of weekly status unemployment, in the case of

PDUR, also, there are large inter-district variations in both the States. In Punjab it varies between as low as 5.84 per cent in Amritsar and as high as 28.48 per cent in Hoshiarpur. Similarly, in Haryana it varies between 5.71 per cent in Hissar and as high as 34.74 per cent in Sonepat. There appears to be no systematic relationship between PDUR of the district and the level of agricultural development. For example, in Punjab, Amritsar, Bhatinda and Faridkot are low productivity districts and also have low value of PDUR. But Ferozepur, Ludhiana and Sangrur are high productivity districts, but have lower rate of PDUR as compared to the State average. On the other hand, among the districts having high rate of unemployment there are low productivity districts such as Hoshiarpur and Ropar, as well as high productivity districts, such as Jalandhar, Kapurthala, Patiala and Gurdaspur. A similar picture emerges for Haryana. For example, below average unemployment districts include high productivity districts of Ambala and Karnal as well as low productivity districts of Gurgaon, Hissar and Rohtak. On the other hand, high unemployment districts include Bhiwani and Jind, low productivity districts, as well as Kurukshetra and Sonepat, high productivity districts. The correlation between the PDUR for all male workers and the level of agricultural development of the district for a cross-section of 22 districts of Punjab and Haryana works out to be .159 which is statistically insignificant. Therefore, unemployment among wage labourers prevailing in different districts of Punjab and Haryana does not have any definite relationship with the level or agricultural development of the district. Thus, our hypothesis that the rate of unemployment among rural wage labourers is inversely related to the level of agricultural development of the district is not borne out by the facts whether we take weekly status unemployment or person-days unemployment rate.

Work Availability

Since there are large inter-district variations in the unemployment rate consequently there are also fairly large inter-district variations, in both Punjab and Haryana, in the number of days as average wage labourer gets work (see columns 4 of Tables 4.5 and 4.6). On an average a male wage labourer gets work for about 289 (79.19 per cent of 365) days in Punjab and for 303 (83.05 per cent of 365) days in Haryana. Once again there appears to be no relationship between the number of days a wage labourer gets work and the level of development of the district. The correlation between number of days an average wage labourer gets work in a district and the level of agricultural productivity of the district works out to be -0.177 which is statistically insignificant. This means the new agricultural technology has not significantly effected the availability of work for wage labourers in Punjab and Haryana. The possible explanations of this lack of correlation would be given later.

Unemployment Among Casual Labourers

The unemployment rates discussed above pertain to all male wage labourers including attached as well as casual labourers. However, whatever unemployment exists, it exists among casual workers only, because attached labourers are fully employed in terms of time criterion at least. Therefore, unemployment among casual workers is bound to be higher than among all male workers. Tables 4.7 and 4.8 contain the unemployment prevailing among male casual workers of different districts of Punjab and Haryana, respectively. Person-days unemployment rate among casual workers under assumption-I in Punjab is 33.82 per cent as compared to 22.8 for all workers whereas it is 29.12 per cent for Haryana as compared to 16.95 per cent for all workers. However, if we go by person-days unemployment rates calculated under assumption-II, which is more near to reality, the PDUR among casual workers is of the order of 27.89 per cent in Punjab (16.58 per cent for all male workers) and 23.59 per cent in Haryana (13.32 per cent for all male workers). The normative rate of unemployment among male casual workers works out to be 19.70 per cent in Punjab and 13.99 per cent in Haryana which means on an average a casual worker gets work for 241 days in Punjab and 258 days in Haryana.

Column 4 of Tables 4.7 and 4.8 give the district-wise figures for the number of days an average casual worker gets work in Punjab and Haryana, respectively. One finds that, in both Punjab and Haryana, there are very large inter-district variations in the number of days a casual worker gets work. In Punjab it varies between as low as 178.57 days in Patiala and as high as 315 days in Amritsar. Similarly, in Haryana it varies between merely 161 days in Sonepat and as high as 314.81 days in Hissar. Incidentally, both Patiala and Sonepat where the work availability to casual workers is minimum in Punjab and Haryana, respectively, are above average productivity districts in their respective States. On the other hand, both Amritsar and Hissar, where the work availability is maximum, are below average productivity districts in their respective States. In fact there appears to be a negative relationship between the availability of work to casual labourers and the level of agricultural development of the district. For example, in Punjab most of the low productivity districts, such as Amritsar, Bhatinda and Faridkot, are having above average availability of work for casual workers. On the other hand, in most of the high productivity districts, like, Jalandhar, Kapurthala, Patiala and Gurdaspur, this figure is below the State average. However, there are exceptions too. For instance, Hoshiarpur and Ropar are low productivity districts and also have low work availability figures and Ludhiana and Ferozepur are high productivity and high work availability districts. A more or less similar picture emerges from Table 4.8 for Haryana. With the exception of Karnal all other high productivity districts, such as Ambala, Kurukshetra and Sonepat, are having below average work availability. On the other hand, in most of the low productivity

TABLE 4.7: Person-Days Unemployment Rate (PDUR) in Punjab (Male Casual Workers)

District/ State	PDUR		Normative unemploy-ment with 300 days as full employment norm	Average No. of days work is available in a year
	Assumption-I	Assumption-II		
1	2	3	4	5
Amritsar	13.42	9.23	5.05	315.15
Bhatinda	32.69	26.26	18.30	245.01
Faridkot	30.30	24.13	15.43	253.72
Ferozepur	31.71	25.20	17.14	248.58
Gurdaspur	35.86	31.03	22.17	233.48
Hoshiarpur	37.17	32.09	23.76	228.41
Jalandhar	36.45	29.45	22.88	231.34
Kapurthala	34.56	28.11	20.59	238.23
Ludhiana	27.07	20.00	11.51	265.47
Patiala	50.94	45.52	40.47	178.57
Ropar	41.88	34.81	29.47	211.58
Sangrur	41.59	35.11	29.12	212.64
Punjab	33.82	27.89	19.70	240.89

TABLE 4.8: Person-Days Unemployment Rates (PDUR) in Haryana (Male Casual Workers)

District/ State	PDUR		Normative unemploy-ment with 300 days as full employment norm	Average No. of days work is available
	Assumption-I	Assumption-II		
(0)	(1)	(2)	(3)	(4)
Ambala	31.30	25.74	16.64	250.09
Bhiwani	32.74	27.10	18.39	244.83
Gurgaon	22.00	18.27	5.36	283.92
Hissar	13.52	10.05	-4.94	314.81
Jind	39.29	32.00	26.33	221.00
Karnal	24.44	17.29	8.32	275.05
Kurukshetra	46.94	39.54	35.62	193.14
Mohindergarh	23.31	19.05	6.95	279.15
Rohtak	16.00	11.98	-1.92	305.76
Sonepat	55.72	50.33	46.26	161.20
Haryana	29.12	23.59	13.99	258.03

districts, such as Gurgaon, Hissar, Mohindergarh and Rohtak, these figures are well above the State average. The correlation between the number of days an average casual worker gets work in a district and the level of agricultural development of the district defined as productivity per acre for a cross section of 22 districts of Punjab and Haryana works out to be -0.380 which is statistically significant at 5 per cent level of significance. Thus, we find that there is a negative relationship between the number of days a casual worker gets work and the level of agricultural development of the district. We should also recall our earlier findings in this chapter that proportion of attached labourer in total wage labourers is positively, though insignificantly, related with the level of agricultural development of the region and that agricultural development has not significantly effected the overall work availability to wage labourers. Seen in this context it appears that wherever the new agricultural technology has been more successful, it has changed the periodicity of crop rotation in such a way that most of the work has been concentrated in a few peaks of relatively shorter duration. This situation, on the one hand, appears to have changed the employers labour mix in favour of attached labourers to have some kind of assured supply during the peak seasons and to avoid high cost of casual labourers during the busy peaks and, on the other hand, it has simultaneously reduced the number of days work is available to a casual worker. But concentration of work in a few peaks is also likely to give, at least temporarily, a greater bargaining power to casual labourers during peak seasons. This is likely to push-up wages of casual workers during peak seasons. This is exactly what has happened as would be discussed in the next chapter. Nonetheless, at least a few things are clear here. First, that new agricultural technology seems to have changed the composition of wage labour in favour of attached workers. Secondly, it has reduced the work availability for casual workers in terms of number of days and, thirdly, it has not significantly effected the overall work availability, for all the workers (including attached workers) and hence rate of unemployment prevailing among all male wage labourers.

Unemployment Among Female Labourers

After having discussed the rate of unemployment prevailing among male wage labourers of different districts of Punjab and Haryana now we shall briefly discuss the unemployment prevailing among female workers. Unlike male workers which are divided into attached and casual categories, all female workers are casual workers only. Tables 4.9 and 4.10 give us the district-wise weekly status unemployment rates prevailing among female workers of Punjab and Haryana, respectively. Tables 4.11 and 4.12 contain person-days rate of unemployment (PDUR) calculated under various assumptions, which prevail among female workers in different districts of Punjab and Haryana, respectively. Since the number of female workers in each district in our sample is small in both the States, some times as small as three to five only, as in the case of Bhatinda, Kapurthala and Sangrur in Punjab, the estimates of unemployment rate at the district level are not likely to be reliable. Therefore, we shall confine our discussion to the unemployment rates prevailing at the State level only.

The most striking conclusion which emerges, while going through these tables, is that whether we take weekly status unemployment or person-days rate of unemployment, the unemployment prevailing among female labourers is much higher as compared to male casual workers. In terms of weekly status about 45 per cent of all female workers are unemployed. The corresponding figure for Haryana is

34.17 per cent. Going by the person-days rate of unemployment females are unemployed for about 50 per cent of their labour time in Punjab and for about 40 per cent in Haryana. Even if we consider the normative rate of unemployment with 225 days as full employment norm, still the PDUR is 27.57 per cent in Punjab and 12.55 per cent in Haryana.[89] Our estimated person-days unemployment figures for females are totally contrary to the results obtained by NSS data which show that the rate of unemployment among female labourers is zero or negligible in Punjab and Haryana. For example, according to 27th Round of NSS relating to the year 1972-73 the person-days rate of unemployment among female labourers for all rural population is only 1.2 per cent in Punjab and only one per cent in Haryana.[90] Similarly, 25th Round of NSS relating to the year 1970-71 put the rate of unemployment among female landless farm labourers at zero in Punjab and 11.20 per cent in Haryana.[91] Further, according to NSS in Haryana the unemployment rate among female labourers came down from 11.20 per cent in 1970-71 to only one per cent in 1972-73 despite the fact that 1970-71 was a bumper crop year for the State whereas 1972-73 was not so good a year in terms of agricultural production. The index of agricultural production (with 1960-61 = 100) stood at 173.3 in 1970-71 and it came down to 152.7 in 1972-73.[92]

On an average a female worker gets work for about 163 days in a year in Punjab and for 197 days in Haryana. We are not able to go into the question of its relationship with the level of agricultural development of the district because of unreliability of our district level estimates but we can say at least a few things. First, that unemployment rates prevailing among female labourers of both Punjab and Haryana are fairly substantial, impressions, to the contrary, being given by NSS data notwithstanding. Secondly, as in the case of males, the females unemployment rate is higher in Punjab as compared to Haryana. That may partly explain the lower incidence of female labour participation in Punjab as compared to Haryana because many of them may involuntarily withdraw from the labour force due to lack of perception of employment opportunities.

In fact our PDUR for females is more akin to what Bardhan (1984) calls potential unemployment rate (PUR), than to the NSS rate of person-days unemployment for females. Bardhan argues that unemployment rate, calculated by NSS, overlooks the phenomenon of discouraged drop-outs which takes the form of withdrawal from the current labour force often into domestic work. In his alternative measure which he calls potential unemployment rate (PUR), he presumes that if a person is in the labour force by usual status, then any withdrawal from the labour force in the reference week should more properly be counted as unemployed days, even though she may not have explicitly reported her availability for work to the survey investigator. Using his alternative criterion on NSS sample of rural West Bengal for 1977-78, Bardhan finds that whereas unemployment rate according to NSS criterion works out to be 10.02 per cent, his PUR is 40.20 per cent, i.e., four times larger than the first estimate.[93] Since we have also made similar assumption while calculating total supply of female labour, therefore, our PDUR for females should be interpreted with caution.

TABLE 4.9: Unemployment/Under-employment in Punjab (Female Workers)

District/ State	Total female workers	Fully employed	Moderately under-employed	Severely under-employed	Unemp-loyed
(0)	(1)	(2)	(3)	(4)	(5)
Amritsar	48 (100.00)	12 (25.00)	3 (6.25)	6 (12.50)	27 (56.25)
Bhatinda	3 (100.00)	—	1 (33.33)	1 (33.33)	1 (33.33)
Faridkot	12 (100.00)	4 (33.33)	4 (33.33)	—	4 (33.33)
Ferozepur	11 (100.00)	5 (45.45)	2 (18.18)	—	4 (36.36)
Gurdaspur	19 (100.00)	9 (47.37)	1 (5.26)	1 (5.26)	8 (42.11)
Hoshiarpur	6 (100.00)	2 (33.33)	1 (16.67)	—	3 (50.00)
Jalandhar	11 (100.00)	4 (36.36)	2 (18.18)	1 (9.09)	4 (36.36)
Kapurthala	5 (100.00)	2 (40.00)	—	—	3 (60.00)
Ludhiana	12 (100.00)	9 (75.00)	—	—	3 (25.00)
Patiala	16 (100.00)	9 (56.25)	—	2 (12.50)	5 (31.25)
Ropar	9 (100.00)	4 (44.44)	1 (11.11)	2 (22.22)	2 (22.22)
Sangrur	5 (100.00)	2 (40.00)	—	—	3 (60.00)
Punjab	164 (100.00)	62 (37.80)	20 (12.19)	18 (10.28)	74 (45.12)

TABLE 4.10: Unemployment/Under-employment in Haryana (Female Workers)

District/ State	Total female workers	Fully employed	Moderately under-employed	Severely under-employed	Unem-ployed
(0)	(1)	(2)	(3)	(4)	(5)
Ambala	10 (100.00)	3 (30.00)	—	—	7 (70.00)
Bhiwani	17 (100.00)	9 (52.94)	2 (11.76)	3 (17.65)	3 (17.65)
Gurgaon	21 (100.00)	14 (66.67)	1 (4.76)	2 (9.52)	4 (19.05)
Hissar	54 (100.00)	21 (38.89)	13 (24.07)	5 (9.26)	15 (27.78)
Jind	6 (100.00)	3 (50.00)	—	—	3 (50.00)
Karnal	17 (100.00)	8 (47.06)	3 (17.65)	3 (17.65)	3 (17.65)
Kurukshetra	10 (100.00)	3 (30.00)	4 (40.00)	2 (20.00)	1 (10.00)
Mohindergarh	12 (100.00)	4 (33.33)	2 (16.67)	1 (8.33)	5 (41.67)
Rohtak	23 (100.00)	13 (56.52)	4 (17.39)	—	6 (26.09)
Sonepat	30 (100.00)	1 (3.33)	3 (10.00)	4 (13.33)	22 (73.33)
Haryana	199 (100.00)	79 (39.70)	32 (16.08)	20 (10.05)	68 (34.17)

To test the proposition that females withdraw from the labour force when they do not perceive any work for them, we regressed the female rate of work participation for 22 districts of Punjab and Haryana on unemployment prevailing among male casual workers and the proportion of wage labour in total agricultural workers. Our hypothesis is that if the unemployment prevailing among male labourers is high the likelihood is that females will not perceive work for them and consequently may not report themselves in the labour force. Similarly, where the male wage labourers are plentiful in relation to the total labour force, females would not perceive much work for them and are likely to drop out of the labour force. Thus we hypothesise that

$$Y = a - b_1 U - b_2 E + U$$

Where

Y = Female rate of work participation

U = Unemployment prevailing among male casual worker; and

E = Proportion of wage labourer in total agricultural workers.

U = Disturbance term confirming to some probability distribution with zero mean and constant variance. The estimated equation is as follows:

$$Y = 57.967 - 0.358U - 1.624E$$
$$(4.569)^{*} \quad (1.174)^{@} \quad (3.078)^{*}$$

$$R^2 = .380, F = 5.84 \; DF = 19$$

TABLE 4.11: Person-Days Unemployment Rates (PDUR) in Punjab (Female Workers)

District/ State	PDUR		Normative unemploy-ment rate with 225 days as full employment norm	Average No. of days work is available
	Assumption-I	Assumption-II		
Amritsar	70.84	64.42	46.08	121.33
Bhatinda	66.67	61.12	46.08	121.33
Faridkot	47.62	39.73	15.26	190.66
Ferozepur	45.16	39.44	9.66	203.27
Gurdaspur	49.63	44.63	18.51	183.37
Hoshiarpur	54.77	50.00	26.81	164.67
Jalandhar	51.95	46.38	22.74	174.91
Kapurthala	60.00	56.25	35.29	145.60
Ludhiana	29.77	23.38	-13.63	255.67
Patiala	38.40	34.29	0.34	224.25
Ropar	42.86	37.94	7.56	208.00
Sangrur	62.86	58.07	39.92	135.20
Punjab	55.23	50.25	27.57	162.97

* Significant at one per cent level of significance.

@ Figures in brackets are t-values.

TABLE 4.12: Person-Days Unemployment Rates (PDUR) in Haryana (Female Workers)

District/ State	PDUR		Normative unemploy-ment rate with 225 days as full employment norm	Average No. of days work is available
	Assumption-I	Assumption-II		
Ambala	70.00	67.19	48.53	109.20
Bhiwani	31.94	27.03	-10.12	247.76
Gurgaon	27.22	23.98	-17.76	264.95
Hissar	41.80	35.86	5.85	211.85
Jind	50.00	46.16	19.11	182.00
Karnal	35.30	30.00	-4.68	235.53
Kurukshetra	35.72	28.58	-4.00	234.00
Mohindergarh	52.38	47.37	22.97	173.33
Rohtak	32.30	27.33	-9.53	246.43
Sonepat	85.24	82.87	76.12	53.73
Haryana	45.95	40.66	12.55	196.76

The estimated regression coefficients have expected sign. The influence of *U* is not statistically significant within the acceptable confidence limits. However, the coefficient of *E* (proportion of agricultural labourer in total agricultural workers) is highly significant. The value of R^2 is not very high and that is understandable because we could not take into account numerous other social, cultural and demographic factors, which influence the rate of female work participation, but our hypothesis, that lack of work perception derive potential female workers out of the labour force, is borne out by the facts.

To sum-up, our results show that about 86 per cent of all male adults in Punjab and about 85 per cent in Haryana participate in work. The figure for the working age group of 15 - 59 is expectedly higher, being 89.24 per cent for Punjab and 88.00 per cent for Haryana. Unlike male labourers, in the case of female labourers, however, there are wide variations in the rate of work participation between the two States as well as across districts within each State. Whereas in the case of Punjab rate of female work participation is only 10.72 per cent, in the case of Haryana it is roughly three times higher as compared to Punjab. The new technology has not affected the rate of male participation but it has adversely effected the rate of female participation. Because of the reasons discussed above the rates of female participation as hypothesised by us turn out to be negatively related to the level of agricultural development of the area.

Our results regarding attached casual composition of wage labourers show that about two-fifths of all male workers are working as attached labourers in both Punjab and Haryana. The rest three-fifths are casual workers. Our study, though not conclusive tends to confirm the results of some earlier studies, like, Bhalla (1976) and Bardhan and Rudra (1981), that new technology has some bias in favour of attached labourers. The proportion of attached labourers to total wage labourers and the level of agricultural development are positively correlated but the relationship is statistically insignificant. However, there is a definite negative relationship between the proportion of attached labourer and the level of unemployment. Thus, contrary to the common pre-supposition that it is the need for insurance against unemployment which primarily determines the incidence of tied labour contracts, it appears that it is the tighter labour market conditions which lead to more tied labour contracts. Thus, it is primarily the demand conditions which have led to the dominance of long-term labour contracts.

Our analysis of the unemployment prevailing among wage labourers of Punjab and Haryana shows that whether we go by weekly status unemployment or person-days rate of unemployment under various assumptions, the incidence of unemployment is marginally higher in Punjab as compared to Haryana. The weekly status unemployment figures are 11.09 per cent for Punjab and 9.82 per cent for Haryana. In terms of person-days, on an average a male wage labourer remains, unemployed for 16.58 per cent days in Punjab and 13.32 per cent days in Haryana. Thus, an average wage labourer gets work for about 289 days in a year in Punjab and 303 days in Haryana. Strangely enough there does not seem to be any relationship between the availability of work for the wage labourers and the level of agricultural development of the district. Thus, new agricultural technology does not seem to have significantly affected the employment prospects of wage labourers. In fact when we analyse the unemployment prevailing among casual workers separately, we find that an average casual worker gets work only for 241 days in a year in Punjab and for 258 days in Haryana. There is also a negative relationship between the number of days a casual workers gets work and the level of agricultural development of the district. It appears that new agricultural technology, by changing the composition of wage workers in favour of attached labourers, have significantly reduced work availability for casual workers in terms of number of days, although it has not significantly effected the overall employment prospects of all the wage labourers.

Contrary to results given by NSS the incidence of unemployment among female labourers in both Punjab and Haryana is quite high. In fact it is higher than those among male workers. Between the two States it is higher in Punjab as compared to Haryana. It appears that comparatively low rate of female participation in Punjab, apart from other factors, can also be partly attributed to the higher rate of unemployment prevailing among both male and female casual wage labourers of Punjab, as our regression, results show that many of them may involuntarily withdraw from the labour force due to lack of perception of employment opportunities.

III

In the preceding section we discussed the rate of male and female work participation, the attached-casual composition of wage labourer and the unemployment and under-employment prevailing among male and female wage labourers of Punjab and Haryana and their relationship with the level of agricultural development of the region. In this section we shall try to analyse the factors which explain the inter-district variations in unemployment prevailing among wage labourers of Punjab and Haryana.

Determinants of Unemployment

As we understand it, unemployment is nothing but the difference between total supply of and demand for labour. When expressed as a percentage of the total labour supply it gives us the rate of unemployment. Therefore, while identifying the factors which are likely to affect the rate of unemployment among wage labourers we shall be concentrating on identifying those structural factors which are likely to play a significant role in determining the demand for and supply of wage labourers in the rural labour market.

The structural factors which we have in mind include the demographic pressure on land, the extent of inequality in the distribution of land and other productive assets and the technology of cultivation. For any given size of population in an area, the supply of wage labour (i.e., the size of labour force which has to depend on wage employment for its livelihood) will depend, to a large extent, on the average amount of land and other productive assets per capita and on the distribution of these resources among the population. The smaller the amount of land per capita and more unequal its distribution, the larger is likely to be the proportion of population which will not be able to make a living by applying family labour to land at its command and, therefore, will have to seek wage employment to supplement its income.

The effect of changes in demographic pressure on land on demand for hired labour is, however, quite different from that of a change in land distribution. A higher demographic pressure means an across-the-board increase in the supply of family labour relative to land so that, other things remaining the same, it will tend to lower the demand for hired labour. Contrary to this, a more unequal distribution of land implies that a larger proportion of land is being operated by relatively big farmers. On the one hand, it will have the effect of increasing total supply of wage labourers because land is concentrated in a fewer hands and a larger proportion will have to depend on their labour power to earn their livelihood. On the other hand, it will have the effect of lowering the supply of family labour relative to total requirements on bigger holdings and consequently will lead to a generation of higher demand for hired labour by the bigger owners. Its overall impact on unemployment, however, will depend upon its supply increasing and demand boosting effects. A higher proportion of wage labourers in total agricultural workers will also have the effect of increasing labour supply *vis-a-vis* demand and, therefore, is likely to have positive relationship with unemployment.

As far as the technology of cultivation is concerned the major element of the new agricultural technology which is likely to have negative impact on the demand for labour is the use of tractor for ploughing and mechanical equipment for harvesting and threshing, etc. Therefore, mechanisation of agricultural operations is likely to reduce the demand for hired labour and hence is likely to have positive relationship with unemployment.

The wage labourers are not a homogeneous category. A large proportion of wage labourers consists of scheduled castes and scheduled tribes. This component of wage labourers suffer from some special social disadvantages in terms of their access to land and other productive resources and opportunities. As a result, they have to depend mainly on wage labour only. Consequently they cannot afford to remain unemployed and would be prepared to work even if the reward for that work is very low. The relative strength of scheduled castes and scheduled tribes in total wage labourers tend to make the supply curve of labour more inelastic and this will have the consequence on rate of unemployment, other things remaining the same.

Variations in the magnitude of alternative opportunities for employment outside agriculture will also alter the supply position of agricultural labour and is likely to have negative impact on rate of unemployment prevailing among rural wage labourers. Lastly, the unemployment prevailing among wage labourers is also likely to be negatively related with the prevailing wage rate because wages will be higher only where demand for labour *vis-a-vis* supply is more. Keeping the above discussion in mind we hypothesise that :

$$U = f(S_t, I, E, P_{sc}, M, N, W)$$

Where

$U =$ Unemployment prevailing among wage labourers
$S_t =$ Demographic pressure on land
$I =$ Index of inequality in the distribution of land holdings
$E =$ Proportion of wage labourers in total agricultural labourers
$P_{sc} =$ Proportion of scheduled castes in total wage labourers
$M =$ Number of tractors per thousand hectares of cropped area
$N =$ Employment opportunities outside agriculture
$W =$ Wage rate of casual workers

Expressing it in the form of a linear equation we get

$$U = a + b_1S_t + b_2I + B_3E + b_4P_{sc} + b_5M - b_6N - b_7W + U$$

Where $b_1, b_2 \ldots b_7$ are regression coefficients and U is a stochastic term which, we assume, will confirm to some probability distribution with zero mean and constant variance.

We have estimated this equation with the help of district level data since most of these variables are available at the district level. It will also give us sufficient number of observations. Before presenting our results, however, we shall briefly discuss how these variables have been measured. District-wise person-days rate of unemployment (PDUR under assumption-II) prevailing among all male wage labourers has been taken as dependent variable whose variations are to be explained. Demographic pressure on land has been measured as number of persons per acre of cropped area. For this purpose total number of agricultural workers according to 1971 Census for each district has been divided by the total cropped area of the respective district taken from *Statistical Abstracts of Punjab and Haryana.* Number of tractors per thousand hectares of cropped area is our *M*. Variable (*E*) has been measured by dividing the number of male agricultural labourers by total agricultural workers (i.e., Cultivators + agricultural labourer) taken from 1971 Census for each district. Proportion of scheduled castes in agricultural wage labourers (P_{sc}) for different districts has been derived from 1971 Census. Percentage of workers employed in non-agricultural activities for each district (*N*) has been taken from the *Statistical Abstracts of Punjab and Haryana.* Index of inequality in land-holdings distribution for different districts (*I*) have been calculated by taking data on land-holdings for 1971-72 for Punjab and Haryana. The basic data used in estimating this equation is given in appendix Table 4.A.1. The estimated equation is as follows:

$$
\begin{array}{llllll}
U & = & 3.743 & +52.925S_t & +38.307I & -0.584E \\
 & & (0.705)@ & (1.090)^{***} & (0.518) & (0.994)^{***} \\
 & & +0.647P_{sc} & +1.510M & -0.391N & -5.733W \\
 & & (2.163)^{*} & (1.301)^{***} & (1.466)^{**} & (2.197)^{*} \\
 & & R^2 = .448 & F = 7.22 & DF = 14 &
\end{array}
$$

Thus our model explains about 45 per cent of total inter-district variations in unemployment prevailing among wage labourers of Punjab and Haryana. Although the total variance explained is rather small but considering the fact that unemployment is a multi-dimensional phenomenon and cannot be reduced very meaningfully to a single figure, the performance of our model is fairly satisfactory. All

---

@ Figures in parentheses are *t*-values

* Significant at 5 per cent level of significance

** Significant at 10 per cent level of significance

*** Significant at 20 per cent level of significance

variables except E are having expected sign but only proportion of scheduled (P_{sc}), alternative employment opportunities outside agriculture, and prevailing wage rate are statistically significant within the acceptable confidence limits. Demographic pressure on land, inequality in land holdings and extent of mechanisation are having expected signs but are statistically insignificant.

The meaning of our results is clear. First of all alternative employment opportunities outside agriçulture does help in bringing down the unemployment prevailing among rural wage labourers. But more important than this is the finding that the type of agricultural growth which is taking place in Punjab and Haryana aggravates the problem of unemployment among wage labourers. The relative preponderance of scheduled caste households among wage labourers (suffering from special social and economic disadvantages in terms of their access to land and other productive resources and opportunities) further reinforces this tendency. Concentration of land in a fewer hands by pushing more and more people into the ranks of rural proletariat swells their number. Whenever increasing number of wage earners compete for limited number of jobs in the rural labour market, unemployment is bound to go up.

What are the implications of our results? Agricultural growth particularly of the type which is taking place in Punjab and Haryana (accompanied by large-scale mechanisation of farm operations) cannot solve the problem of rural unemployment. Even if it has increased the total demand for wage labourers, it has also changed the periodicity of crop rotation in such a way that most of the work has been concentrated in a few critically time bound peaks of relatively shorter duration so that the work availability to a wage labourer in terms of number of days has gone down and consequently the unemployment rates have gone up. However, concentration of work in a few busy seasons is likely to give, at least temporarily, a greater bargaining power to wage labourers during peak seasons. This is likely to push up wages of agricultural labourers during peak seasons. This is exactly what has happened as would be discussed in the next chapter, but at least one thing is clear that new agricultural technology with increasing component of mechanisation has reduced the work availability to local labourers in terms of number of days. Our results also suggest that demographic pressure on land has to be relieved to some extent by creating more job opportunities outside agriculture. Land concentration in a fewer hands has to be broken and under-privileged sections of rural population have to be given access to land and/or other productive assets and opportunities so that some of them can withdraw from the rural labour market thereby relieving some of the pressure on land. Simultaneous action on two fronts, i.e., creation of job opportunities outside agriculture sector and radical agrarian reforms to break concentration of land holdings in a few hands and giving access to land and other productive assets to socially under-privileged sections of rural population, is called for, if the lot of rural poor is to be improved.

NOTES

1. Census of India 1961, p. 35. The instructions went on to explain that "if on the check or the revision round such a person is found to be unemployed no change in the original entry should be made" and that "a person who is working but was absent from his work during the fifteen days preceding the day on which enumerated or even exceeding the period of fifteen days due to illness or other causes should be treated as worker."
2. NSS criteria varied from round to round. In the 11th, 12th and 13th rounds, both one day and one week, immediately preceding the day of enquiry, were chosen for reference and a person was treated as 'employed' if he had gainful work on that day. A person not having gainful work would be classified as 'unemployed' if he was either 'seeking work' or fell into the category of 'not seeking but available for work'. Since 14th round, however, the criterion of being in work has been to have worked 'at least' one day during the reference week. Further, beginning with the 16th round, persons below the age of 15 or aged 60 years or more have been excluded from the figure of the unemployed even if they are actively seeking work. For a detailed review of the concepts of employment and unemployment adopted by the NSS see Sudhir Bhattacharya, (1970). "A Note on Employment and Unemployment Concepts Adopted in the National Sample Survey" *Report of the Committee of Experts on Unemployment Estimates"*, Planning Commission, Government of India, Appendix 1, pp. 33-38.
3. *Ibid.*, Appendix ii by P. Visaria, p., 86.
4. *Ibid.*, p. 31.
5. *Ibid.*, p. 17.
6. *Ibid.*, p. 17.
7. M.L. Dantwala (1972). "Approaches of Growth and Employment", *Economic and Political Weekly*, 7, 51, November 16, p. 2462.
8. Raj Krishna (1973). "Unemployment in India", *Indian Journal of Agricultural Economics*, XXVIII, 1, pp. 1-24.
9. *Ibid.*, p. 6.
10. V.M. Dandekar and N. Rath (1971). *Poverty in India*, Indian School of Political Economy, p. 137.
11. *Ibid.*, p. 138.
12. *Ibid.*, p. 138.
13. Raj Krishna (1973). *Op. cit.*, pp. 4-6.

14. A.K. Sen (1973). "Poverty, Inequality and Unemployment", *Economic and Political Weekly*, 8, Special Number August 1973, pp. 1457-64.
15. *Ibid.*, p. 1458.
16. I.Z. Bhatty (1973). "Unemployment: Questions of Measurement and Mitigation" *Yojna*, 17, 1, January 26, pp. 71-80.
17. *Ibid.*, p. 80.
18. Y.K. Alagh (1979). "Indian Planning in the Eighties", *Economic and Political Weekly*, 14, Special Number, August, pp. 1273-82.
19. *Ibid.*, p. 1274.
20. S.K. Rao (1973). "Measurement of Unemployment in Rural India", *Economic and Political Weekly*, 8, 39, Review of Agriculture, pp. A78 - A90.
21. See *NSS Report No. 114*, Table 3.16.1.
22. Rao (1973). *Op. cit.*, p. A87.
23. Joan Robinson (1936). "Disguised Unemployment", *Economic Journal*, 46, June, pp. 225-37.
24. J.L. Buck (1930). *Chinese Farm Economy*, The University of Chicago Press, Chicago.
25. Doreen Warriner (1939). *Economics of Peasant Farming*, Oxford University, Press, London.
26. P.N. Rosenstein-Rodan (1943). "Problems of Industrialisation of Eastern and South-Eastern Europe", *Economic Journal*, 53, pp. 202-11.
27. United Nations (1951). *Measure for the Economic Development of Underdeveloped Countries*, Department of Economic and Social Affairs, New York.
28. R. Nurkse (1953). *Problems of Capital Formation in Underdeveloped Countries*, Oxford University Press, p. 35.
29. Arthur Lewis (1955). *The Theory of Economic Growth*, George Allen and Unwin Ltd.
30. P.N. Rosenstein-Rodan (1957). "Disguised Unemployment and Underdevelopment in Agriculture", *Monthly Bulletin of Agricultural Economics and Statistics*, 6, pp. 1-7, July-August.
31. H. Leibenstein (1959). "The Theory of Underemployment in Backward Economies", *Journal of Political Economy*, LXV, pp. 91-103, April.
32. A.K. Sen (1960). *Choices of Techniques*, Basil Blackwell & Moth Ltd., Oxford, p. 14.
33. Doreen Warriner (1948). *Land and Poverty in Middle East*, Royal Institute of International Affairs, London.
34. Doreen Warriner (1955). *Land Reform and Economic Development*, Fiftieth Anniversary Commemoration Lectures, National Bank of Egypt, Cairo.
35. T.W. Schultz (1956). "The Role of Government in Promoting Economic Growth" in Leonard D. White (ed), *The State of the Social Science*, University of Chicago Press, Chicago, p. 375.
36. J. Viner (1957). "Some Reflections on the Concept of Disguised Unemployment", *The Indian Journal of Economics*, 38, 148, July, p. 18.
37. R.S. Eckaus (1955). "Factor Proportions in Underdeveloped Countries", *American Economic Review*, 45, pp. 539-65, September.
38. Harvey Leibenstein (1957). *Op. cit.*

39. John W. Mellor and Robert D. Stevens (1956). "The Average and Marginal Product of Farm Labour in Underdeveloped Economies", *Journal of Farm Economics*, 38, pp. 780-91, August.
40. A.K. Sen (1960). *Op. Cit.*
41. Paul Wonnacott (1962). "Disguised and Overt Unemployment in Underdeveloped Economies", *Quarterly Journal of Economics*, (May), 76, pp. 279-97.
42. N. Georgescu - Roegen (1963). "Economic Theory and Agrarian Economics", *Oxford Economic Papers*, February, 12, pp. 1-40.
43. H. Myint (1964). *The Economics of Developing Countries*, Hutichinson, London.
44. Pradhan H. Prasad (1970). *Growth with Full Employment*, Allied Publishers, Bombay.
45. A.K. Sen (1975). *Employment Technology and Development*, Claredon Press, Oxford.
46. John W. Mellor and Robert D. Stevens (1956). *Op. cit.*
47. N.K. Sarkar (1957). "A Method of Estimating Surplus Labour in Peasant Agriculture in Overpopulated Underdeveloped Countries", *Journal of Royal Statistical Society*, 20.
48. Shakuntala Mehra (1966). "Surplus Labour in Indian Agriculture", *Indian Economic Review*, I, 1, (New Series), pp. 111-29.
49. Prafulla Sanghavi (1969). *Surplus Manpower in Agriculture and Economic Development*, Asia Publishing House, Bombay.
50. Ashok Rudra (1973). "Direct Estimation of Surplus Labour in Agriculture", *Economic and Political Weekly*, 8, Annual Number, February, pp. 277-80.
51. Kanta Ahuja (1975). Measurement of Rural Labour Surplus, A Ph.D. Thesis, University of Rajasthan; also see by the same author, (1978). *Idle Labour in Village India*, Manohar.
52. Harry T. Oshima (1958). "Underemployment in Backward Economies; An Empirical Comment", *Journal of Political Economy*, 66, pp. 259-64.
53. T.W. Schultz (1964). *Transforming Traditional Agriculture*, Yale University Press.
54. B. Hansen (1966). "Marginal Productivity Wage Theory and Subsistence Wage Theory in Egyptian Agriculture", *Journal of Development Studies*, 2.
55. D.W. Jorgenson (1967). "Surplus Agricultural Labour and Dual Economy", *Oxford Economic Papers*, November.
56. C.H. Hanumantha Rao (1965). *Agricultural Production Functions Costs and Returns*, Asia Publishing House, Bombay.
57. G.R. Saini (1969). "Resource Use Efficiency in Indian Agriculture" *Indian Journal of Agricultural Economics*, XXIV, 2, April-June.
58. P.K. Bardhan (1973). 'Size, Productivity and Returns to Scale. An Analysis of Farm Level Data in Indian Agriculture" (Mimeo).
59. Raj Krishna (1973). *Op. cit.*, p. 4.
60. Tarlok Singh (1945). *Poverty and Social Change*, Longmans Green & Co. Ltd., Calcutta.
61. N.V. Sovani (1959). "Potential Out-Migrants and Removable Surplus Population in Three Districts of Orissa (India)" in International Union for the Scientific Study of Population, *Proceedings of the International Population Conference*, Vienna, London.
62. N.A. Majumdar (1961). *'Some Problems of Underemployment'*, Popular Book Depot, Bombay.

63. J.P. Bhattacharjee (1961). "Underemployment Among Indian Farmers. Analysis of its Nature and Extent Based on Data for Bihar", *Artha Vijnana*, 3, 3.
64. A. Quayum (1962). "Agricultural Underemployment in Uttar Pradesh", *Economic Weekly*, 15, 51 & 52, December 22, pp. 1961-66.
65. Theodore W. Schultz (1964). *Op. cit.*
66. *Ibid.*, p. 67.
67. S. Mehra (1966). *Op. cit.*
68. A.K. Sen (1967). "Surplus Labour in India: A Critique of Schultz's Statistical Test" *Economic Journal*, 77, 1, March, pp. 154-61. Also see by the same author, "Rejoinder to Theodore W. Schultz's "Reply" in the same issue, pp. 163-65.
69. S. Mehra (1966). *Op. cit.*
70. A. Rudra (1973). *Op. cit.*
71. K. Ahuja (1978). *Op. cit.*
72. A.K. Sen (1975). *Op. cit.*, p. 130.
73. Ashok Rudra (1973). *Op. cit.*, p. 279.
74. K. Ahuja (1978). *Op. cit.*, p. 70.
75. N.A. Khan (1963). "Some Reflections on the Census of 1961" I and II, *Indian Economic Journal*, 10, 3 and 4, January and April.
76. J.N. Sinha (1964). "Comparability of 1961 and 1951 Census Economic Data", *Artha Vijnana*, 6, 4.
77. Pravin Visaria (1965). "Comparability of 1961 and 1951 Census Economic Data: A Comment", *Artha Vijnana*, 7.
78. N.K. Namboodri (1956). "A Contribution to the Study of Factors Associated with Working force Participation Rates", *Asian Economic Review*, 9, 1, November.
79. J.N. Sinha (1965). "Dynamics of Female Participation in Economic Activity in a Developing Economy" in *Papers Presented by Indian Authors to the World Population Conference*, Belgrade, Yugoslavia, pp. 253-62.
80. R.C. Chandra (1967). "Female Working Force of Rural Punjab — 1961", *Manpower Journal*, 2, 4, January-March, pp. 47-62.
81. Pravin Visaria (1970). "Employment and Unemployment in India: A Review of Selected Statistics" *Report of the Committee of Experts on Unemployment, Estimates*, Appendix 11, pp. 43-144.
82. See for example K.S. Gnansekharan (1960). "Labour Force Projection for India 1951-76" *Artha Vijnana*, 2, 1, pp. 1-13; and also A.M. Khusro (1962). *Economic Development with No Population Transfers*, Asia Publishing House, Bombay.
83. Sheilla Bhalla (1976). "New Relations of Production in Haryana Agriculture", *Economic and Political Weekly*, 11, March.
84. P.K. Bardhan and A. Rudra (1981). "Terms and Conditions of Labour Contracts in Agriculture : Results of Some Survey in West Bengal 1979", *Oxford Bulletin of Economics and Statistics*, 43, February.
85. See for example Kanta Ahuja (1978). *Op. Cit.*
86. For example person-day unemployment rate of 16.58 per cent for Punjab would mean person-days employment rate of 83.42 per cent which is equal to 289 (79.19 per cent of 365) days. Therefore, 100 per cent or total labour supply would be 289 x 100/83.42=346.44 days which is 94.91 per cent of 365 or 5.09 per cent less than total labour supply under assumption-I. A similar procedure has been adopted for calculating decrease in labour supply under assumption-II for Haryana.
87. Raj Krishna (1976). *Op. cit.*, p. 36.

88. J.N. Sinha (1978). "Rural Employment Planning : Dimension and Constraints", *Economic and Political Weekly*, 13, Annual Number, February, p. 297.
89. The full employment norm of 225 days for female workers has also been used by Kanta Ahuja. See for example Kanta Ahuja (1978). *Op. Cit.*
90. See for example NSS 27th Round Reports 255/1 - 255/8.
91. See 25th Round Report 270 and also *Unemployment at a Glance*, 1977.
92. See for example Table 2.26 in Chapter 2 of our study.
93. Pranab K. Bardhan (1984). *Land Labour and Rural Poverty : Essays in Development Economics*, Oxford University Press, Delhi, pp. 35-6.

5

INCOME LEVELS AND WAGE RATES OF NON-CULTIVATING HOUSEHOLDS

IN THIS chapter we propose to study the income levels and composition of income of non-cultivating rural labour households for different districts and regions of Punjab and Haryana. Here we shall also study the wage rates and their mode of payments in different districts and regions and shall try to analyse the determinants of wage rate. The idea is that if the benefits of agricultural development have trickled down to the non-cultivating sections of the rural population also then it is expected to be reflected in their higher income. This chapter is divided into two sections. Section I deals with income levels and its composition. Section II deals with wage rates and variations in them. A wage determination model has been evolved and empirically tested in this section.

I

In this section we shall discuss the income level and the composition of income of rural wage labour and other non-cultivating households for different districts and regions of Punjab and Haryana. The hypotheses being tested in this section are :

(i) The level of their income is positively related with the level of development of the area, and

(ii) the non-wage component of income in their total income becomes stronger as we move from less developed to more developed districts.

Before taking up these hypotheses, however, we shall briefly discuss the relative importance of various sources in the total household income of wage labour and other non-cultivating households for different districts and regions of Punjab and Haryana and shall analyse the inter-district variations in them.

Before we analyse income, the concept of income that has been used here may be clarified. In our study income means actual income of the non-cultivating households from various sources, such as income from wages and salaries and income from non-wage sources. The wage income includes income from both farm and non-farm work of all the earning members, i.e., men, women and children, of the household. Non-wage income includes income from dairying, poultry and rearing of sheep, goats, pigs, fowls, rabbits, or any other livestock. Income from other 'household enterprises' other than farming, rearing and maintenance of livestock and poultry is also included in this category. Income from 'other sources' such as pension, remittances, rent and interests is also included in it. Finally, income from land leased out, if any, and net agricultural income, if the household undertakes any cultivation, are included in this category. But our concept of income does not include the benefits, if any, received by households from government expenditure on education, health and other social and economic services for the simple reason that it is extremely difficult to correctly allocate the differential benefits of such expenditures to households in a cross-section study.[1] For arriving at average household income for the district for wage labour and other non-cultivating households we have added incomes from all the sources discussed above for that category of households and divided it by number of households in that category for the district. Per capita income for the district for different categories has been arrived at by dividing the average household income for the category by the average size of the household for the respective category. Similar procedure has been adopted for arriving at household and per capita income of different regions and the States of Punjab and Haryana. However, before testing the hypothesis regarding trickle-down of agricultural growth, the relative importance of various sources in the annual incomes of wage labour and other non-cultivating households of Punjab and Haryana are first discussed briefly.

Tables 5.1 and 5.2 give source-wise income of 'wage labour households' for different districts and regions of Punjab and Haryana, respectively. For an average wage labour household in Punjab income from wage employment constitutes about 78 per cent of total household income. Within districts, however, there are large variations.

The proportion of income from wage employment varies from as low as 66.03 per cent in Hoshiarpur to as high as 86.86 per cent in Amritsar. In two-thirds of the districts, however, income from wages constitute more than three-fourth of the annual household income. The second major source of income for wage labour households in Punjab is the category called 'income from other sources' which includes income from pension, remittances, rent and interest. On an average about 12 per cent of the total household income comes from these sources. Once again, however, there are large inter-district variations. Income from 'other sources' varies from as low as 5.48 per cent in Ferozepur to as high as 20.71 per cent in Hoshiarpur. The higher proportion of income from 'other sources' in total household income in districts, like, Hoshiarpur, Jalandhar and Kapurthala, appears to be primarily the result of high remittances from abroad as these districts which together constitute 'Doaba' region of Punjab account for highest number of emigrants from the State. The third major source of income for wage labour households in Punjab is income from 'dairying, poultry and other livestock'. For the State, as a whole, this source accounts for 8.31 per cent of the total incomes, although once again there are large inter-district variations. Income from land leased out accounts for less than one per cent of total household income of wage labour households. Net income from agriculture constitutes only one-fourth of one per cent. Such a meagre income from land and agriculture shows that wage labour households in Punjab are not only asset poor in terms of land but they do not have access to land even as tenants. Income from 'other household enterprises' constitutes less than one per cent of total household income for the State as a whole. On an average a wage labour household in Punjab earns an annual income of Rs. 3,839 which gives a per capita annual income of Rs. 690.46 or a monthly per capita income of Rs. 57.54.

As in the case of Punjab wage labour households, in the case of Haryana, also, about four-fifths of the income comes from wage employment. Similarly, there are large inter-district variations and it ranges from as low as 66.45 per cent in Sonepat to as high as 86.70 per cent in the case of Ambala. But, unlike Punjab, the second major source of income for wage labour households in Haryana is "dairying, poultry and other livestock" which contribute 13.74 per cent of their total income. Thus, an average wage labour household in Haryana is better off than its Punjab counterpart in terms of animal wealth. Income from 'other sources', which includes income from pension and

TABLE 5.1: Source-wise Annual Household Income : Punjab (Labour)

(Rs.)

District/ Region	Income from land leased out	Net agri-culture income	Income from other H.H. enterprises	Income from other, sources	Income from dairying popultry & other live-stocks	Total non-wage income	Income from wa-ge emp-loyment	Total household income	Annual per capita income	Per capita income from wages	Produc-tivity male agricul-tual workers
(0)	(1)	(2)	(3)	(4)	(5)	(6)	(7)	(8)	(9)	(10)	(11)
Amritsar	—	—	3 (0.08)	290 (7.48)	216 (5.57)	509 (13.14)	3,365 (86.86)	3,874 (100.00)	718.73	624.30	3182
Bhatinda	18 (0.47)	—	—	334 (8.66)	293 (7.60)	645 (16.73)	3211 (83.27)	3856 (100.00)	683.69	569.32	3415
Faridkot	9 (0.24)	11 (0.30)	22 (0.59)	320 (8.67)	402 (10.90)	764 (20.72)	2,924 (79.28)	3,688 (100.00)	655.06	519.36	3993
Ferozepur	153 (3.98)	13 (0.34)	118 (3.06)	211 (5.48)	148 (3.85)	643 (16.71)	3,204 (83.29)	3,847 (100.00)	780.32	649.89	5076
Gurdaspur	21 (0.65)	25 (0.77)	47 (1.45)	430 (13.25)	85 (2.62)	608 (18.74)	2,637 (81.26)	3,245 (100.00)	576.37	468.38	3641
Hoshiarpur	136 (3.03)	32 (0.71)	56 (1.25)	928 (20.71)	370 (8.26)	1,522 (33.97)	2,958 (66.03)	4,480 (100.00)	869.90	574.37	3064
Jalandhar	61 (1.71)	—	—	608 (17.00)	94 (2.63)	763 (21.33)	2,814 (78.67)	3,577 (100.00)	628.64	494.55	4250

Co.

TABLE 5.1 — *Contd.*

(0)	(1)	(2)	(3)	(4)	(5)	(6)	(7)	(8)	(9)	(10)	(11)
Kapurthala	6 (0.16)	17 (0.46)	—	758 (20.30)	100 (2.68)	881 (23.59)	2,853 (76.41)	3,734 (100.00)	614.14	469.24	4158
Ludhiana	41 (0.94)	8 (0.18)	52 (1.19)	493 (11.26)	695 (15.87)	1,289 (29.44)	3,089 (70.56)	4,378 (100.00)	801.83	565.75	4832
Patiala	—	—	18 (0.47)	502 (13.00)	433 (11.22)	953 (24.69)	2,906 (75.30)	3,859 (100.00)	618.42	465.70	4669
Ropar	—	21 (0.59)	106 (2.97)	278 (7.80)	249 (6.99)	654 (18.36)	2,908 (81.64)	3,562 (100.00)	694.34	566.86	3086
Sangrur	1 (0.03)	5 (0.13)	—	385 (10.20)	586 (15.52)	977 (25.87)	2799 (74.13)	3,776 (100.00)	649.91	481.75	4564
Region I	23 (0.59)	3 (0.07)	17 (0.43)	484 (12.36)	334 (8.52)	861 (21.99)	3,055 (78.01)	3,916 (100.00)	688.22	536.91	4143
Region II	37 (0.98)	7 (0.18)	28 (0.74)	321 (8.47)	371 (9.79)	764 (20.16)	3,025 (79.84)	3,789 (100.00)	682.70	545.04	4249
Region III	60 (1.59)	27 (0.72)	61 (1.62)	591 (15.69)	221 (5.87)	960 (25.49)	2,806 (74.51)	3,766 (100.00)	702.61	523.50	3310
Punjab	37 (0.96)	10 (0.26)	31 (0.81)	457 (11.90)	319 (8.31)	854 (22.25)	2,985 (77.75)	3,839 (100.00)	690.46	536.87	4030

Note: Figures in parentheses are percentage of the total in column No. 8.

TABLE 5.2: Source-wise Annual Household Income: Haryana (Labour)

District/ Region	Income from land leased out	Net agri- culture income	Income from other H.H. enterprises	Income from other, sources	Income from dairying popultry & other live- stocks	Total non-wage income	Income from wa- ge emp- loyment	Total household income	Annual per capita income	Per capita income from wages	Produc- tivity male agricul- tual workers
(0)	(1)	(2)	(3)	(4)	(5)	(6)	(7)	(8)	(9)	(10)	(11)
Ambala	—	—	—	17	402	419	2,731	3,150	592.10	513.34	2,055
				(0.54)	(12.76)	(13.30)	(86.70)	(100.00)			
Bhiwani	—	—	144	666	587	1397	2,824	4,221	767.45	513.45	989
			(3.41)	(15.78)	(13.91)	(33.09)	(66.90)	(100.00)			
Gurgaon	—	—	32	108	378	518	3,164	3,682	596.76	512.80	1,094
			(0.87)	(2.93)	(10.27)	(10.07)	(85.93)	(100.00)			
Hissar	—	12	86	1	627	726	3,639	4,365	702.89	585.99	1,300
		(0.27)	(19.97)	(0.02)	(14.36)	(16.63)	(83.37)	(100.00)			
Jind	—	—	30	383	220	633	2,266	2,899	407.16	318.26	1,743
			(0.10)	(13.21)	(7.59)	(21.84)	(78.16)	(100.00)			
Karnal	18	—	—	146	376	540	2,450	2,990	542.65	444.64	2,450
	(0.60)			(4.88)	(12.57)	(18.06)	(81.94)	(100.00)			
Kurukshetra	—	—	16	455	379	850	2,386	3,236	541.14	398.99	2,778
			(0.49)	(14.06)	(11.71)	(26.27)	(73.73)	(100.00)			

Contd.

TABLE 5.2 — *Contd.*

(0)	(1)	(2)	(3)	(4)	(5)	(6)	(7)	(8)	(9)	(10)	(11)
Mohindergarh	52 (1.02)	—	91 (1.79)	490 (9.66)	960 (18.92)	1593 (31.40)	3,481 (68.60)	5,074 (100.00)	838.67	575.37	1,120
Rohtak	—	18 (0.36)	77 (1.54)	351 (7.02)	871 (17.43)	1317 (26.35)	3,680 (73.64)	4,997 (100.00)	755.97	556.73	1,596
Sonepat	—	—	18 (0.65)	313 (11.29)	599 (21.61)	930 (33.55)	1,842 (66.45)	2,772 (100.00)	442.81	294.25	2,050
Region I	5 (0.16)	—	8 (0.26)	228 (7.52)	425 (14.01)	666 (21.96)	2,367 (78.04)	3,033 (100.00)	528.39	412.37	2,391
Region II	—	10 (0.24)	70 (1.70)	177 (4.30)	569 (13.81)	826 (20.05)	3,294 (79.95)	4,120 (100.00)	635.80	508.33	1,448
Region III	10 (0.25)	—	69 (1.69)	309 (7.59)	533 (13.10)	921 (22.63)	3,148 (77.37)	4,069 (100.00)	679.99	525.54	1,155
Haryana	4 (0.11)	4 (0.11)	43 (1.18)	222 (6.10)	500 (13.74)	773 (21.25)	2,865 (78.75)	3,638 (100.00)	597.37	470.44	1,634

Note: Figures in parentheses are percentages of the total in column No. 8.

remittances, accounts for about six per cent. In fact this source of income is important only in 'jat' dominated districts of Bhiwani, Mohindergarh, Rohtak, Sonepat, Kurukshetra and Jind. The explanation for this, perhaps, lies in the fact that people from these districts have age old tradition of serving in the army which give rise to income from pension and remittances. Income from 'other household enterprises' constitutes only slightly more than one per cent. Total income from land and agriculture constitutes one-half of one per cent of their total income which means in terms of landed assets a Haryana wage labourer is even more poor than its Punjab counterpart. On an average a wage labour household in Haryana earns Rs. 3,638 per annum which is about five per cent lower than its Punjab counterpart. However, because of the large average size of the family in Haryana (6.09) as compared to Punjab (5.56) its per capita annual income of Rs. 597.37 is about 15 per cent lower than its counterpart in Punjab.

Tables 5.3 and 5.4 show source-wise annual household income of other non-cultivating households for different districts and regions of Punjab and Haryana, respectively. A look at these tables reveals that in the case of other non-cultivating households the pattern of income generation is vastly different from those of wage labour households. In the first place income from wage employment in their case accounts for less than one-fifth of their total income and more than four-fifths comes from non-wage sources. In Punjab among the non-wage sources 'household enterprises' alone account for more than half of their total annual income. Another 15.43 per cent is contributed by 'other sources' such as pension and remittances. Once again Hoshiarpur, Jalandhar and Kapurthala, along with Ludhiana and Patiala, are the districts which have higher proportion of their income compared to the state average coming from 'other sources'. Incidentally income from land leased out constitutes the fourth major source of income for this category of households. About eight per cent of their income comes from land. However, net income from agriculture constitutes only one-fifth of one per cent for this category also. On an average a non-cultivating rural labour household is much better off than its counterpart in the 'wage labour' category in terms of landed asset holdings. Income from dairying, poultry and other livestocks constitutes 7.15 per cent of their total income. However, there are large inter-district variations in it. On an average a household belonging to the category of 'other non-cultivating rural labour households' earns an annual income of Rs. 5,869 which is about 53 per cent higher than the income of an average wage labour household in Punjab.

TABLE 5.3: Source-wise Annual Household Income: Punjab (Other Non-Cultivating Households)

(Rs.)

District/ Region	Income from land leased out	Net agri-culture income	Income from other H.H. enterprises	Income from other, sources	Income from dairying popultry & other live-stocks	Total non-wage income	Income from wa-ge emp-loyment	Total household income	Annual per capita income	Per capita income from wages	Produc-tivity male agricul-tual workers
0	1	2	3	4	5	6	7	8	9	10	11
Amritsar	398	—	3,501	616	168	4,683	1,705	6,388	1,376.72	367.45	3,182
	(6.23)	—	(54.81)	(9.64)	(2.63)	(73.30)	(26.69)	(100.00)			
Bhatinda	368	—	5,793	327	579	7,067	1,454	8,521	1,306.69	223.01	3,415
	(4.32)		(67.98)	(3.84)	(6.79)	(82.94)	(17.06)	(100.00)			
Faridkot	142	—	4,500	379	399	5,420	663	6,083	1,046.99	113.33	3,993
	(2.33)		(73.97)	(6.23)	(6.56)	(89.10)	(10.90)	(100.00)			
Ferozepur	1031	—	2,866	196	741	4,834	584	5,418	969.23	104.47	5,076
	(19.03)		(52.90)	(3.62)	(13.67)	(89.22)	(10.78)	(100.00)			
Gurdaspur	449	—	1,492	1,121	135	3,197	584	3,781	741.37	114.50	3,641
	(11.87)		(39.46)	(29.65)	(3.57)	(84.55)	(15.45)	(100.00)			
Hoshiarpur	467	25	2,823	1,470	398	5,183	1,650	6,833	1,377.62	332.66	3,064
	(6.83)	(0.36)	(41.31)	(21.51)	(5.82)	(75.85)	(24.15)	(100.00)			

Contd.

TABLE 5.3 — *Contd.*

(0)	(1)	(2)	(3)	(4)	(5)	(6)	(7)	(8)	(9)	(10)	(11)
Jalandhar	288	79	1,962	1,233	156	3,718	1,477	5,195	1,014.65	288.47	4,250
	(5.54)	(1.52)	(37.77)	(23.73)	(3.00)	(71.57)	(28.43)	(100.00)			
Kapurthala	192	—	1,804	749	532	3,277	1,333	4,610	1,008.75	291.68	4,156
	(4.16)		(39.13)	(16.25)	(11.54)	(71.08)	(28.92)	(100.00)			
Ludhiana	633	—	2,643	1,443	704	5,423	1,688	7,111	1,383.46	328.40	4,832
	(8.90)		(37.17)	(20.29)	(9.90)	((76.26)	(23.74)	(100.00)			
Patiala	670		1,875	978	296	3,819	1,446	5,265	1,028.32	282.42	4,669
	(12.73)		(35.61)	(18.58)	(5.62)	(72.54)	(27.46)	(100.00)			
Ropar	100	—	2,810	625	762	4,297	1,139	5,436	1,383.21	289.82	3,086
	(1.84)		(51.69)	(11.50)	(14.02)	(79.05)	(20.95)	(100.00)			
Sangrur	859	—	2,063	1,494	643	5,059	818	5,877	940.32	130.88	4,564
	(14.62)		(35.10)	(25.42)	(10.94)	(86.08)	(13.92)	(100.00)			
Region I	441	22	2,488	1,015	318	4,284	1,203	5,487	1,110.73	243.52	4,143
	(8.03)	(0.40)	(45.34)	(18.50)	(5.79)	(78.07)	(21.92)	(100.00)			
Region II	567	—	3,974	606	584	5,731	933	6,664	1,094.25	153.20	4,249
	(8.51)		(59.63)	(9.09)	(8.76)	(86.00)	(14.00)	(100.00)			
Region III	384	10	2,324	1,162	376	4,256	1,146	5,402	1127.76	239.25	3,310
	(7.11)	(0.18)	(43.02)	(21.51)	(6.96)	(78.79)	(21.21)	(100.00)			
Punjab	472	12	2,959	906	420	4,769	1,100	5,869	1107.35	207.55	4,030
	(8.04)	(0.20)	(50.42)	(15.43)	(7.16)	(81.26)	(18.74)	(100.00)			

Note: Figures in parentheses are percentages of the total in column No. 8.

TABLE 5.4: Source-wise Annual Household Income: Haryana (Other Non-Cultivating Households)

(Rs.)

District/ Region	Income from land leased out	Net agri-culture income	Income from other H.H. enterprises	Income from other, sources	Income from dairying popultry & other live-stocks	Total non-wage income	Income from wa-ge emp-loyment	Total household income	Annual per capita income	Per capita income from wages	Produc-tivity male agricul-tual workers
(0)	(1)	(2)	(3)	(4)	(5)	(6)	(7)	(8)	(9)	(10)	(11)
Ambala	190	—	2,334	411	578	3,513	1,228	4,741	840.00	217.73	2,055
	(4.00)		(49.23)	(8.67)	(12.19)	(74.10)	(29.90)	(100.00)			
Bhiwani	7	—	1,307	1,585	952	3,851	2,604	6,455	994.61	401.23	989
	(0.11)		(20.25)	(24.55)	(14.75)	(59.66)	(40.34)	(100.00)			
Gurgaon	18	—	3,112	191	462	3,783	1,260	5,051	876.91	220.13	1,094
	(0.36)		(61.61)	(3.78)	(9.15)	(74.89)	(24.95)	(100.00)			
Hissar	24	—	5,106	1,370	1,004	7,504	1,707	9,211	1638.96	303.73	1,300
	(0.26)		(55.43)	(14.87)	(10.90)	(81.46)	(18.53)	(100.00)			
Jind	—	—	2,575	467	268	3,310	875	4185	783.70	163.85	1,743
			(61.53)	(11.16)	(6.40)	(79.09)	(20.91)	(100.00)			
Karnal	35	10	1,996	284	533	2,860	1,066	3,926	672.26	182.53	2,450
	(0.89)	(0.25)	(50.89)	(7.23)	(13.57)	(72.85)	(27.15)	(100.00)			
Kurukshetra	129	—	3,190	342	245	3,906	1,165	5,071	940.81	216.14	2,778
	(2.54)		(62.91)	(6.74)	(4.83)	(77.03)	(22.97)	(100.00)			

Contd

TABLE 5.4 — *Contd.*

(0)	(1)	(2)	(3)	(4)	(5)	(6)	(7)	(8)	(9)	(10)	(11)
Mohindergarh	108	—	1,288	478	951	2,825	2,076	4,901	872.06	369.39	1,120
	(2.20)		(26.28)	(9.75)	(19.40)	(57.64)	(42.36)	(100.00)			
Rohtak	34	—	1589	1,883	836	4,342	1,300	5,642	1,002.13	230.91	1,596
	(0.60)		(28.16)	(33.37)	(14.82)	(76.96)	(23.04)	(100.00)			
Sonepat	42	—	2,993	468	747	4,250	919	5,189	854.38	151.90	2,050
	(0.81)		(57.90)	(9.05)	(14.55)	(82.22)	(17.78)	(100.00)			
Region I	97	3	2,635	372	515	2,622	1,005	4,717	824.65	191.43	2,391
	(2.05)	(0.06)	(55.86)	(7.88)	(10.92)	(76.79)	(12.21)	(100.00)			
Region II	21	—	3,174	1,290	736	5,221	1,330	6,551	1,182.49	240.07	1,148
	(0.32)		(48.45)	(19.69)	(11.23)	(79.70)	(20.30)	(100.00)			
Region III	45	—	2,100	605	734	3,484	1,834	5,318	904.42	311.90	1,155
	(0.85)		(39.29)	(11.37)	(13.80)	(65.51)	(34.49)	(100.00)			
Haryana	60	1	2,668	716	639	4,084	1,354	5,438	954.03	237.54	1,634
	(1.10)	(0.02)	(49.06)	(13.17)	(11.75)	(75.10)	(24.90)	(100.00)			

Note: Figures in parentheses are percentages of the total in Column No. 8.

In the case of 'other non-cultivating households' of Haryana about one-fourth of their income comes from wage employment and the rest three-fourths from non-wage sources. Like Punjab, in Haryana, also, amongst the non-wage sources 'household enterprises' alone contribute about half of their total annual income. Income from 'other sources' which include pension and remittances accounts for 13.17 per cent of their total annual income. 'Dairying, poultry and other livestock' account for another 11.75 per cent. But unlike Punjab, land and agriculture are not important sources of income even for this category of households in Haryana. Together these two sources account for slightly more than one per cent of their total annual income. On an average a household in the category of 'other non-cultivating households' in Haryana earns an annual income of Rs. 5,438 which is approximately eight per cent lower than its counterpart in Punjab. Once again, however, because of the largeer family size of this category in Haryana (5.70) as compared to Punjab (5.30), its per capita income is about 16 per cent lower than its counterpart in Punjab.

After having discussed the importance of various sources in the annual income of 'wage labour' and 'other non-cultivating households' of Punjab and Haryana, we shall now briefly discuss whether the household or per capita income of these categories have any relationship with the level of agricultural development of the districts to see if the benefit of agricultural development have trickled-down to the non-cultivating sections of rural population also or not. If the trickle-down effect is present then we should expect a positive relationship between the per capita income of the category and the level of agricultural development of the districts. The evidence so far on this question 'from rural India' is not unambiguous. Of course, in general growth in agricultural output tends to generate some forces improving the income of wage labourers. Generally, yield increasing and land improvement factors increase the demand for hired labour and this is, by and large, also the case with the biological innovations which are part of the new agricultural technology. By shortening the duration of the crop cycle and increasing the importance of timeless of each operation, the new technology also increases the bargaining power of wage labourers at some crucial points of time. In spite of all this, as we have discussed in Chapter 1, some studies have pointed out that in India the new technology may have adversely affected the relative share of wage labour in output.[2] What is more controversial however, is the question of absolute immiserisation of agricultural labourers. Before turning to the evidence on this question let us first enumerate the possible ways in which the income generating forces mentioned above could have been counter-acted and the 'trickle-down' process of agricultural growth blocked as far as agricultural wage labourers are concerned.

One possible way trickle-down can be blocked is the effect of adoption of labour displacing machinery, which is incidentally considerable in area of our study. A second factor is that there have been heavy influx of labour in the agricultural labour market in some high growth regions thereby depressing their wages. The immigration of labour in Punjab and some parts of Haryana from backward districts of Bihar and eastern Uttar Pradesh is a case in point. Third, and probably more significantly, there have been over-crowding in many regions of the labour market as a result of the growth process itself. For example, increased profitability of self-cultivation by land-owners may lead to eviction of small tenants who join the rank of wage earners. A decrease in the number of operational holdings in Punjab by about 3.8 lakhs during 1971-81 as discussed in Chapter 2 points towards this tendency. Again the demand pattern of the new rural rich, who are themselves the creature of the agricultural development, may shift away from local handicraft and services to mass-produced urban consumer goods thereby pushing the village artisans in the already over-crowed agricultural labour market.

The empirical evidence on the question of absolute poverty of agricultural labour in rural India is, however, scanty. Perhaps the most recent and also most detailed evidence on this issue is a study by Bardhan (1984).[3] Bardhan discussed this issue by examining statistical evidence from two sources of data:

(i) Rural Labour Enquiries for the period 1964-65 and 1974-75, and
(ii) NSS data for 1963-64 and 1977-78.

The first set of data suggests a 16 per cent decline in annual wage incomes of agricultural labour households for the whole of rural India. This decline is observed in all States including the highest growth region of Punjab-Haryana, except Uttar Pradesh.[4] There are, however, two limitations in drawing conclusions from this data and both are recognised by Bardhan. First, 1974-75 is not a good agricultural year as compared to 1964-65 and, secondly, income does not cover non-wage income.

The estimates based on NSS data for 1963-64 and 1977-78 suggest that the proportion of labour household below the poverty line for rural India as a whole (poverty being defined as Rs. 15 per capita at 1960-61 prices) increased somewhat from 52 per cent to 56 per cent despite the fact that over this period net domestic product from agriculture (at 1960-61 prices) went up by about 43 per cent.[5] Bardhan also pursues a much more disaggregative analysis by using NSS cross-section data for (i) agricultural labour households of West Bengal in 1977-78, and (ii) 55 agro-climatic regions of NSS for early 1970s. The probability of an agricultural labour households falling below poverty line in rural West Bengal seems to be higher if the household is located in a district where agricultural production has grown at a faster rate. Bardhan attributes this result to a higher rate of tenant eviction in the advanced districts. Parthasarthy (1984), however, challenges Bardhan's these findings and points out that if backward districts are found to be those with higher rates of growth then the association of high poverty may be more with backwardness of the district than the rate of growth.[6] Unlike the results obtained from West Bengal data, Bardhan's analysis at the NSS region level shows a positive association between the rate of growth of crop production and the level of living of the wage-earnings households.[7] Therefore, the overall evidence on the question of 'trickle-down' effects of agricultural growth on the poverty of agricultural wage labour households is mixed and not unambiguously comforting.

In this study we shall test if there is any relationship between the per capita income of an average wage labour household and the level of agricultural development of the districts defined as productivity per male agricultural worker. We believe that productivity per male agricultural workers is a better indicator of the level of agricultural development than productivity per acre to test the trickle-down hypothesis because it not only takes into account how much is being produced in an acre but also how many workers are producing it. The trickle down hypothesis will be tested by taking a cross section of 22 districts of Punjab and Haryana. The average annual per capita income of wage labour households and productivity per male agricultural worker for different districts of Punjab and Haryana are given in column numbers 9 and 11 of Tables 5.1 and 5.2, respectively. A look at these Tables reveal that there appears to be no systematic relationship between the average per capita income of the wage labour households and the level of productivity per male agricultural workers. For example, in Punjab there are high productivity high income districts, such as Ferozepur and Ludhiana, and low productivity low income districts such as Bhatinda, Faridkot, Gurdaspur and Ropar. But then there are also high productivity low income districts such as Jalandhar, Kapurthala and Patiala as well as low productivity high income districts. A more or less similar picture emerges for Haryana from Table 5.2. If, however, we consider all the 22 districts together then we find that generally per capita income is higher in Punjab districts where the productivity per labour is also higher as compared to Haryana districts. When we calculate the correlation coefficient between the per capita income and the labour productivity of the districts for a cross-section of 22 districts of Punjab and Haryana it works out to be 0.105 which is statistically insignificant. Thus, we find that trickle-down hypothesis, though indicated, is not quite established with income data in the case of wage labour households.

As in the case of wage labour households, in non-cultivating households, also, there appears to be no systematic relationship between the level of their per capita income and the level of productivity per worker of the districts as is evident from column numbers 9 and 11 of Tables 5.3 and 5.4. The correlation in their case works out to be 0.134 which again is statistically insignificant.

To test our second hypothesis, i.e., whether the non-wage component of the income becomes stronger as we move from less-developed to more developed districts, we shall analyse the proportion of non-wage income in the total household income of wage labour and other non-cultivating households of Punjab and Haryana. A look at column number 6 of Tables 5.1 and 5.2 would reveal that there appears to be no systematic relationship between proportion of non-wage income in the total household income of wage labour households and the level of agricultural development of the district in either of the two States. Our impression of non-systematic relationship is confirmed when we calculate correlation between the two series for a cross section of 22 districts. It works out to be -0.040 which is statistically insignificant.

In the case of other non-cultivating households, however, there appears to be some systematic pattern between the proportion of their non-wage income and the level of productivity per male agricultural worker of the district. For example, it is generally higher in Punjab districts where the labour productivity is also higher as compared to

Haryana. The figure for Punjab is 81.26 per cent as compared to 75.10 per cent in Haryana. The correlation between the proportion of non-wage component of income in the total income of other non-cultivating households and the level of productivity per-male agricultural worker for a cross-section of 22 districts of Punjab and Haryana works out to be 0.449 which is significant at 5 per cent level of significance. Thus, there emerges a positive relationship between the proportion of non-wage income of other non-cultivating households and the level of agricultural development of the district defined as productivity per male agricultural worker.

It appears that agricultural development, wherever it took place, has created some opportunities for self-employment outside agriculture in allied activities such as machinery repairing and servicing and supply of various other agricultural inputs, etc. Increased income of farmers as a result of agricultural growth has also created demand for new urban produced goods and new kind of services within the village. That section of rural population which is making use of these opportunities and is catering to the demands of modern agriculture in these areas has experienced a shift in their pattern of income generation away from wage employment. As a result the proportion of non-wage income in the total household income has become stronger in these areas.

To sum-up, our analysis of the income data of wage labour and other non-cultivating households indicates that there has been some percolation of the benefits of agricultural growth to this non-cultivating sections of the rural society also. The relationship is statistically insignificant and thus the trickle-down hypothesis, though indicated is, not quite established on the basis of income data. Also the hypothesis that the proportion of non-wage income becomes stronger, as we move from less-developed to more developed areas, is not borne out by our analysis of the income data for the wage labour households. However, there is a positive relationship between the non-wage component of income and the level of agricultural development of the district defined as productivity per male agricultural workers in the case of primarily self-employed, non-wage, non-cultivating rural households. The income figures of wage labour households, however, are likely to be highly unstable and the trickle-down hypothesis should more appropriately be tested with consumption data which are more stable and reliable. That we shall take up in the next chapter. Currently we move on to the next section to analyse wages and the factors determining wage rates.

II

Wage Rate and its Determinants

In the preceding section we have seen that about four-fifths of the income of wage labour households in both Punjab and Haryana comes from the sale of their labour power, i.e., wages and salaries. This component of their income is the product of number of days the members of a family get work and the prevailing wage rate. The work availability and rate of unemployment prevailing in various districts of Punjab and Haryana and their correlates have been discussed in the preceding chapter. In this section we shall discuss the wage rate of agricultural labourers, both attached and casual, prevailing in various districts of Punjab and Haryana and shall try to explain the inter-district variation in them. Our hypotheses are :

(i) wages are positively related to the level of agricultural development of the district; and
(ii) that wages are negatively related to the proportion of wages paid in cash.

Alternative theories of wage determination are also discussed in this section. We have also evolved a wage determination model in terms of demand and supply forces. This has been empirically tested with the help of district level data and the results are discussed and interpreted in this section. However, first we shall discuss the wage rates of attached and casual agricultural labourers for different districts of Punjab and Haryana and try to explain inter-district variations in them.

Tables 5.5 and 5.6 give district-wise daily and annual wage rate of attached agricultural labourers and their break up in terms of cash and kind or perquisites. A look at these tables would reveal that wage varies significantly between the districts. In Punjab it ranges from Rs. 1,850 per annum in Gurdaspur to Rs. 2,518 per annum in Bhatinda district. The daily wage varies from Rs. 5.06 per day in Gurdaspur to Rs. 6.90 per day in Bhatinda. The State average daily wage comes to Rs. 5.95 and annual to Rs. 2,174 which is slightly higher than Haryana's Rs. 5.69 per day or Rs. 2,077 per annum. In Haryana, it ranges from Rs. 1,789 (Rs. 4.90 per day) in Sonepat to Rs. 2,430 (Rs.

6.66 per day) in Hissar per annum. There seems to be no relationship between productivity per acre and wage rate paid to an attached labourer. For example, in Punjab some high productivity districts, like, Ludhiana Jalandhar and Gurdaspur, are having annual or daily wage of attached labourers which is below the state average. On the other hand, Bhatinda, Hoshiarpur and Ropar are low productivity districts but are having much higher wage than the average wage rate. Similar is the case with Haryana. Interestingly, there does not seem to be any direct relationship between productivity of land and wage rate of attached agricultural labourers. The correlation between the wage rate of attached agricultural labourer and the level of agricultural development of the district works out to be +0.286 which is statistically insignificant.

TABLE 5.5: District-wise Wage Rate of Attached Agricultural Labourer (Punjab)

District/ State	Cash (Rs.)	Kind (Rs.)	Perquisites (Rs.)	Total (Rs.)	Annual average (Rs.)	Productivity Per acre (Rs.)
Amritsar	1.22 (18.37)	3.87 (58.28)	1.55 (23.34)	6.64 (100.00)	2,423.50	1,848.8
Bhatinda	1.01 (14.63)	4.58 (66.37)	1.31 (18.99)	6.90 (100.00)	2,517.97	1,335.8
Faridkot	4.05 (73.77)	0.77 (14.02)	0.67 (12.20)	5.49 (100.00)	2,004.08	1,720.8
Ferozepur	2.95 (46.16)	2.06 (32.23)	1.38 (21.60)	6.39 (100.00)	2,334.88	1,900.0
Gurdaspur	2.71 (53.56)	1.94 (38.34)	0.41 (8.10)	5.06 (100.00)	1,850.05	2,050.4
Hoshiarpur	5.37 (83.38)	0.43 (6.67)	0.64 (9.94)	6.44 (100.00)	2,355.00	1,646.8
Jalandhar	3.76 (68.24)	1.26 (22.86)	0.48 (8.71)	5.51 (100.00)	2,010.83	2,242.7
Kapurthala	4.50 (72.00)	0.66 (10.56)	1.09 (17.44)	6.25 (100.00)	2,282.20	2,122.4
Ludhiana	3.34 (57.98)	2.08 (36.11)	0.34 (5.90)	5.76 (100.00)	2,120.03	2,165.8
Patiala	3.71 (61.12)	2.06 (33.94)	0.29 (4.78)	6.07 (100.00)	2,215.62	2,016.0
Ropar	2.52 (39.75)	2.44 (38.48)	1.38 (21.77)	6.34 (100.00)	2,312.60	1,855.8
Sangrur	2.85 (49.74)	2.33 (40.66)	0.55 (9.60)	5.73 (100.00)	2,091.67	1,869.3
Punjab	2.76 (46.38)	2.44 (41.01)	0.75 (12.61)	5.95 (100.00)	2,174.28	1,864.2

Note: Figures in parentheses are percentages.

TABLE 5.6: District-wise Wage Rate of Attached Agricultural Labourer (Haryana)

District/ State	Cash (Rs.)	Kind (Rs.)	Perquisites (Rs.)	Total (Rs.)	Annual average (Rs.)	Productivity Per acre (Rs.)
Ambala	1.98 (36.13)	2.25 (41.05)	1.25 (22.81)	5.48 (100.00)	1,999.76	1,860.4
Bhiwani	5.48 (100.00)	—	—	5.48 (100.00)	2,000.00	731.9
Gurgaon	1.62 (30.57)	3.32 (62.64)	0.36 (6.79)	5.30 (100.00)	1,935.38	1,094.0
Hissar	2.94 (44.64)	2.54 (38.14)	1.18 (17.72)	6.66 (100.00)	2,430.04	1,101.0
Jind	1.14 (20.39)	3.58 (64.04)	0.87 (15.56)	5.59 (100.00)	2,040.40	1,261.0
Karnal	3.32 (65.87)	1.20 (23.81)	0.53 (10.52)	5.04 (100.00)	1,841.22	1,921.9
Kurukshetra	2.87 (49.59)	2.05 (34.00)	1.11 (18.41)	6.03 (100.00)	2,202.43	1,932.0
Mohindergarh	3.47 (69.82)	0.80 (16.10)	0.70 (14.08)	4.97 (100.00)	1,815.00	785.4
Rohtak	4.34 (74.82)	0.57 (9.83)	0.89 (15.34)	5.80 (100.00)	2,117.00	1,174.9
Sonepat	3.35 (68.37)	0.43 (8.77)	1.12 (22.86)	4.90 (100.00)	1,788.85	1,672.8
Haryana	2.63 (46.22)	2.12 (37.26)	0.94 (16.52)	5.69 (100.00)	2,076.98	1,269.7

Note: Figures in parentheses are percentages.

About 46 per cent of the wages of attached agricultural labourers in both Punjab and Haryana are paid in cash, the rest in kind or perquisites. But there are very large inter-district variations. There appears to be some relationship between the proportion of wage paid in cash and the wage rate of the district. For instance, in Punjab State, Bhatinda and Amritsar, the two highest wage districts, are also the one where the proportion of wage of attached agricultural labourers paid in cash is the lowest. On the other hand, Jalandhar, Ludhiana and Faridkot districts are below average wage districts but have very high proportion of wage paid in cash. But there are exception also. A similar pattern can also be observed in Haryana. We have calculated the correlation for a cross section of 22 districts of Punjab and Haryana between the proportion of wage paid in cash and the wage rate to see if there is any systematic relationship between the two. The correlation is

-0.396 which is statistically significant at five per cent level of significance. Thus, there is a negative relationship between the proportion of wage paid in cash and the wage rate but there is no systematic relationship between the wage rate of attached labourer and productivity per acre of the district.

After analysing the district-wise wage rates of attached agricultural labourers we shall now analyse the wage rates of male casual workers. Tables 5.7 and 5.8 give the operation-wise break-up of daily wage rates of male casual workers for various districts of Punjab and Haryana. Column 6 in these tables give the average daily wage rate. Column 7 gives the average number of days a casual worker get work and the last column gives the average annual earnings of a male casual worker for the district.

TABLE 5.7 Operation-wise Wage Rate of Male Casual Workers (Punjab)

District/ State	Rs. Per Day							
	Sowing	Ploughing	Harvesting	Others	Non-Agricultural	Average daily wage	No. of man days available	Average annual earnings per male casual worker
(0)	(1)	(2)	(3)	(4)	(5)	(6)	(7)	(8)
Amritsar	7.75	6.36	8.38	7.65	5.93	7.61	315.15	2,398.29
Bhatinda	7.00	8.10	11.03	8.09	6.98	8.83	245.01	2,163.43
Faridkot	9.00	8.53	9.28	8.10	9.17	8.82	253.72	2,237.81
Ferozepur	10.00	8.95	9.26	8.34	8.18	8.69	248.58	2,160.16
Gurdaspur	6.00	5.30	7.86	7.00	6.27	6.81	233.48	1,589.99
Hoshiarpur	—	7.25	10.25	7.12	7.48	8.12	228.71	1,857.12
Jalandhar	—	9.00	8.34	7.69	7.92	7.89	231.34	1,825.27
Kapurthala	6.75	6.00	10.46	6.55	8.89	8.42	238.23	2,005.89
Ludhiana	7.84	7.33	9.74	9.06	9.29	9.10	265.47	2,415.78
Patiala	—	5.83	8.73	7.26	7.26	7.58	178.57	1,353.56
Ropar	—	—	6.74	6.76	7.29	8.00	211.58	1,692.64
Sangrur	5.57	7.28	8.98	7.73	8.14	8.12	212.64	1,726.63
Punjab	7.71	8.76	9.12	7.87	7.49	8.12	240.89	1,956.08

The difference between the average daily wage rate of the two States as well as inter-district variation in wages are much larger in the case of casual labourers as compared to attached labourers. While differences between the average daily wage of attached agricultural labourer between Punjab and Haryana is only of 26 paise, the difference in the wage rate of casual agricultural workers between the two States is of the order of Rs. 2.30, i.e., a difference of about 40 per cent. As a result, although the average number of days a casual worker gets work are fewer in Punjab as compared to Haryana, yet the average annual earnings of a male casual worker in Punjab are significantly higher than that of his counterpart in Haryana. We also find that in both the States the annual earnings of a casual worker are slightly less than that of an attached labourer, but then an attached labourer works throughout the year whereas a casual workers work on an average for 241 days in Punjab and 258 days in Haryana. As a result an attached labourer earns a much lower wage per day although his overall earnings are larger than a casual worker because he works for a much longer period.

TABLE 5.8: Operation-wise Wage Rate of Male Casual Workers (Haryana)

District/ State	Rs. Per Day							
	Sowing	Ploughing	Harvesting	Others	Non-agriculture	Average daily wage	No. of man-days available	Average annual earnings per male casual worker
(0)	(1)	(2)	(3)	(4)	(5)	(6)	(7)	(8)
Ambala	6.50	5.75	7.00	6.39	5.58	6.03	250.00	1,508.04
Bhiwani	—	5.85	5.33	4.61	3.88	4.94	244.83	1,209.46
Gurgaon	5.00	6.55	5.56	4.45	4.92	5.05	283.92	1,433.79
Hisaar	6.22	6.34	6.97	6.02	6.33	6.35	314.81	1,999.04
Jind	7.00	6.15	5.89	4.62	5.46	5.62	221.00	1,242.02
Karnal	6.01	6.10	5.98	6.32	6.61	6.20	275.05	1,705.31
Kurukshetra	6.76	—	5.77	6.53	7.50	6.42	193.14	1,239.95
Mohindergarh	7.00	5.50	5.13	5.92	6.22	5.79	279.15	1,616.28
Rohtak	7.63	6.14	5.87	4.56	5.78	5.77	305.76	1,764.23
Sonepat	—	—	4.25	4.68	5.71	5.16	161.20	831.79
Haryana	6.13	6.21	6.05	5.49	5.64	5.82	258.03	1,501.73

There appears to be a positive relationship between the wage rate of casual workers and the level of development of the districts. For example, in Punjab the high productivity districts, like, Kapurthala, Ferozepur, Ludhiana and Sangrur, are also having wage rate above the state average. On the other hand low productivity districts of Hoshiarpur, Ropar and Amritsar are having below average wage rate of casual workers. This appears consistent with our hypothesis, although there are some exceptions also. In Haryana the relationship appears to be still more clear-cut. For example, the three high productivity districts of Ambala, Karnal and Kurukshetra are having above average wage rate. On the other hand, all five low productivity districts — Bhiwani, Mohindergarh, Gurgaon, Rohtak and Jind — are having wage rate which is below the state average. The only exceptions are Sonepat and Hissar. By and large, the wage rates of male casual workers seem to support our hypothesis that wages are positively related to the level of agricultural development of the district. The correlation between the wage rate of male casual workers and the level of agricultural productivity per acre of the districts for a cross-section of 22 districts of Punjab and Haryana works out to be 0.616 which is statistically significant at one per cent level of significance. Thus we find that our hypotheses that wage levels are positively related to the level of agricultural development of the district and negatively related to the proportion of wages paid in cash are, by and large, supported by the empirical evidence.

Determinants of Wage Rates

While agricultural productivity of the district does effect the wage rate it is certainly not the only important factor in explaining the variations in wage rates across districts. There are a host of other demographic, institutional and socio-economic factors which are likely to have a bearing on the level of wages of agricultural workers. Therefore, in the following pages we shall try to explain the determinants of wage rate. For this purpose we shall take wage of male casual worker as representing the wage level. Our understanding is that while an attached labourer is sometimes employed to have some amount of assured labour supply during the peak season, although his services may not be properly utilised throughout the year, a casual labourer is employed only when he is really required. Thus, average daily wage of a casual worker is a better indicator of the existing conditions of demand and supply than the wage of an attached labourer. Before, however, we discuss the determinants of wage rate in terms of our model, we shall briefly discuss the alternative theories of wage determination and empirical evidence available on this issue from rural

India.

Alternative Theories of Wage Determination: Empirical Evidence from Rural India

Thanks largely to the works of Lewis (1954),[8] Nurkse (1953)[9] and Ranis and Fei (1961)[10], it was widely believed that the supply of labour in under-developed thickly populated countries is almost perfectly elastic and that real wage rate in such economies is institutionally determined roughly corresponding to the subsistence needs of the workers. This view was seriously questioned by the findings of Bardhan (1970[11] and 1973),[12] Jose (1974),[13] Krishnaji (1971)[14] and the empirical evidence put forward by them that real wage rate as well as their direction and rate of movement over time varies a great deal across regions. However, these studies point towards the fact that agricultural labourers' wages are poorly adjusted to and generally lag behind rise in their cost of living.

One important finding of all these studies was that while there was a tendency towards convergence in the inter-state variations in the money wages over the pre-green revolution period, there was a significant divergence in the later period when the already better developed and high wage States experienced a faster growth while agriculturally backward low wage States lagged further behind. The increasing differences in the yield per acre and productivity per worker because of the success of Green Revolution in certain States reflected itself in the widening regional disparity in rural labourers' standard of living. The increased demand for labour generated by more intensive farming and productivity increases in certain regions had a positive impact on the wage rates. Whether the increase in agricultural wages represented a fair share of production growth or whether their per capita income and level of living reached a level even in these areas which ensured a decent living for them is another question but it did explode the myth that wages are institutionally determined and represent the lowest level of subsistence. Attention, therefore, shifted to explaining the observed pattern of wage rates across space and over time. A member of theoretical formulation on the working of rural economy has been advanced and some of these have also been empirically tested.[15]

Perhaps the most influential version of the surplus labour model which try to explain the co-existence of idleness and constant wages is the nutritionally based efficiency wage hypothesis propounded first by Leibenstein (1957)[16] and later supported by Majumdar (1959),[17] Mirrless (1975)[18] and Stiglitz (1976).[19] The model assumes that at low level of income there is a positive relationship between nutritional level and labour effort per unit of time. Given this technically determined income-nutrition effort relationship, there is a unique wage — the efficiency wage — that minimise the cost per unit of labour effort. If farmers in labour surplus economies are to maximise their profits they must hire labour until the marginal value product of total effort hired expressed in efficiency units is equal to the efficiency wage (the theory assumes that labour can be measured in efficiency units). In such a situation some workers will be left unemployed. They will not be hired even if they are willing to work at a lower wage than the efficiency wage because reduction in efficiency associated with lower wages will be so much that it will not be profitable for the farmer to hire them no matter how much wage per unit of time is bid down. Given the goal of profit maximisation, a large number of labourers relative to land, and the assumed technical relationship between level of nutrition and work efficiency, it is clear that unemployment and positive or even high wages will co-exist. Of course, if the marginal product of last labourer hired exceeds the efficiency wage and no more idle labourers are available then the wage rate will rise and the conventional supply and demand relationship will start operating.

The problem with this hypothesis is that in conditions of object poverty, the unemployment equilibrium, described by this hypothesis, cannot exist in the long-run for unemployed workers will have no means of survival and the Malthusian solution will emerge. This question has been tackled by different proponents of this hypothesis in three different ways. Leibenstein (1957)[20] assumes that because of social pressures, landlords will collude to lower wages, sacrificing some of the profits and totals output in order to support more people in the economy. Stiglitz (1967)[21] achieves the same result by assuming that family farms have egalitarian concern about the consumption of family workers but he does not explain what happens to unemployed landless workers with whom the model is really concerned.

The third explanation of this problem has been offered by Rodgers (1975)[22] by assuming that it holds seasonally. At times of the year when labour demand is very low the efficiency wage is the floor below which wage rates do not fall despite high seasonal unemployment. At other times when labour demand is relatively high the conventional supply demand framework holds. But restricting nutrition wage theory to the slack season labour market phenomenon clearly limits its empirical importance.

Rodgers tried to test the nutrition-wage framework by deducing some of the implications of this hypothesis and then comparing how they tally with the data collected by him from selected agricultural labourers in seven villages in the Kosi area of Bihar. His major deductions are :

(a) a measure of wage stability can be expected at the most efficient wage,
(b) that employers pay attention to workers' actual consumption so that workers with more dependents will need higher nutritionally based wage than unattached workers,
(c) that it will lead to more tying of labour to particular employers, and
(d) the perquisites (meals) will be an important component of the wage which, according to Rodgers, is designed to weigh the labourers intra-family distribution of food in his favour.

In five of the seven villages he studied, the daily wage paid remained stable through large part of the year rising moderately and briefly during the peak season. The degree of wage variation was much less than that of employment variation across season. Also, a major part of the daily wage was supplied in the form of meals to be consumed by the labour at work. In four out of the five villages, a considerable portion of the labourers were tied to their employers. He also found that in one of the villages the Muslim labourers with a high dependency ratio because of the customary non-participation of the women folk in work, were getting a higher total wage compared with the tribal and the lower caste labourers with lower dependency ratio. Thus, Rodgers concluded "there is a broad measure of agreement between labour market behaviour in the Kosi area and that predicated by the nutritionally based theory".[23] However, as we shall discuss in the succeeding pages, Bardhan gave alternative explanation to most of these phenomenons.

Kalpana Bardhan (1977)[24] criticises both his data base as well as his method of hypothesis testing. Bardhan points out that the two villages in Rodger's study which had considerable variation in wage rates in spite of as low an average caloric intake per consumption unit as in the five other villages, are having different cropping pattern from the rest. The set of five villages have traditionally intensive rotation with autumn and winter paddy and jute, resulting in sharp peaks in demand for labour. Therefore, the greater prevalence of tied labour can partly be attributed to more varied crop rotation in these five villages which generated a more steady stream of labour demand compared with the two sparsely cropped villages. In a situation where there is a steady flow of labour requirement over the greater part of the working season, there can be any number of reasons for labour tying arrangements apart from the employer's rational concern for the continued maintenance of the number of work units required at peak seasons. For example, an old hand saves the training cost in time and it often works out to a lower wage rate even in the conventional term. She quotes Rudra's findings for a very different and capitalist farming set up of Punjab to prove her point that the core volume of the stream of farm employment generated by a particular cropping pattern is very likely to be an important consideration in a farmer's decision in the first place and having done so ensured subsistence for work efficiency is important but perhaps not of prime consideration.

Again the custom of paying a part of the wage in the form of meals at work is a fairly common practice in rural areas and there are many reasons for it other than the employer's desire to minimise the cost of a work unit by tilting the distribution of food in favour of the labourer *vis-a-vis* his dependents. Bringing food from home is hard when one has to start for work before dawn or when there is not any food at home. In fact, Chandra (1975)[25] describes as a common mid-day sight some one from the labourer's family taking back home a part of his lunch for the starving rest of his family. In a less miserable situation letting the workers go home for lunch is obviously wasteful for the employer. Even short term labourers are usually given meals at work, to save time rather than out of the employer's decision about productive nutrition.

Rodgers observation of an inverse relationship between average wage for a labourer and the earner's dependency ratio may not be the result of unilateral decision on the part of employers until it is proved that the composition of operation performed by the workers with different dependency ratio is the same. It could very well be that worker with a high dependency ratio manages to specialise in operations which are more paying and for which he happens to have advantage over other labourers by way of physical strength and/or training. The cause of the higher wage rate would then partly be his own decision, capacity or special asset.

Apart from Kalpana Bardhan's criticism of Rodger's study, the whole concèpt of nutritionally based wages has been criticised on analytical grounds. The main difficulty, as Vaidyanathan (1980) puts it, is "the notion of minimum nutritional requirement is too fussy".[26] Studies by Sukhatme (1978)[27] and many others have shown that people of the same sex and engaged in similar activities are able to maintain fairly normal health with very different levels of food intake. In such a situation it is impossible to define any unique minimum dietary standard. Again it is not clear whether the wage rate is supposed to be determined by the worker's own subsistence requirements or that of his family. In either case, however, given the wide variations in family size, dependency ratio and intensity of employment, as well as less than absolute control of the worker over the intra-family income distribution, it is difficult to see how a particular uniform wage rate can ensure that all workers or their families get the minimum. Moreover, it is the combination of wage rate and total employment over the year which determines whether or not the worker (or his family) is able to get the minimum subsistence. So, there can be no unique relation between minimum subsistence and the wage rate. Lastly, the very fact that very large percentage of agricultural labour households, in fact, are below subsistence level, is enough evidence to prove that the labour market does not operate in a way which ensures a minimum subsistence to all members of the class of agricultural labourers.

An alternative approach to explain the determination of rural wages in terms of demand for and supply of labour has also been followed by quite a few scholars. Mishra (1970),[28] Vaidyanathan 1971),[29] K. Bardhan (1978),[30] Lal (1974),[31] Bardhan (1979a[32] and 1979b),[33] Evanson and Binswanger (1979),[34] Rosenzweig (1979)[35] and Vaidyanathan (1980)[36] are some of the studies which try to explain inter-regional variations in agricultural wage rate in the conventional supply demand framework and try to show that market mechanism does work. The basic method followed in most of these studies has been to select on *a priori* grounds certain indicators of supply and demand parameters that are likely to affect agricultural wage rates and then applying multiple regression analysis.

Mishra (1970) relates inter-district variations in agricultural wages in Gujarat for the year 1960-61 with three demand factors, i.e., per capita rural income indicating agriculture's "paying capacity", proportion of area under crops requiring more than 100 man-days per hectare and proportion of net sown area irrigated and with one supply factor, i.e., the proportion of agricultural labour in rural work force. Surprisingly, he finds wage rate negatively related with the demand factors but unrelated with the supply factor. Mishra takes wage data from AWI whose reliability is suspect.

Vaidyanathan (1971) using NSS data tries to relate the ratio between agricultural labourers consumption level (taken as a proxy for income level) and the cultivator's consumption level with a demand factor, i.e., average income level of cultivating households and a supply factor represented by the proportion of agricultural labour households taken from the census data. Vaidyanathan finds expected signs, i.e., a positive correlation of labour's relative level of living with the demand factor and negative with the supply factor. K. Bardhan (1973) uses State level wage data from 11th and 12th rounds of NSS for 1956-57 and 25th round for 1970-71. She also uses some village level data from village surveys conducted by the Agro-Economic Research Centre, University of Delhi, from Punjab, Haryana and Western U.P. For indicating labour demand parameters, she used, alternatively, the intensity of irrigation, the intensity of cropping, the variance of agricultural production around the trend and extent of assured irrigation. Among the supply parameters she used were (a) the non-agricultural wage rates reflecting employment opportunities available to rural poor, and (b) the proportion of rural population or workers who were primarily dependent on agriculture for wage employment or the coefficient of concentration of cultivated area among landless and size group of farm households or the degree of indebtedness of agricultural labour households which is expected to influence labourer's bargaining strength in the wage determination process. Bardhan's underlying argument is that the more the labour market is flooded by those with very little or no land and the smaller the group of large farmer-employers, the weaker is likely to be the bargaining position of labourers. Similarly, indebtedness to farmer/money-lenders for consumption loans quite often leads to adverse employment contracts or labour tying arrangements and its high incidence in a region may indicate labourers bargaining weakness. Her results show that inter-regional variations in wage rate are quite significantly associated with differences in irrigation or cropping intensity or use of HYVs and other factors affecting the productivity of land and, hence, demand for labour, and negatively to production variability index, the relative size of agricultural labourer's in rural work-force. In fact, the explanatory power of her model in relation to data for the sample of villages of Punjab, Haryana and U.P. is quite impressive, the value of R^2 being 0.79.

Lal (1974) deflated the money wage rates over time by Agricultural Labourer's cost of Living Index and tried to relate inter-State variations in the index of real wage rate to changes in demand variable indicated by cereal output and supply variable indicated by the size of agricultural labour force. Although his coefficients had the expected sign, the proportion of variation in real wage rate explained by them was rather small.

A major objective of studying labour market is to be able to analyse quantitatively the impact of change in labour demand or labour supply on the level of employment and of wage rates. Changes in demand for agricultural labour may be induced by changes in output, market conditions or because of changes in technology of production. On the other hand, changes in labour supply can arise from population growth or inter-sectoral or inter-regional migration. Bhalla (1976),[37] for example, shows that wages cannot be considered fixed even when they appear to be determined by institutional arrangements; both the choice of institutional arrangements and their evolution are responsive to changes in supply and demand. Thus, a quantitative analysis of the impact of shifts in supply and demand on employment, wages and earnings has been the focus of attention of Rosenzweig (1979), Bardhan (1979a) and Evanson and Binswanger (1979). Bardhan and Rosenzweig estimate the supply of demand functions for labourers jointly in a simultaneous equation general equilibrium system treating the distribution of land as exogenously given but treating wages and employment as endogenous variables.

The Evanson-Binswanger study, on the other hand, estimates, the demand in India for labour as well as for some other major factors of agricultural production, i.e., land, bullocks and fertilizer. Using a profit maximisation model they obtain estimates of responsiveness of labour demand to changes in wage rates, output price and other factor prices. They find the elasticity of demand for labour with respect to the wage rate in the region of –0.2 to –0.7 and with respect to output price in the range of 0.1 to 0.4. Thus, all three of these papers challenge the basic assumption of the surplus labour models and suggest that reductions in labour supplied will significantly increase wages and that the variability in wage rate over time and across space is explained to a considerable degree by variations in demand for and supply of labour. In short, these studies show that the market mechanism does work efficiently after all.

In a subsequent article, Bardhan (1979) using large scale survey data of rural West Bengal collected by NSS for the year 1972-73 disproves subsistence or nutrition-based efficiency wage theory and shows that the agricultural wage rate (either for casual or permanent wage labourers) is sensitive to demand and productivity conditions, like irrigation, the agricultural development index of the district, age of the worker (possibly indicating higher productivity of experienced workers) and the relatively busy seasons. Although he observes from his data that landed casual farm labourers are paid at a lower rate and also finds a positive association between the casual farm wage rate and the number of dependents per earner in the worker's family; two observations which are consistent with the non-competitive version of efficiency theory of wages, but Bardhan offers alternative explanations of these two phenomena in terms of the more encumberment in the landed casual labourer's supply of labour service at the crucial time and recruitment costs involved, respectively. He also refutes the competitive wage equals marginal productivity theory which, according to Bardhan, "is particularly incapable of explaining the persistence of unemployment among extremely poor farm labourers whose appetite for voluntary unemployment (or leisure preference) is not likely to be great."[38] This theory, according to Bardhan, also "pays insufficient attention to frequent cases of monoposony power that the employer comes to exert in the village labour market and in particular to the high premium the employer places on quick and ready availability of labour during some peak operations leading him to various formal or informal labour tying arrangements."[39] Bardhan builds his own model incorporating the employer's monoposony power (represented by more concentration of land distribution in the village), recruitment cost, wage variations in response to demand productivity factors and involuntary unemployment; and finds it consistent with his data.

Vaidyanathan (1980) reiterates that the supply and demand do play a role in determination of wage rate but they do not play exclusive role is clear from the fact that there prevails sizable unemployment at the ruling wage rate. However, he feels that this phenomenon cannot be explained satisfactorily by minimum nutrition needs of the workers' theory. Vaidyanathan argues that although it is true that workers must live before they can work and, therefore, wage rage must be positive even if the market clearing wage is zero, yet there is enough evidence that people of the same age and sex and engaged in similar activities can work and maintain more or less normal health with very different levels of food intake, hence no unique or uniform wage can be specified.[40]

In his model, Vaidyanathan postulates that other things being equal wage rate will have positive relationship with market clearing wage rate which in turn shall be determined by factors, like, demand for and supply of labour and prevailing level of unemployment. The market clearing wage is likely to be positively related to factors which increase productivity of land and negatively to demographic pressure on land and segmentation in the labour market. He tests his model by using State level data taken from NSS for early 1960s and finds that more than 80 per cent of the variations in wage rates are explained by the model and all the explanatory variables have expected signs. Judged by the statistical criterion, demographic pressure and productivity of land turn out to be the dominant factors in explaining variations in wage rates. Vaidyanathan also tested his model taking village level data from intensive type studies of rural labour done by the Labour Bureau in 1967-70. He divides the villages into three groups (a) those having proximity to the urban areas, (b) villages covered by intensive development effort and (c) under-developed villages. The result show that except in group (a) villages, the proportion of variance explained both for wages and unemployment is significant and coefficient for wage in general has the expected sign. However, only a few coefficients pass the statistical test of significance.

Role of Supply and Demand: A Restatement

A major problem with all the studies discussed above except that of Vaidyanathan (1980) is that these studies focus exclusively on the wage rate. Since there is considerable unemployment in the rural areas and since wage rate and unemployment are inter-related any attempt to explain wage rate without taking into account the degree of unemployment is bound to be unsatisfactory. Secondly, in most of these studies supply of labour is defined as consisting of both family and wage labour. Since family labour does not enter the market and since determinants of the supply of and demand for the two categories are not identical, it would be perhaps better to specify the model in terms of wage labour rather than of total labour. These two points, however, have been taken care of by Vaidyanathan (1980). It is particularly important for a study which deals dealing with only agricultural wage labour. Therefore, we shall broadly follow Vaidyanathan but shall specify supply and demand factors according to the conditions existing in area of our study.

To begin with, for the sake of convenience, we assume that in rural economy (a) agriculture is the only activity in rural areas, (b) there are two categories of labour, i.e., family labour and wage labour, and (c) that family labour is forthcoming to the extent cultivators consider it necessary and economical so that there is no voluntary unemployment in this category. Whatever unemployment exists under the above assumptions, it would be confined to the wage labour class only and would equal the excess of supply of wage labour over the demand for it at the ruling wage rate.

For any given population and wage rate, the supply of wage labour, i.e., the size of the labour force which has to depend on the wage employment for its livelihood, varies great deal depending on the average amount of land and other productive resources per capita and on the distribution of these resources within the population. The smaller the amount of productive resources per head the more unequal its distribution, the larger is likely to be the proportion of population likely to depend on wage employment. However, the effect of change in demographic pressure and change in land distribution on demand for hired labour is quite different. Whereas a higher demographic pressure means an across-the-board increase in the supply of family labour, relative to land so that other things being equal, it will lead to a general lowering of the demand for hired labour, on the other hand, a more unequal distribution of land implies that a larger proportion of land is being operated by relatively big farmers so that supply of farm family labour relative to total labour is less. As a result it will lead to a general rise in the demand for wage labour.

Total labour requirement is the other major determinant of demand for hired labour because after adjusting for the supply of family labour it determines the demand for hired labour. This in turn depends on the level of agricultural technology, like, intensity of cultivation and technique of cultivation. Intensity of cultivation is a function of the extent and quality of irrigation, the use of fertilizer per unit of area, proportion of area under HYVs and other land augmenting inputs. The extent of human labour will also be influenced by the type of technique used in various farming operations, e.g., the use of tractors for ploughing, mechanical harvesting and threshing generally reduces the requirement for human labour.

The wage-unemployment relationship is determinate for any given configuration of structural factors but changes in any of these will disturb it, e.g., if demographic pressure alone increases it is possible to say with a fair amount of certainty that wage rate will fall subject to the minimum floor whether determined institutionally in accordance with minimum subsistence needs or otherwise, because it increases the supply of labour and decreases the demand for it. But when the inequality of land distribution increases, as already discussed, the supply of wage labour rises and so does demand. Hence the net outcome on wage rates and unemployment is indeterminate and would depend, mostly, on the relative shifts in the position and slope of supply and demand curves. While all this complicates tracing behaviour of wages-unemployment relationship under different combinations of structural characteristics, it does not vitiate the central proposition that, for any given combination of structural features, wage rate and unemployment are negatively related. If the market works well wages should settle at the market clearing wage rate, for any higher wage rate will leave some people unemployed who are likely to try and find work by offering themselves at a lower wage rate. But the persistence of unemployment shows that the market conditions do not quite conform to this model. Minimum subsistence needs may be one such factor setting the floor. However, as noted earlier, there is no way of defining objectively the minimum needs' level itself. Therefore, the variability in the minimum level also makes it difficult to predict the exact relation between wage rate and unemployment. Barring the complication arising from uncertain role of minimum survival needs in determining wage rates and unemployment, generally ruling wage rate moves in step with the market clearing wage which reflects the balance between supply and demand.

So far we have assumed that agriculture is the only activity in rural areas and that there are only two categories of labour, i.e., the family labour and the wage labour. But even if these assumptions are dropped it does not materially affect basic framework. For example, variations in the magnitude of opportunities for employment outside agriculture can be viewed either as altering the position of overall demand curve for wage labour or of the position of supply curve for wage labour. Similarly the existence of a class of wage labour, which combines self-employment on owned land with wage employment for others, can be viewed as the factors modifying the position and shape of the supply curve. Thus, these aspects of the real world situation can be accommodated within the framework of supply-demand formulation. Alternatively these can be treated as part of the determinants of workers' bargaining power.

Our discussion so far has also assumed that market is an impersonal and neutral mechanism but it is far from reality. In fact, in the labour market there is interaction between two unequals. In a predominantly agrarian economy, the opportunities for alternative non-agricultural work for rural wage labour are so limited and the resources (except their own labour) at their command are so meagre that they have to, perforce, seek employment with cultivators. Working as wage labour with cultivators is thus the sole or at any rate the major source of their incomes. Those who employ them, on the other hand, being better off in terms of income and wealth, are not nearly as hard pressed. The employers are, therefore, much better placed to influence the terms at which labourers are employed. Some researchers have tried to capture it by using such indices as relative numerical strength of workers and employers or proportion of socially under-privileged segments, such as Scheduled Castes and Scheduled Tribes, in the wage labour class.[41] Though not entirely satisfactory, we shall use proportion of agricultural labour in total rural agricultural workers as an index of their bargaining power (weakness).

Some large farmers hire attached labour and provide house sites and advance credit and other facilities. To the extent they are successful such employers usually get labour cheaper than other farmers. The use of economic power of well-off employers in certain cases leads to some kind of bonded labour. This segments the labour market into at least two distinct parts: one, in which employers set their own terms and another in which forces of supply and demand determine the outcome. Segmentation of labour also divides the ranks of workers thereby weakening their effort to organise trade unions to press for better terms. Labourers who are dependent on their employers for credit and house sites, fodder for their cattle or some other fringe benefits would be rather circumspect in joining trade union activities. Chances of unionisation are also less when workers are socially heterogeneous. For example, it is sometimes suggested that when all wage labourers are Harijans and all Harijans are labourers, the prospects of their combining to advance their common interest are likely to be much greater than when the labourers are drawn from diverse caste groups there by making it easier for the employers to divide them.

The Model

We have argued earlier that supply and demand factors determine the market clearing wage. Barring the complications arising out of the pressure of trade unionism representing the relative bargaining strength of workers in the market and segmentation in the labour market, it is reasonable to assume that the actual wage rate will be positively correlated with the market clearing rate. The greater the difference between the market clearing rate and the actual wage rate, for whatever reasons, the higher will be unemployment between wage labourers. The market clearing wage is likely to be negatively related to demographic pressure on land. It should be positively related to factors which increase productivity of land, like extent of irrigation, use of fertilizers and proportion of area under high yielding varieties. Since most of these factors are likely to be very highly correlated to each other putting them separately as explanatory variables would give rise to the problem of multi-collinearity. Hence, we have decided to use productivity per acre as a surrogate variable for these different productivity augmenting factors. Segmentation in the labour market is likely to depress the average wage rate. However, the impact of index of inequality in land holding distribution on wage rate as already discussed is unpredictable. These hypotheses can be expressed symbolically as follows:

Let

U = unemployment prevailing among wage labour
W = actual wage rate
$\overline{W}$ = market clearing wage rate
S_t = total supply of labour
S_w = supply of wage labour
$D_{w'}$ = demand for wage labour
O = output per acre
P_{Nsc} = index of segmentation in the labour market

I = index of inequality in the distribution of land holdings

E = index of relative numerical strength of wage labour in total agricultural labourers.

Then
$$W = f_1(\overline{W},\ P_{Nsc},\ E,\ U) \qquad \ldots \quad (5.1)$$

$$\overline{W} = f_2(S_\omega,\ D\omega) \qquad \ldots \quad (5.2)$$
$$S_\omega = f_3(S_t,\ I,\ W) \qquad \ldots \quad (5.3)$$
$$Dw = f_4(S_t,\ I,\ O,\ W) \qquad \ldots \quad (5.4)$$

Substituting (5.3) and (5.4) into (5.2) we get

$$\overline{W} = f_2(S_t,\ I,\ W,\ O) \qquad \ldots \quad (5.5)$$

Substituting (5.5) into (5.1) and expressing the function wholly in terms of exogenous variable we get

$$W = f_1((S_t,\ I,\ O,\ U,\ P_{Nsc},\ E) \qquad \ldots \quad (5.6)$$

Taking log of both sides

$$\text{Log}\,W = a - b_1 \text{Log}\,S_t + b_2 \text{Log}\,I + b_3 \text{Log}\,O - b_4 \text{Log}\,U$$
$$- b_5 \text{Log}\,P_{Nsc} - b_6 \text{Log}\,E.$$

We expect wage to be negatively associated with S_t, U, P_{Nsc} and E and positively with O. The effect of I on wage rate is indeterminate and it can be either way depending upon the relative strength of its supply increasing and demand boosting effects.

The empirical testing of the model has been done with district-level data since most of these variables can be had at the district level. It will also give us sufficient number of observations. Before we proceed further, however, a word about how we have measured different variables will be in order. District-wise average wage rate of casual agricultural labour in our data have been taken as wage rate whose variations are to be explained. Supply of total labour has been measured as number of workers per acre of cropped area. For this purpose total number of agricultural workers according to 1971 Census of each district have been divided by the total cropped area of the respective district taken from *Statistical Abstracts of Punjab and Haryana* for the year 1975-76. Index of inequality in land-holding distribution has been calculated from census of Land Holdings for 1971-72 for Punjab and Haryana.[42]

Output per acre figures have been arrived at by adding the output in rupee terms for each district of 12 major crops, which covers more than 85 per cent of gross cropped area of Punjab as well as Haryana and dividing it by the total area under these crops. The crops covered are rice, jowar, bajra, maize, wheat, barley, gram, groundnut, oilseeds, sugarcane, potato and cotton. Our district-wise estimates of person-days rate of unemployment (PDUR) among casual labourers under assumption-II in the previous chapter have been used as unemployment rate for the present purpose. Proportion of agricultural labourers in the total agricultural workers taken from 1971 Census has been taken as a proxy for relative strength (weakness) of agricultural workers. Proportion of non-scheduled castes among agricultural labourers has been taken as an index of segmentation in the labour market. Our hypothesis is that the higher the extent of segmentation in the labour market, the less the chances of workers joining hands for their common cause and hence lower the wages. It is because of this reason that we expect a negative relationship between wage rate and index of segmentation in the labour market P_{Nsc}. The basic data used for testing our model are given in appendix Table 5.A-1.

The estimated equation of inter-district cross section based on our model is given below:

$$\text{Log } W = \underset{(.159)}{0.308} - \underset{(2.387)^{**}}{0.553 \log S_t} + \underset{(1.601)^{***}}{0.357 \log O} + \underset{(2.547)^{**}}{1.161 \log I}$$

$$- \underset{(.504)}{0.033 \log U} + \underset{(.867)}{0.210 \log E} - \underset{(3.403)^{*}}{0.400 \log P_{Nsc}}$$

$R^2 = .757$ $\quad F = 7.807$

$DF = 15$ $\quad DW$ Statistics $= 1.42$

Our model seems to do quite well in terms of the proportion of variance in wages explained. It explains more than 75 per cent variance in the wage rates. All variables except E, i.e., proportion of agricultural labourers in total agricultural workers, are having expected signs.

* Significant at 1 per cent level of significance

** Significant at 2.5 per cent level of significance

*** Significant at 10 per cent level of significance

Variable E, in any case, is statistically insignificant. Judged by the criterion of statistical significance, demographic pressure on land and segmentation of labour market are dominant variables which tend to depress wage rates. On the other hand, demand factors, like, productivity of land and inequality in the distribution of land-holdings, are important which tend to push up wage rate. Rate of unemployment is, expectedly, having negative relationship with wage rate but it is statistically insignificant.

What is the meaning of our results? First of all it is clear that increased agricultural productivity does help in improving wage rates but more important than this is the finding that the demographic pressure on land and segmentation in the labour market significantly depress wages. That means if wage rates of agricultural labourers and, hence, their incomes and conditions of living are to be improved, agricultural growth alone cannot do it. Population pressure on land have to be relieved to some extent and some people have to be moved out of agriculture and given productive jobs in other sectors. Thus, industrial development of an area should go hand in hand with the agricultural growth to improve the economic lot of the poor. Agricultural growth alone cannot raise wages.

Second implication of our results is that, other things remaining the same, the greater the homogeneity or sense of oneness among agricultural labourers, the better the chances of their coming together and joining hands for the common cause. We tested only the impact of social homogeneity or division among labourers. Although social homogeneity does play a role in bringing the labourers together but it is not the only factor which binds them together. Unity among labourers can also be fostered by making them class conscious. This brings out clearly the important role which rural labour organisations and their leaders can play in uniting the labourers as a class and getting them their due share in the increased agricultural productivity. Thus, our study points out the important need to strengthen the labour organisations in rural areas to get them a better deal.

A word of caution is necessary here. While wage rate appears to be quite sensitive to demand and supply factors this, however, should not be interpreted that wages are being determined in a competitive market or marginal productivity determines labour demand. This is because the existence of involuntary unemployment, and the phenomenon of labour-tying cannot be explained in terms of marginal productivity theory of wages.

NOTES

1. A distribution of income after adjusting for Government expenditures is known as post-re-distribution income. For a detailed analysis on this see, T. Barna (1948). *The Distribution of Income Through Public Finance* Oxford University Press, London, pp. 21-4.
2. See for examples Chapter I.
3. Pranab K. Bardhan (1984). "Poverty of Agricultural Labourers and Trickle-Down in Rural India", In *Land, Labour and Rural Poverty: Essays in Development Economics*'. Oxford University Press, Delhi, pp. 188-90.
4. *Ibid.*, p. 191.
5. *Ibid.*, p. 192.
6. G. Parthasarthy (1984): "Land, Labour and Poverty", *Economic and Political Weekly*, XIX, December 15, p. 2119.
7. Bardhan (1984), *Op. cit.*, p. 197.
8. Lewis, W. Arthur (1954): *Economic Development with Unlimited Supplies of Labour*, Manchester School of Economics and Social Studies, 22.
9. Ragner Nurkse (1953): *Problems of Capital Formation in Underdeveloped Countries*, Oxford University Press, London.
10. G. Ranis and J. Fei (1961): "A Theory of Economic Development", *American Economic Review*, 51.
11. P.K. Bardhan (1970): "The Green Revolution and Agricultural Labourers", *Economic and Political Weekly*, 5, Annual Number.
12. —— (1973): "Variations in Agricultural Wages: A Note", *Economic and Political Weekly*, 8, May 26.
13. A.V. Jose (1974): "Trends in Real Wage Rates of Agricultural Labourers", *Economic and Political Weekly*, VI, 13, Review of Agriculture, March, 30.
14. N. Krishnaji (1971): "Wages of Agricultural Labour," *Economic and Political Weekly*, VI, 39, Review of Agriculture, September 25.
15. See for example Kalpana Bardhan (1977): "Rural Employment, Wages and Labour Markets in India. A Survey of Research", *Economic and Political Weekly*, 12, June 25, July 2 and July 9.
16. H. Leibenstein (1957): *Economic Backwardness and Economic Growth*, John Wiley and Sons, New York.
17. Dipak Majumdar (1959): "The Marginal Productivity Theory of Wages and Disguised Unemployment", *Review of Economic Studies*, 26.
18. James, A. Mirrless (1975): "A Pure Theory of Under Developed Economies" in Lloyed G. Reynold (ed.) *Agriculture in Development Theory*, Yale University Press.
19. Joseph, E. Stiglitz (1976): "The Efficiency Wage Hypothesis, Surplus Labour and the Distribution of Income in LDC's" *Oxford Economic Papers*, 28, 2, pp. 185-207.
20. H. Leibenstein: (1957) *Op. cit.*
21. J.E. Stiglitz (1976): *Op. cit.*
22. G.B. Rodgers (1975): "Nutritionally Based Wage Determination in the Low-Income Labour Market", *Oxford Economic Papers*, 27, I, March.
23. *Ibid.*, p. 79.

24. K. Bardhan (1977), *Op. cit.*, pp. 1102-4.
25. N.K. Chandra and Associates (1975): *Survey of Peasant Organisations in West Bengal*, Mimeo.
26. A. Vaidyanathan (1980): "Unemployment and Wages in an Agrarian Economy", *Centre for Development Studies Working Paper No. 120*, December, p. 2.
27. P.V. Sukhatme (1978): "Assessment of Adequacy of Diets at Different Economic Levels", *Economic and Political Weekly*, 13, Special Number, August.
28. V.N. Mishra (1970): "Labour Market in Agriculture: A Study of Gujarat Districts", *Indian Journal of Agricultural Economics*, 25, 3, pp. 8-15.
29. A. Vaidyanathan (1971): Quoted in K. Bardhan (1977), *Op. cit.*, p. 1073.
30. K. Bardhan (1973): "Factors Affecting Wage Rates for Agricultural Labour", *Economic Political Weekly*, 8, 26 (Review of Agriculture), June 30.
31. D. Lal (1974): "Agricultural Growth, Real Wages and the Rural Poor in India", Mimeo.
32. P.K. Bardhan (1979a): "Determinants of Supply and Demand for Labour in a Poor Agrarian Economy: An Analysis of Household Survey Data from Rural West Bengal, " in Binswanger H.P. and M.K. Rosenzweig (ed.) (1984): *Contractual Arrangements, Employment and Wages in Rural Labour Market in Asia*, Yale University Press, pp. 242-62.
33. —— (1979b): "Wages and Employment in a Poor Agrarian Economy: A Theoretical and Empirical Analysis", *Journal of Political Economy*, 87, 3, June, pp. 479-500.
34. Robert, E. Evanson and Hans, P. Binswanger (1979): "Estimating Labour Demand Functions for Indian Agriculture" Binswanger and Rosenzweig (ed.); *Op. cit.*, pp. 263-79.
35. Mark K. Rosenzweig (1979): "Determinants of Wage Rate and Labour Supply Behaviour in the Rural Sector of a Developing Country", *Ibid.*, pp. 211-41.
36. A. Vaidyanathan (1980): *Op. cit.*
37. Sheilla Bhalla (1976): "New Relation of Production in Haryana Agriculture", *Economic and Political Weekly*, 11, March.
38. P.K. Bardhan (1979b): *Op. cit.*, p. 486.
39. *Ibid.*, p. 480.
40. A. Vaidyanathan (1980): *Op. cit.*, p. 22.
41. K. Bardhan (1973): *Op. cit.*
42. Landholding Census Figures for 1971-72 had to be taken because 1976-77 Census of Land Holdings was not conducted in Punjab.

6

CONSUMPTION PATTERN AND LEVELS OF LIVING OF NON-CULTIVATING HOUSEHOLDS

IN THE preceding chapter we have analysed the income levels and wage rates and tried to explain the regional variations in wages. In this chapter we propose to analyse the consumption pattern and levels of living of wage labour and other non-cultivating rural households of Punjab and Haryana. The idea behind this is that if the fruits of agricultural development have in fact percolated down to the non-cultivating labour households also, who are not cultivators themselves, but are either directly involved in agriculture, like, agricultural labourer, or are providing various kinds of services in rural areas, then these should be reflected somewhere in their consumption pattern and living standards. In that case we should also expect a lower proportion of households below the poverty line in more developed areas and vice versa.

This chapter is divided into three sections. In section I, we shall analyse the consumption pattern of households of these two categories and the extent of their dependence on market purchases for food and other necessities of life. Here we shall also analyse the regional differences, if any, in their consumption patterns. In Section II, we have estimated the expenditure elasticities of various items of consumption of these two categories. We have experimented with a number of functional forms. The functions giving the best fit in terms of statistical criterion laid down and fulfilling the requirements of consumption theory have been selected for each commodity or group of commodities and have been tried at regional as well as State levels. Results obtained on the basis of selected functions have been discussed in this section. In Section III we have tried to measure the extent of poverty prevailing among labour and other non-cultivating households of Punjab and Haryana. For this purpose we have used the ordinary head count method. Our hypothesis is that the higher the level of agricultural development of the region the lower the extent of poverty in that area.

Before we actually discuss the consumption pattern of rural labour and other non-cultivating households at least one point needs to be clarified. Most of the attached labourers and many of the casual workers also are given two times tea and two meals a day by the employer with whom they work. The estimated value of this food was recorded in questionnaire as 'perquisites'. Thus, the recorded monthly expenditure of the household does not include this part of consumption which the working members of the household had consumed outside during the period they were working. If, however, these members had in fact eaten from the family kitchen during this period, the family expenditure would have risen to that extent. Thus 'perquisites', if any, of the working members have been included in the consumption of their respective household expenditure. Since perquisites consist of food only, its recorded value has been distributed on food items in the same proportions in which the rest of the family members' total expenditure on food is distributed.

It is worth mentioning here that unlike in the previous two Chapters, the analysis in the first two sections of this chapter is carried out at the region level instead of at the district level. The reason for this is that for calculating expenditure elasticities the number of households in both the categories, i.e., wage labourers as well as other non-cultivating households, have to be further sub-divided into a fairly large number of consumption categories (fifteen in our case) in terms of their per capita consumption. If the analysis had been carried out at the district level it would not have been possible to have sufficient number of observations in each expenditure class. In fact in some small districts, like, Kapurthala and Mohindergarh, from which the number of observations in our sample is small, it would not have been possible to have any observations in some expenditure classes. The other alternative was to carry out the analysis at the State level only ignoring the regional variations. But we did not opt for the latter alternative because we also did not want to ignore the regional variations, if any, in the consumption pattern of wage labour and other non-cultivating households of Punjab and Haryana. So, to avoid the fallacies of the small sample and to retain the regional aspect in tact, we have carried out the analysis at the regional level. For this purpose as discussed earlier both Punjab and Haryana have been divided into three, more or less, homogeneous agricultural regions. Thus the analysis in the first two sections of this chapter has been carried out at the region as well as State levels. However, in Section III where the 'trickle-down' hypothesis is tested to observe any relationship between the extent of poverty prevailing among wage labour and other non-cultivating households and the level of agricultural development of the region, once again the analysis at the district level is carried out.

I

Consumption Pattern

In this section we shall analyse the consumption pattern of wage labour and other non-cultivating rural households of Punjab and Haryana and determine whether there exist any significant differences between the consumption behaviour of these two categories or within each category across regions which are at different levels of development and, if so, what is the pattern of such variations. The analysis will indicate how the consumption pattern behaves in a *ceteris peribus* set up.

Tables 6.1 and 6.2 show the item-wise distribution of average monthly per capita expenditure of wage labour and other non-cultivating households of different regions of Punjab and Haryana. A few points emerge from these tables very clearly.

A lion's share of the total expenditure of both the categories in both the States goes to food items. However, for both these categories the relative share of food in total expenditure is lower in Punjab than that of their counterparts in Haryana. While a labour household in Punjab spends on an average 75 per cent of its total expenditure on food items, its counterpart in Haryana spends more than 82 per cent of its total expenditure on food alone. For the other non-cultivating households the figures are 70.6 and 77.1 per cent for Punjab and Haryana, respectively. Between these two categories the proportion is lower for other non-cultivating households than labour households in both the States. This can be attributed to the higher total per capita expenditure of both the categories in Punjab as compared to their counterparts in Haryana and higher for 'others' as compared to labour households in both the States. This accords very well with the postulates of

TABLE 6.1: Item-wise Average Monthly Per Capita Consumption of Punjab

(Rs.)

Sl. No.	Items	Region-1		Region-2		Region-3		Punjab	
		Labour households	Other non-cultivating households	Labour households	Other non-cultivating households	Labour households	Other non-cultivating households	Labour Households	Other Non-Cultivating Households
(1)	(2)	(3)	(4)	(5)	(6)	(7)	(8)	(9)	(10)
1.	Cereals and Cereal Products	14.1	14.1	15.8	13.2	16.0	15.5	15.1	14.2
		(28.0)	(21.4)	(29.8)	(24.1)	(31.5)	(24.5)	(29.4)	(23.2)
2.	Gram and Pulses	1.8	2.2	1.3	1.7	2.2	2.7	1.7	1.6
		(3.6)	(3.3)	(2.5)	(3.2)	(4.3)	(4.4)	(3.3)	(2.6)
3.	Milk & Milk Products	11.1	16.7	12.6	14.5	9.5	13.2	11.2	15.0
		(22.0)	(25.4)	(23.8)	(26.4)	(18.7)	(20.9)	(21.8)	(24.5)
4.	Edible Oils	2.3	2.7	1.5	1.5	2.0	2.5	1.9	2.3
		(4.6)	(4.1)	(2.8)	(2.8)	(3.9)	(4.0)	(3.7)	(3.8)
5.	Meat, Egg & Fish	0.4	0.4	0.4	0.1	0.2	0.7	0.3	0.7
		(0.8)	(0.6)	(0.8)	(0.2)	(0.4)	(1.2)	(0.6)	(1.1)
6.	Vegetable, Fruits & Nuts	2.1	3.4	1.9	2.3	2.6	3.7	2.1	3.4
		(4.2)	(5.2)	(3.6)	(4.4)	(5.1)	(5.9)	(4.1)	(5.6)
7.	Sugar & Gur	4.8	5.2	5.0	4.6	4.2	4.2	4.7	4.7
		(9.5)	(7.9)	(9.4)	(8.5)	(8.3)	(6.7)	(9.2)	(7.7)
8.	Salt & Spices	1.2	1.2	1.2	1.2	1.6	1.6	1.3	1.3
		(2.4)	(1.8)	(2.3)	(2.4)	(3.2)	(2.6)	(2.5)	(2.1)

Contd.

TABLE 6.1 — *Contd.*

(1)	(2)	(3)	(4)	(5)	(6)	(7)	(8)	(9)	(10)
9.	Total Food	37.8 (75.0)	46.4 (70.5)	39.1 (73.8)	39.8 (72.0)	38.3 (75.4)	44.9 (79.7)	38.5 (74.90)	43.2 (72.6)
10.	Beverages, *Paan*, Tobacco & Intoxicants	2.6 (5.2)	3.0 (4.6)	3.1 (5.8)	2.3 (4.3)	2.8 (5.5)	2.6 (4.0)	2.8 (5.4)	2.8 (4.6)
11.	Fuel & Light	2.9 (5.8)	3.7 (5.2)	2.5 (4.7)	3.2 (5.8)	3.2 (6.3)	4.3 (6.9)	2.8 (5.4)	3.7 (6.0)
12.	Clothing	2.7 (5.4)	4.8 (7.3)	2.9 (5.5)	2.5 (4.6)	2.6 (5.1)	5.2 (8.3)	2.8 (5.4)	4.1 (6.7)
13.	Footwear	0.6 (1.2)	1.4 (2.1)	0.7 (1.3)	0.7 (1.3)	0.7 (1.4)	0.2 (0.4)	0.7 (1.4)	0.7 (1.4)
14.	Miscellaneous	3.7 (7.3)	5.8 (8.8)	4.2 (7.9)	5.7 (10.4)	3.1 (6.1)	4.2 (6.7)	3.7 (7.2)	5.4 (8.8)
15.	Rent & Taxes	0.1 (0.2)	0.5 (0.8)	0.1 (0.2)	0.1 (0.2)	0.1 (0.2)	0.6 (1.0)	0.1 (0.2)	0.1 (0.2)
16.	Durables	0.0 (0.0)	0.4 (0.6)	0.1 (0.2)	0.8 (1.5)	0.1 (0.2)	0.6 (1.0)	0.1 (0.2)	0.5 (0.8)
17.	Total Non-Food	10.0 (19.8)	16.4 (24.9)	10.5 (19.8)	13.1 (23.7)	9.7 (19.1)	16.1 (25.2)	10.1 (19.6)	15.2 (24.8)
18.	Total	50.4 (100.00)	65.8 (100.00)	53.0 (100.00)	55.3 (100.00)	50.8 (100.00)	63.5 (100.00)	51.4 (100.00)	61.2 (100.00)

Note: Figures in Parentheses are percentages.

TABLE 6.2: Item-wise Average Monthly Per Capita Consumption of Haryana (Rs.)

Sl. No.	Items	Region-1		Region-2		Region-3		Haryana	
		Labour households	Other non-cultivating households	Labour households	Other non-cultivating households	Labour households	Other non-cultivating households	Labour households	Other non-cultivating households
(1)	(2)	(3)	(4)	(5)	(6)	(7)	(8)	(9)	(10)
1.	Cereals and Cereal Products	17.2 (39.2)	16.2 (30.5)	16.4 (39.4)	15.7 (32.1)	17.7 (38.8)	15.9 (33.0)	17.0 (39.3)	16.0 (31.7)
2.	Gram and Pulses	1.6 (4.3)	2.0 (3.8)	1.2 (2.9)	1.2 (2.5)	1.8 (3.9)	1.8 (3.7)	1.5 (3.5)	1.7 (3.4)
3.	Milk & Milk Products	9.4 (21.4)	12.0 (22.5)	11.8 (28.4)	15.2 (31.1)	9.2 (20.2)	13.2 (27.4)	10.3 (23.8)	13.2 (26.1)
4.	Edible Oils	1.7 (3.9)	2.1 (3.9)	0.7 (1.7)	0.9 (1.8)	1.1 (2.4)	1.2 (2.5)	1.2 (2.3)	1.4 (2.8)
5.	Meat, Egg & Fish	0.1 (0.2)	0.1 (0.2)	0.1 (0.2)	0.1 (0.2)	0.3 (0.7)	0.1 (0.2)	0.2 (0.5)	0.1 (0.2)
6.	Vegetable, Fruits & Nuts	1.7 (3.9)	2.5 (4.7)	1.2 (2.9)	1.9 (3.9)	2.3 (5.0)	2.4 (5.0)	1.6 (3.7)	2.2 (4.4)
7.	Sugar & Gur	3.5 (8.0)	3.9 (7.3)	2.4 (5.8)	2.9 (5.9)	1.6 (3.5)	1.7 (3.5)	2.7 (6.3)	2.9 (5.8)
8.	Salt & Spices	1.1 (2.5)	1.1 (2.1)	1.1 (2.6)	1.1 (2.2)	1.3 (2.9)	0.9 (1.9)	1.1 (2.5)	1.1 (2.2)

Contd.

TABLE 6.2 — *Contd.*

(1)	(2)	(3)	(4)	(5)	(6)	(7)	(8)	(9)	(10)
9.	Total Food	36.2	40.0	34.8	38.7	35.4	37.7	35.5	39.0
		(82.5)	(75.2)	(83.6)	(79.1)	(77.6)	(78.2)	(82.2)	(77.1)
10.	Beverages, *Paan*, Tobacco & Intoxicants	1.6	1.8	1.5	1.5	1.3	1.1	1.5	1.5
		(3.6)	(3.4)	(3.6)	(3.1)	(2.9)	(2.3)	(3.5)	(3.0)
11.	Fuel & Light	2.0	2.0	1.5	2.2	1.9	2.2	1.8	2.1
		(4.6)	(3.8)	(3.6)	(4.5)	(4.2)	(4.6)	(4.2)	(4.2)
12.	Clothing	2.2	6.3	2.1	3.1	2.9	3.5	2.3	4.5
		(5.0)	(11.8)	(5.0)	(6.3)	(6.4)	(7.3)	(5.3)	(8.9)
13.	Footwear	0.7	1.1	0.8	1.5	1.0	1.3	0.8	1.2
		(1.6)	(2.1)	(1.9)	(3.1)	(2.2)	(2.7)	(1.8)	(2.4)
14.	Miscellaneous	1.1	1.9	0.7	1.4	1.5	0.9	1.0	1.4
		(2.5)	(3.6)	(1.7)	(2.9)	(3.3)	(1.9)	(2.3)	(2.8)
15.	Rent & Taxes	0.1	0.3	0.0	0.0	0.1	0.1	0.1	0.1
		(0.2)	(0.6)	(0.0)	(0.0)	(0.2)	(0.2)	(0.2)	(0.2)
16.	Durables	0.0	0.0	0.2	0.2	1.4	1.5	0.3	0.5
		(0.0)	(0.0)	(0.5)	(0.4)	(3.1)	(3.1)	(0.7)	(1.0)
17.	Total Non-Food	6.1	11.3	5.2	8.6	8.9	9.7	6.2	10.1
		(13.9)	(21.3)	(12.5)	(17.6)	(19.5)	(20.0)	(14.4)	(20.0)
18.	Total	43.9	53.2	41.6	48.9	45.6	48.2	43.2	50.6
		(100.00)	(100.00)	(100.00)	(100.00)	(100.00)	(100.00)	(100.00)	(100.00)

Note: Figures in parentheses are percentages.

consumption theory which states that the higher the total per capita expenditure of a person the lower the proportion of its total expenditure on food.

In both Punjab as well as in Haryana, the single most important item in the food budgets of wage labour households is 'cereals and cereal products' followed by 'milk and milk products' and 'sugar and gur'. The fourth and fifth places are taken by 'beverages, *paan*, tobacco and intoxicants' and 'vegetables, fruits and nuts' in Punjab and in reverse order in Haryana.[1] A greater expenditure on 'beverages, *paan*, tobacco and intoxicants' in Punjab is despite the fact that because of social customs a large section of population in Punjab does not consume *paan* and tobacco. A proportionately higher expenditure on this group of items in the budgets of Punjab labour households would actually mean a far higher per capita expenditure on alcoholic drinks. The items next in importance in their food budgets are edible oils; gram and pulses; and salt and spices in both the States. Per capita expenditure on edible oils is higher in Punjab for both the categories as compared to their counterparts in Haryana. Expenditure on 'gram and pulses' and 'salt and spices' is more or less the same in both the States. Meat, eggs and fish come last in both the States, the expenditure on this group of items being only about half a per cent of the total per capita expenditure.

Within the category of non-food items the priorities in Punjab and Haryana differ. In the case of Punjab it is 'miscellaneous goods and services' (which includes medicines, education, conveyance, laundry and toilet goods, etc.) which account for highest proportion of expenditure on non-food items, followed by clothing and fuel and light. In the case of Haryana, it is clothing, fuel and light and then 'miscellaneous'. Most of the items included under 'miscellaneous' are luxuries and semi-luxuries for the poor people which perhaps only the Punjab labourers who are in a slightly better off position in terms of total per capita expenditure can afford. Even on clothing and 'fuel and light' the per capita expenditure is higher in Punjab as compared to Haryana. Footwear accounts for another 1.5 to 2 per cent of the total per capita expenditure. Expenditure on 'rent and taxes' and 'durables' by this category is negligible in both the States.

In the case of other non-cultivating households, the pattern of priorities in both Punjab and Haryana is exactly the same as in the case of wage labour households, the only exception being, 'milk and milk products' replacing 'cereals and cereal products' as the most important item in their budgets in Punjab.

One striking difference which comes out very prominently between Punjab and Haryana for both the categories is that, whereas in the case of 'cereal and cereal products' it is not only the percentage of expenditure which is lower in Punjab as compared to Haryana for both the categories of households, but even in absolute terms it is lower in Punjab than in Haryana. This is because on almost all other food items, for both the categories, the per capita expenditure is higher in Punjab as compared to Haryana. In other words we can say that in Punjab both categories of households are increasingly replacing cereals by other better food items.

At the regional level there is a remarkable similarity in the pattern of priorities within both the States, with occasionally two adjoining items on the priority list interchanging their ranks. But broad patterns at the regional level are the same as at the State level. The regional pattern of proportion of expenditure on cereals as well as total foods accords very well with the postulates of consumption theory which states that the proportion of expenditure on food decreases as income rises. This is true for both the categories in both the States. In short, we can say that in both Punjab and Haryana, the consumption basket of wage labour as well as other non-cultivating households is heavily food-oriented, more so in Haryana as compared to Punjab, which is a relatively better off State.

In terms of per capita expenditure on an average a Punjab labourer spends Rs. 51.4 per month, whereas his counterpart in Haryana has a lower per capita monthly expenditure of Rs. 41.6 only. Similarly, an average other non-cultivating household in Punjab has a per capita expenditure of Rs. 61.2 per month whereas for Haryana the figure is Rs. 50.6. Therefore, both the categories of non-cultivating rural households are comparatively better off in Punjab as compared to their counterparts in Haryana.

As already mentioned, the per capita expenditure on cereals is higher in Haryana for both the categories as compared to Punjab but for almost all other food items it is higher in Punjab as compared to Haryana. For all food items taken together the per capita expenditure of both the categories is higher in all the regions of Punjab as compared to Haryana regions. Similarly, for all the non-food items per capita expenditure is higher in Punjab as compared to Haryana for both the categories.

Dependence on Market Purchase

To have an idea of the dependence of these two categories of rural labour households on market purchases for their food requirements, we have calculated the percentage of cash purchase component out of total expenditure on the commodity for nine commodities or commodity groups for which we have break-up of their expenditure on these items in terms of cash and kind. The kind part may be home grown as well as wages received in kind for certain operations, like, wheat harvesting, etc., or food taken by working members outside the house. Percentages of cash purchase in total for these nine items are given in Tables 6.3 and 6.4.

A look at these tables shows that non-cultivating households in Punjab and Haryana are very heavily dependent on market purchase for their food requirements. In the case of wage labourers of both the States more than 80 per cent of their total cereals requirements are met through market purchases. For the rest of the food items, except for 'milk and milk products', for all other food items they are almost entirely dependent on market purchase. In case of 'milk and milk products', however, about three-fourths of their total consumption of milk is home grown and about one-fourth of it is purchased from market. Thus, for total foods, about two-thirds of it is the cash purchase components and the rest one-third is either home grown or represent wages, etc., received in items of grains and perquisites of the working members. Major part of the expenditure on fuel and light, however, is in kind. This is because many of the labour households own cattles and their large proportion of expenditure on fuel and light in kind is because they use home-made dung cakes as fuel and also collect some twigs and other firewood from the fields.

Dependence of the 'other non-cultivating households' category on market purchase for their food requirements is only marginally less than that of labourers. About 63 per cent of their total food requirements are met through cash purchases. The cash purchase component of this category in fuel and light is higher than that of labour households. Thus, it is a measure of the extent of monetisation of rural economies of Punjab and Haryana that non-cultivating households even in rural areas depend on market to the extent of two-thirds of their total food requirements. This has some important implications. Because of their greater dependence on market for food, this section is more vulnerable to inflationary pressure than the better

TABLE 6.3: Percentage of Cash Purchases in Punjab

Sl. No	Item	Wage labour households				Other non-cultivating households			
		Region-I	Region-II	Region-III	All Punjab	Region-I	Region-II	Region-III	All Punjab
(1)	(2)	(3)	(4)	(5)	(6)	(7)	(8)	(9)	(10)
1.	Cereals	80.00	85.91	78.60	81.56	73.86	82.07	71.07	76.35
2.	Gram & Pulses	84.93	98.11	99.48	92.42	96.18	97.63	97.26	96.89
3.	Milk & Milk Products	27.74	19.99	32.13	25.87	31.14	21.91	28.78	28.82
4.	Edible Oils	94.65	99.57	96.07	96.15	97.70	99.14	98.15	98.22
5.	Meat, Egg and Fish	87.02	96.32	94.70	91.42	84.37	79.36	88.51	83.93
6.	Vegetables, Fruits & Nuts	86.34	76.43	92.55	85.48	92.85	92.37	95.49	93.22
7.	Sugar and Gur	91.96	94.34	98.48	94.18	93.71	96.61	96.39	95.22
8.	Total Foods	64.95	63.38	69.27	65.47	62.75	60.92	66.52	62.78
9.	Fuel & Light	28.69	34.03	22.53	28.58	49.95	36.62	27.39	40.42

TABLE 6.4: Percentage of Cash Purchases in Haryana

Sl. No.	Item	Wage labour households				Other non-cultivating households			
		Region-I	Region-II	Region-III	All Haryana	Region-I	Region-II	Region-III	All Haryana
(1)	(2)	(3)	(4)	(5)	(6)	(7)	(8)	(9)	(10)
1.	Cereals	75.07	83.33	90.63	81.21	73.56	92.76	92.18	84.09
2.	Gram & Pulses	96.33	94.73	100.00	96.63	98.74	96.76	96.71	97.79
3.	Milk & Milk Products	19.01	28.16	10.96	21.91	26.11	21.26	12.14	20.81
4.	Edible Oils	90.40	93.34	96.94	92.21	94.92	99.64	83.47	93.57
5.	Meat, Egg and Fish	97.08	100.00	82.03	93.28	100.00	100.00	100.00	100.00
6.	Vegetables, Fruits & Nuts	98.64	92.80	73.90	90.47	98.96	96.14	78.01	92.43
7.	Sugar and Gur	88.82	96.26	96.08	92.24	95.33	96.74	100.00	96.46
8.	Total Foods	62.04	63.69	66.52	63.50	63.29	62.81	60.98	62.57
9.	Fuel & Light	39.05	46.36	37.50	41.26	49.96	42.52	35.69	43.86

off rural section of cultivating households. It also means that if the rural poor are so heavily dependent on market for their food requirements, there is a strong need to strengthen the public distribution system in rural areas also.

It may be concluded that consumption patterns of wage labour as well as other non-cultivating rural households are heavily food-oriented. There are no significant regional differences in the patterns of their consumption expenditure. On the average both these categories are better off in Punjab as compared to their Haryana counterparts. Region-wise analysis of their consumption patterns shows that their behaviour is by and large in accordance with the postulates of consumption theory. However, both these sections are very heavily dependent on market purchase for their food requirements. Thus, they are more prone to the inflationary trend than the better off section of cultivators.

II

Engel Elasticities of Expenditure

We analysed the consumption expenditure and consumption pattern of rural wage labour and other non-cultivating households of Punjab and Haryana and its region-wise break up in the previous section. In this section we shall estimate the expenditure elasticities of various items for these two categories separately.

Discussions of the consumer behaviour have all along been enthrilling empirical economists. This is one of the few instances in economics where empirical findings preceded the actual formulation of the theory of consumption function. The quantitative analysis of the effects of income on consumer behaviour developed fully 70 years before income became important variable in the formal theory of consumption.

Broadly speaking two approaches have been followed in the analysis of household consumption behaviour. One based on aggregate time series data on quantities, prices of commodities consumed and on aggregate income; and, the other, based on income and expenditure of a cross-section of individual households in a given period of time. However, the empirical work in the field of consumption behaviour has been largely devoted to the second type of approach usually known as

Engel functions. An Engel function purports to uncover a *ceteris paribus* relationship between consumption of a particular commodity and income on the basis of cross section data. These types of studies are also referred to as family budget studies.

Review of Literature

The earlier known reference to the collection of household budget data in economic literature dates back to 1790s.[2] Stimulated for this task by the distress of the working class at that time, David Davies, a British clergyman, collected data of 127 budgets of very poor families which he reported in detail in 1795.[3] His purpose, however, was not any systematic study of family budgets but to solicit sympathy and assistance for the poor labouring families. Interestingly, however, the chief proposal of this very first study was the enactment of a minimum wage law.

In 1797 Eden published budget of 60 agricultural families and 26 non-agricultural families.[4] However, neither Davies nor Eden made any summary of their budgets. To them budget data were merely a particular form of historical data, to be summarised much as quantitative historical data had traditionally been summarised.

Two developments are believed to have opened the modern era of budgetary studies.[5] The first was the wave of unrest, largely socialistic in aspirations, that swept Europe in the late 1840s. The agitation and violence of the working classes led to an increasing concern for their economic condition and thus to the collection of economic data including budgetary data. Studies of budgets were also made in Saxony and Prusia in 1848. In 1855, a Belgian study by Edward Duepetiaux was published with full details on almost 200 budgets.[6]

The second development was the popularisation of statistical analysis of collections of social data. The contributions to the mathematical theory of probability by Laplace, Cournot, Poisson, Gauss and others provided an expanding technique of analysis.These two developments led to the careful collection and scientific analysis of socio-economic data.

The first and the most famous of all statistical analysis of budgets was made in 1857 by Ernest Engel.[7] Engel studied the conditions of production and consumption in the Kingdom of Saxony in which he formulated an empirical law concerning the relation between income and expenditure on food. Engel's law, as it has since become known, states that 'the poorer a family the greater the proportion of its total expenditure on food'.[8] This was the first empirical generalisation from the budget data. Since that date the law has by now been verified literally hundreds of times.[9]

Between Engel's study in 1857 and 1920s the number and scope of budget studies increased incessantly and it's not possible to comment here on each and every study. Yet reference may be made to Del Vecchio (1912)[10] and William Ogburn's (1919)[11] works. Two very comprehensive works in the field of consumer demand which appeared in the '30s were monographs by Allen and Bowley (1935)[12] and Henry Schultz (1938).[13] In 1950s, there appeared a large number of quite comprehensive studies on demand analysis and consumer behaviour. Studies by Herman Wold in association with Lars Jureen in (1953),[14] Richard Stone (1954),[15] and by Prais and Hauthakker (1955)[16] are the most important ones, to name a few.

Some theoretical and statistical investigations of the quality problem have also been undertaken by Hauthakker and Prais (1952),[17] Hauthakker (1952),[18] Hauthakker (1953)[19] and Thiel (1953).[20] In these studies an increase in quality has been found to be associated with an increase in the average price paid for a commodity and separate calculations of income elasticities of quality and income elasticities of quantity bought are presented.

Perhaps the most systematic of all these studies is the one by Prais and Hauthakker (1955)[21] based on the budgets of more than 3,500 working class and middle class households in United Kingdom for the years (1937-39). After trying five functional forms the authors arrive at the conclusion that a semi-log function is generally more suitable for food items. For non-foods a constant elasticity function in the form of double-log gives better results. The study also distinguishes the specific effects of household composition and economies of scale from the income effect. The effect of quality variation on the income elasticities of most food items were found significant. The elasticity of quantity bought of a commodity with respect to income is less than the elasticity of expenditure of that commodity at any given level of income and that this gap goes on increasing as income rises. The study also points out that while the use of total expenditure as a proxy for total income gives good results in the case of food items, in the case of non-foods, such as consumer durables, this approximation is not altogether adequate. The relative over-attention given in this study to food stuffs as compared to non-foods is partly attributed to this reason.

In yet another study, Hauthakker (1957) derived Engel curves for expenditure groups based on data from each of 40 surveys from 17 countries and found that the Engel's Law — that the proportion of household expenditure on food declines as household income rises — holds good.[22] Interestingly the function used in this, as in many others, was essentially the same as used by Engel in his original paper, namely, Log-log relationship between the specific expenditure and total expenditure. Generally most studies also provide strong support for what is known as Schwabe's law, namely, that the per cent of income spent for housing declines as income rises, although using permanent income concept Margaret Reid (1958) finds that high quality housing in reality is one of the main luxuries of consumers.[23]

Efforts have also been made in some studies to ascertain the determinants of not only food expenditure but also a wide range of household purchases, such as housing, clothings, house furnishing and services, etc.[24] These studies show that these consumer purchases are influenced by a wide variety of socio-economic characteristics but, nevertheless, the proportion of variance in individual household purchases explained by these numerous factors is small, often in the order of 0.3 or less. These studies also confirm the earlier findings on income elasticity, yielding low elasticities for food and housing, elasticities close to unit for clothing and education, and higher elasticities for various types of recreation, personal care, and other services.

Although serious econometric analysis of the household budgets started in 1930s elsewhere in the world, yet hardly any attempt was made in India prior to 1950 to analyse consumer behaviour partly because of the general stability of consumption pattern but mainly because of the non-availability of consumption data.[25] With the launching of planning in early 1950s the need of projecting future demand for various goods was felt and this necessitated study of consumer behaviour in the country. The availability of data of household consumption on nation-wide basis since the setting up of the national Sample Survey Organisation (NSSO) in 1950 further stimulated interest in this field.

Since 1950s quite a large number of interesting investigations into the consumer behaviour in India have been carried out by research workers. Among the individual researchers, studies by Verma (1959),[26] Biswas and Bose (1962),[27] Mathur (1962),[28] Balota (1964),[29] Sinha (1966),[30] Iyengar (1967),[31] Singh (1968),[32] Rudra (1969),[33] Maitra (1969),[34] Bhattacharya and Maitra (1970),[35] Gupta (1973),[36] Radhakrishna (1977),[37] Mahajan (1980)[38] and Mahajan and Mahajan (1981)[39] are some of the more important ones. Apart from these above-mentioned individual researchers there are two other published studies on consumer behaviour in India. The first one is a collection of papers by research workers of the Indian Statistical Institute, Calcutta. The second, 'Long Term Projections of Demand and Supply of Selected Agricultural Commodities, 1960-61 to 1975-76', is the result of the study made by the National Council of Applied Economic Research, New Delhi.

Although it is not possible to comment on all these studies in detail, most of them are based on the NSS cross-section data on household consumption and uncover all-India Engel Functions within the framework of a given price structure separately for rural and urban areas. The studies by Mathur, Radhakrishna and Mahajan are exceptions in this respect insofar as they have also tried to estimate the indifference curve surface by using one variant or the other of Wold's method.

Most of the research workers in this field have used the method of Ordinary Least Squares (OLS) for the purpose of calculating income elasticities but Sreenivasa Iyengar's study is different in this regard. He has employed the method of concentration curves for estimating the expenditure elasticities. But this latter method has been generally found to be unsuitable to deal with two or more explanatory variables and hence has a limited applicability. Balvir Singh has estimated the suitability of a number of Engel functions for western Uttar Pradesh. He has also examined the effect of a number of household characteristics on household expenditure. Ashok Rudra used the linear system developed by Stone for measuring income elasticity from time series data for six commodity groups. The magnitude of elasticity derived by Rudra for foodgrains was the largest and fairly close to one.

Ravi Verma tried double-log and semi-log functions for six regions of India as defined by NSS and found double-log estimates generally greater than those derived from semi-log relationship. Again he found that income elasticities for rural sector were greater than those for urban sector. Between the regions, elasticities for South India and East

India were found to be higher than other regions of rural India. Similarly, Sinha also tried a number of Engel formulations separately for six regions of India for all the major categories of foods and suggested the suitability of the log-log inverse form, with total expenditure in per capita terms as the main determinant of household per capita consumption. However, neither Verma nor Sinha has tested whether the regression equations estimated for different regions are statistically different from each other. Devendra Gupta has compared the consumption pattern of rural and urban areas of Uttar Pradesh and Tamil Nadu and has analysed inter-regional variation and the effects of household size and age of household head on consumption by making use of variance analysis.

Balota investigated the bias in elasticity derived from per family expenditure and income elasticities under various circumstances and concluded that the elasticities obtained by taking the family as a unit might be significantly different from the actual or real income elasticities. Thus, he emphasised the important influence of family size on consumption. Mahajan and Mahajan have investigated the effect of grouping of observations on coefficient of determination in the Engel curve analysis. By using the bi-variate normal and bi-variate log-normal functions they find that, in general, a tenuous or poor correlation between the individual household consumption and income show up as a near perfect correlation as a result of grouping of observations, wrongly implying thereby that income alone can explain the whole of variations in consumption.

After having reviewed briefly the existing literature on the subject, in what follows, we shall discuss the methodology followed in our study, the unit of analysis, the variables taken, the functional form chosen and finally the results obtained.

All the theories prevalent on the relationship between consumption and income postulate consumption as a function of income though the concept underlying these terms may vary substantially. The basic concern of an empirical analysis of family budgets is to isolate the influence of economic determinants, like, income, prices and sometimes level of assets, held on the consumption of a particular commodity, holding constant the effect of other possibly relevant but less important variables, like, age, family composition, location of residence, education, social classes and their habits and various other psychological factors. We assume that these numerous non-economic determinants are unimportant and individually give rise to an error term confirming to some probability distribution. Then the demand D_{ij} of the jth household for the ith commodity can be expressed as :

$$D_{ij} = f_i (Y_j; P_i, \ldots P_n; E_{ij}) \quad (6.1)$$

Where

Y_j is the income of the *J*th family

$P_i \ldots P_n$ are the prices of the *n* commodities,

E_{ij} is a random variable.

If prices are assumed constant and only income is allowed to vary among households, we get the following relationship :

$$Q_1 = f_1 (Y_1); Q_2 = f_2 (Y_2); \ldots Q_n = f_n (Y_n) \quad (6.2)$$

Where

Q is the quantity consumed,

f denotes the functional relationship,

Y is the income.

Equation (6.2) assumes different values depending on the value of *Y* and it is possible to trace a curve in the *n*-dimensional quantity space $(Q_1, Q_2, \ldots, Q_n)$. This curve is known as the Engel Curve named after Ernst Engel.

Unit of Analysis

The preference theory on the basis of which the theoretical Engel Curve is derived treats a single consumer as the unit of analysis. A family budget data on the basis of which the empirical Engel Curve is obtained treats a households as the unit of analysis. There is some difficulty in passing from a single consumer to single household because all purchases are not made by a single person.[40] Even if it is assumed that there is certain unanimity between members of a household, such that household is the unit of decision-making, it only means that per person consumption of any commodity by the household depends on its per person income. But we cannot estimate the Engel function relating to an individual household because only one set of income and quantities is known in a family budget data whereas several different sets of such observations would be required for the purpose. However, the latter situation can be substantially approximated if it is assumed that all households in the family budget have the same preferences and are faced with the same price structure. In that case, the various sets of income and quantity observations, one for each household, would be conceived as equivalent to different sets of such observations relating to a single household. This criterion has been followed in the present study.

An alternative approach would have been to stratify the households according to their family size and composition and derive separate Engel curves for each strata. The problem with this approach is that the larger the number of homogeneous groups, the smaller will be the number of families each group contains and thus the sampling error associated with any estimate of its behaviour will be large unless the group under study is sufficiently large to ensure stability of the estimates. Keeping these things in mind we have instead treated a person as a unit in our analysis.

Independent and Dependent Variables

In family budgets data we have only expenditure data on various commodities and groups, taking expenditure on a commodity or group of commodities as independent variable. Even if one has quantity as well as price data one has to choose expenditure rather than quantity as a matter of practical consideration. For instance, in the case of some composite commodities, such as dairy and poultry products or for certain miscellaneous non-food items, etc., quantity measure may not be meaningful at all. In some studies proportion of expenditure on the commodity has been used as the dependent variable.[41] But this is not considered desirable in the light of the fact that, for some commodities, the proportion has a distinct maximum.

In the case of determining variable, the considerations are rather more complicated. Ideally, income should represent the economic position of the household. But in most family budget studies actual data on income is mainly composed of income received during a short period, usually a month. As such it may not be representative of the true economic position of the household. This recorded income is more likely to include transitory and unexpected elements which are not very relevant for spending decisions. This, in fact, is the case with our data also. The income of the non-cultivating but non-labour households has been derived from their monthly income from various sources. In the case of attached agricultural labour households, the income has been arrived at by adding up yearly wages, monthly income from other sources and weekly earnings of the casually working members of the household during the reference week. In the case of casual labour households, it has been arrived at by adding monthly incomes from other sources to income calculated on the basis of their earnings during the reference week. Given the seasonal variations in the work availability to agricultural labourers, the estimates of household income derived from that are bound to be highly unstable. In this situation, it is only appropriate to take total monthly expenditure instead of total income as a determining variable for deriving the Engel elasticities. This stand is also justified on the assumption that while total expenditure may depend, in a complicated way, on income expectations and the like, the allocation of expenditure among the various commodities depends on the level of total expenditure. This procedure has been universally followed by most of the scholars.

Forms of Engel Function

Broadly speaking three criteria seem to guide the specification of the form of the Engel function,i.e.,

(i) economic plausibility;
(ii) statistical acceptability and
(iii) pragmaticality.

As far as the economic plausibility is concerned two propositions are incorporated into the formulation. These are :

(i) there is an initial income level below which a commodity is not purchased; and
(ii) that there is a satiety level or a maximum beyond which the quantity of the commodity consumed does not exceed, howsoever high is the income.

However, it is clear that all commodities will not have Engel Curves with these properties. The notion of a saturation limit is only applicable to items of expenditure for which there is no greater shift to higher qualities as income rises. Except for certain staple food items, for most other commodities such shift takes place sooner or later with the result that, if expenditure on the commodity is measured on the vertical axis rather than quantity, the satiety level will have upward slope.

Besides this, there is a third point which should be considered in the algebraic formulation of an Engel Curve. This is the constraint imposed on the parameters of the curves so that the sum of all expenditures is equal to income at all income levels. The consequence of this adding-up criterion is that Engel Curves for all commodities cannot have asymptotic values for then there would be some income level at which the whole of the income would not be spent. This criterion leads to the conclusion that, if there are some commodities which have a satiety level, there are others which do not. Therefore, a better representation of the consumer behaviour may be obtained by postulating different forms of Engel Curves for different types of commodities.

Apart from the economic considerations, discussed above, certain statistical considerations have also to be kept in mind. One of these is that the selected function should show a satisfactory fit. It is in this context that a number of alternative forms of Engel function chosen on the basis of economic plausibility are fitted to the same data and the one giving the best fit, out of these, is considered to be the best approximation to the true, but unknown, Engel Curve. The criterion for the overall goodness of fit is the coefficient of determination, i.e., R^2, which is nothing but proportion of explained Sum of Squares (ESS) to the Total Sum of Squares (TSS).

Among the pragmatic considerations governing the choice of the Engel functions are their satisfactory estimation, simplicity both in terms of computation and interpretation of the parameters and comparative prevalence in economic literature.

It is mainly because of the above considerations that there is no consensus in the existing literature as to the shape of Engel Curves and in part the shape decided upon can be determined by the data under analysis. The range of income or total expenditure in the data is specially important in this respect. Stone's equations imply that the relation between expenditure of a group of commodities and total expenditure is linear in logarithms,[42] Wold and Jureen also use this

'others' category is an amorphous group including all sorts of people in the village other than labour and cultivating households. It includes artisans, carpenters, blacksmiths, goldsmiths, milkmen, village retailers, weavers, potters, masons, plumbers, cobblers, barbers and village temple priests, etc. We thought by dividing the households into two categories we will have at least one homogeneous group; other, in any case, is going to be a heterogeneous grouping. We have also analysed data region-wise, using the selected function for each commodity or groups of commodities.

All Engel functions have been estimated by the method of weighted least squares. The number of households in each expenditure group has been used as weights. For the purpose of analysis households in each category have been divided into 15 expenditure classes on the basis of per capita monthly expenditure. The number of households in each expenditure class for different regions of Punjab and Haryana and for the two States are given in appendix Tables 6. A.1 and 6.A.2.

The Results

As mentioned earlier we experimented with eight functional forms with the State level data and on the basis of criteria mentioned above found that function (6) and (8) give the best result in the case of cereals and cereal products for both the categories and in both the States. In the case of all other food items except sugar and gur as well as fuel and light, while function (6) and/or (7) give the best result in the case of labour category, it is invariably function (1) which gives the best results in the case of 'others' category in both Punjab as well as Haryana. It may be noted that changes implied by functions (6) and (7) are more gradual compared to function (1). In the case of sugar and gur function, (4) gives the best results for labour category in both the States but in the case of 'others' function (2) gives the best results. For non-food items like, clothing, footwear and miscellaneous categories and total non-food, function (2) gives the best results for both the categories in Punjab as well as Haryana.

The selected function for each item for the two categories (their adjusted coefficient of determination and expenditure elasticities) are given in Tables 6.5 to 6.8. It may be stated that in the case of cereals and cereal products while functions (6) and (8) gave almost equally good results, our ultimate choice for function (6) has been partly influenced by the fact that this function had been widely used in the earlier studies for this item. In what follows we shall first discuss the results of labour households and then other non-cultivating households.

It is clear from Tables 6.5 and 6.6 that expenditure elasticities for all food items for all the regions of both the States are very high for wage labour households. These are less than one only in the case of 'cereals and cereal products', 'gram and pulses', 'sugar and gur' and 'salt and spices' for all the regions of Punjab and Haryana. In the case of 'edible oils' and 'beverages, *paan*, tobacco and intoxicants' elasticity is greater than one in most regions. For 'milk and milk products', as expected, it is invariably greater than one. Magnitude of elasticity for cereals is in the range of 0.7 to 0.8. There is no systematic relationship between the magnitude of expenditure elasticity for cereals and total per capita expenditure of the region if we take all the regions together. However, within each State there is a relationship, i.e., the higher the total per capita expenditure of the region, the lower is the magnitude of elasticity for cereals. But cereal elasticities are slightly higher for Punjab than for Haryana. It may be partly because of the fact that we have taken expenditure on the commodity and not the quantity as our dependent variable and magnitude of elasticity in this case represents both the quantity elasticity and quality aspect. Similar is the case with 'gram and pulses'. Elasticity for gram and pulses is around 0.9 in the case of Punjab regions and around 0.7 in the case of Haryana regions. One possible explanation for this phenomenon is that proportion of cash purchase component in case of gram and pulses is higher in the case of Punjab labourers as compared to Haryana. In case of 'sugar and gur', elasticity is in the range of 0.6 to 0.7 for Punjab regions but it is slightly higher for Haryana regions. In fact, for Haryana region-II (central Haryana) it is as high as 1.121. There is a very high inverse relationship between the magnitude of elasticity for sugar and gur and the total per capita expenditure of the region. The rank correlations between these two works out to be -0.94.

'Salt and spices' is another item for which elasticity is less than one for all the regions. The elasticity of this item for various regions is in the range of 0.8 to 0.9. Elasticity for edible oils is greater than one in five out of eight cases. For 'milk and milk products' and 'vegetables, fruits and nuts' elasticity is invariably greater than one for all the regions. Elasticity is nearly unit in the case of 'beverages, *paan*, tobacco and intoxicants' group for all the regions of both the States.

TABLE 6.5: Plausible Engel Functions — Punjab Labour

Sl. No.	Items	Functional form	Region-I		Region-II		Region-III		All Punjab	
			R^2	Elasticity	R^2	Elasticity	R^2	Elasticity	R^2	Elasticity
1.	Cereals Cereal Products	6	0.95	0.841	0.96	0.775	0.95	0.821	0.97	0.791
2.	Gram and Pulses	7	0.78	0.994	0.80	0.909	0.92	0.819	0.92	0.929
3.	Milk and Milk Products	6	0.96	1.137	0.93	1.077	0.94	1.097	0.96	1.108
4.	Edible Oils	7	0.90	1.054	0.77	1.071	0.86	0.970	0.94	1.006
5.	Vegetables, Fruits & Nuts	6	0.96	1.142	0.83	1.042	0.88	1.147	0.92	1.103
6.	Sugar and Gur	4	0.93	0.669	0.72	0.574	0.89	0.743	0.88	0.643
7.	Salt and Spices	6	0.95	0.923	0.95	0.798	0.93	0.964	0.97	0.891
8.	Beverages, *Paan*, Tobacco and Intoxicants	7	0.85	0.804	0.98	0.951	0.96	1.067	0.97	0.960
9.	Total Foods	7	0.99	0.931	0.99	0.870	0.99	0.894	0.99	0.920
10.	Fuel and Light	7	0.93	0.862	0.85	0.929	0.93	0.957	0.97	0.948
11.	Clothing	2	0.92	2.045	0.93	2.423	0.96	2.096	0.97	2.074
12.	Footwear	2	0.84	2.165	0.96	1.708	0.77	1.867	0.94	1.590
13.	Miscellaneous	2	0.86	1.169	0.97	1.002	0.89	1.058	0.97	1.032
14.	Total Non-Food	2	0.96	1.814	0.96	1.450	0.96	1.269	0.99	1.345

TABLE 6.6: Plausible Engel Functions — Haryana Labour

Sl. No.	Items	Functional form	Region-I		Region-II		Region-III		All Haryana	
			R^2	Elasticity	R^2	Elasticity	R^2	Elasticity	R^2	Elasticity
1.	Cereals and Cereal Products	6	0.95	0.769	0.79	0.792	0.84	0.769	0.91	0.781
2.	Gram and Pulses	7	0.75	0.726	0.39	0.698	0.34	0.791	0.60	0.706
3.	Milk and Milk Products	6	0.78	1.601	0.79	1.426	0.25	1.791	0.95	1.322
4.	Edible Oils	7	0.85	0.904	0.34	1.446	0.45	0.662	0.70	1.039
5.	Vegetables, Fruits & Nuts	6	0.90	1.123	0.60	1.114	0.82	1.111	0.79	1.136
6.	Sugar and Gur	4	0.79	0.723	0.77	1.121	0.70	0.749	0.85	0.756
7.	Salt and Spices	6	0.68	0.924	0.66	0.984	0.72	0.806	0.87	0.962
8.	Beverages, Paan, Tobacco and Intoxicants	7	0.73	1.027	0.71	1.149	0.60	0.947	0.70	1.057
9.	Total Foods	7	0.99	1.033	0.99	0.976	0.98	0.941	0.99	1.017
10.	Fuel and Light	7	0.77	0.824	0.65	0.673	0.67	0.886	0.53	0.797
11.	Clothing	2	0.69	1.321	0.64	1.222	0.73	1.278	0.62	1.282
12.	Footwear	2	0.64	1.540	0.62	1.352	0.54	1.328	0.62	1.432
13.	Miscellaneous	2	0.74	1.068	0.32	1.358	0.73	1.509	0.53	1.072
14.	Total Non-Food	2	0.96	1.044	0.63	1.011	0.94	1.276	0.92	1.077

Thus, elasticity for total foods, excluding 'beverages group', works out to be around 0.9 in the case of Punjab regions and nearly one in the case of Haryana. It is a reflection of the low level of living of this section of rural population even in the most developed agricultural areas of the country that nearly 70 per cent of any increase in their income, if and where it takes place, is spent on their food budget only.

Among the non-food items, 'fuel and light' is the only commodity for which the elasticity is less than one in all the regions of both the States. Its magnitude is slightly lower for Haryana regions as compared to Punjab regions, but is fairly high for both the States. In fact, there is a very high positive association between the magnitude of elasticity and the level of per capita expenditure of the region. The rank correlation in this case works out to be 0.88. Elasticities for 'clothing', 'footwear' and 'miscellaneous' which includes expenditure on health, medicines, education, travelling, toiletry, laundry and so on, are uniformly greater than one for all the regions in both the States. Like typical luxuries, expenditure elasticity of clothing has a very high positive association with the level of per capita expenditure of the region. The rank correlation between elasticity and per capita expenditure on clothing of the regions is of the magnitude of 0.90. This is also true in the case of 'footwear', though, the association is not as strong as in the case of 'clothing'. The rank correlation in this case is 0.64. In the case of 'miscellaneous' expenditure, although elasticity is greater than one for all the regions, there is no systematic pattern *vis-a-vis* total per capita expenditure of the region.

To sum-up, our analysis of expenditure elasticities for various commodities, of labour households of various regions of Punjab and Haryana, indicates that, except for absolutely basic necessities, like, cereals, pulses, sugar and gur, salt and spices and fuel, every thing, ranging from superior foods to other non-food items, is a luxury for them in all the regions of Punjab as well as Haryana. Even for many of the basic necessities, the expenditure elasticities are quite high. Other food items, like, milk and milk products, edible oils and vegetable, fruits and nuts, are still luxuries for them. More than 70 per cent of any increase in income, if and when it takes place, goes to buy food items only. One consequence of this phenomenon of very high elasticities for food items is that not much is left to be spent on non-food items.

Another conclusion which emerges from the analysis of Tables 6.5 to 6.8 is that the pattern of consumption and the relative importance attached to each item in various regions is virtually the same. If the elasticity is less than one for commodity in one region, it holds good for all the regions. The same is the pattern for most of the items whose elasticity is greater than one. Thus, there are no significant differences in the consumption patterns of labour households among various regions of Punjab and Haryana.

Tables 6.7 and 6.8 contain region-wise elasticities for various items of other non-cultivating rural labour households of Punjab and Haryana. A careful look at these tables show that consumption pattern and magnitude of elasticities of various items for this category of households is roughly the same as in the case of wage labour households. For example, elasticities even for necessities are quite high even for this category. Although these are generally lower as compared to that of wage labour category of the same region. Again for the same items, like, cereals, pulses, sugar and gur, and salt and spices among foods and fuel and light among non-foods, the elasticities are less than one in all the regions of the two States. On the other hand, like,wage labour category, for this category also, elasticities for milk and milk products, clothing and footwear are uniformly greater than one for all the regions. However, certain differences can also be observed. For example, in the case of edible oils while elasticity is greater than one in the case of wage labourers, in at least two Punjab regions which are having higher per capita expenditure, it is less than one in the case of 'other' non-cultivating households. Similarly, going by the elasticity criterion, 'beverages, *paan*, tobacco and intoxicants' is no longer a luxury for this category in the case of Punjab although it continues to be a luxury in the case of Haryana regions. Thus, elasticities for total foods for this category are marginally lower than their corresponding values in the case of wage labourers. Clothing and footwear continue to be luxuries even for this category in both Punjab and Haryana. Elasticity of 'miscellaneous' expenditures for this category is approximately one for both the States.

Thus, we find that the pattern of consumption of other non-cultivating rural households of Punjab and Haryana is broadly the same as that of labour households and that there are no significant differences between the two categories except the ones which are implied by the relatively higher per capita total expenditure of 'other non-cultivating households' as compared to wage labour households in all the regions of Punjab and Haryana.

TABLE 6.7: Plausible Engel Functions — Punjab

(Other Non-Cultivating Households)

Sl. No.	Items	Functional form	Region-I		Region-II		Region-III		All Punjab	
			R^2	Elasticity	R^2	Elasticity	R^2	Elasticity	R^2	Elasticity
1.	Cereals and Cereal Products	6	0.97	0.683	0.96	0.796	0.95	0.753	0.98	0.708
2.	Gram and Pulses	1	0.98	0.747	0.74	0.553	0.99	0.940	0.98	0.994
3.	Milk and Milk Products	1	0.98	1.166	0.92	1.311	0.97	1.048	0.98	1.195
4.	Edible Oils	1	0.96	0.804	0.80	0.884	0.97	1.447	0.98	0.957
5.	Vegetables, Fruits & Nuts	1	0.97	1.238	0.93	0.908	0.99	0.950	0.78	1.003
6.	Sugar and Gur	2	0.98	0.758	0.86	0.635	0.99	0.879	0.98	0.870
7.	Salt and Spices	1	0.98	0.877	0.68	0.553	0.98	0.992	0.99	0.800
8.	Beverages, *Paan*, Tobacco and Intoxicants	1	0.94	0.877	0.70	0.673	0.99	1.123	0.97	0.803
9.	Total Foods	2	0.99	0.907	0.99	0.903	0.99	0.919	0.99	0.907
10.	Fuel and Light	1	0.98	0.871	0.98	1.572	0.96	0.826	0.98	1.025
11.	Clothing	2	0.99	1.529	0.92	1.578	0.95	1.700	0.99	1.745
12.	Footwear	2	0.97	1.464	0.48	1.055	0.97	1.851	0.97	1.563
13.	Miscellaneous	2	0.97	1.959	0.91	1.108	0.99	0.869	0.97	0.935
14.	Total Non-Food	2	0.99	1.287	0.98	1.320	0.99	1.223	0.99	1.273

TABLE 6.8: Plausible Engel Functions — Haryana

(*Other Non-Cultivating Households*)

Sl. No.	Items	Functional form	Region-I		Region-II		Region-III		All Haryana	
			R^2	Elasticity	R^2	Elasticity	R^2	Elasticity	R^2	Elasticity
1.	Cereals and Cereal Products	6	0.98	0.698	0.84	0.740	0.76	0.636	0.91	0.718
2.	Gram and Pulses	1	0.97	0.984	0.79	0.570	0.75	0.810	0.95	0.892
3.	Milk and Milk Products	1	0.97	1.272	0.96	1.280	0.80	1.095	0.96	1.[illegible]11
4.	Edible Oils	1	0.84	0.684	0.95	1.412	0.68	0.787	0.93	0.903
5.	Vegetables, Fruits & Nuts	1	0.95	1.000	0.87	1.132	0.76	1.124	0.98	1.058
6.	Sugar and Gur	2	0.95	0.889	0.97	0.816	0.89	0.925	0.96	0.872
7.	Salt and Spices	1	0.88	0.677	0.83	0.622	0.39	0.910	0.92	0.552
8.	Beverages, *Paan*, Tobacco and Intoxicants	1	0.97	1.123	0.92	1.033	0.70	1.183	0.97	0.978
9.	Total Foods	2	0.99	0.894	0.99	0.963	0.98	0.931	0.99	0.842
10.	Fuel and Light	1	0.83	0.771	0.76	0.978	0.67	0.701	0.92	1.746
11.	Clothing	2	0.94	1.199	0.82	1.463	0.74	1.212	0.97	1.526
12.	Footwear	2	0.82	1.240	0.91	1.515	0.84	1.561	0.93	1.432
13.	Miscellaneous	2	0.89	1.192	0.77	0.834	0.77	1.137	0.95	1.198
14.	Total Non-Food	2	0.98	1.356	0.99	1.148	0.98	1.382	0.99	1.293

III

Poverty and Agricultural Growth

We discussed the consumption pattern and expenditure elasticities of various items of consumption of rural labour and other non-cultivating households of Punjab and Haryana in the first and the second sections respectively. It has been observed that the budgets of non-cultivating households of Punjab and Haryana are heavily food-oriented. The expenditure elasticities of even absolute necessities, like, cereals, are very high. It appears that despite the unprecedented agricultural development which these States have witnessed since late '60s, the mean per capita income and consequently the mean per capita expenditure of non-cultivating rural households have not risen by a large enough magnitude to enable this section of the rural population to satisfy the basic minimum requirements of food and other necessities. Consequently their demand elasticities for food items continue to be fairly high. In this section we propose to measure the magnitude of absolute poverty among landless labour and other non-cultivating rural households of various districts and regions of Punjab and Haryana to see whether the fruits of development have percolated down to this section of the rural society also or not. If the fruits of agricultural development have trickled down to agricultural labourers and other non-cultivating sections of rural society also, it should reflect itself by bringing down the proportion of households below the poverty line in more developed regions or districts. Our hypothesis here is:

> The proportion of wage labour and other non-cultivating households below the poverty line is inversely related to the level of agricultural development of the district.

To test this hypothesis we shall first estimate the proportion of non-cultivating rural households below suitably defined poverty line and then see if there is any relationship between the level of development of the district and the proportion of non-cultivating households below the poverty line.

There are two broad concepts of poverty, i.e., relative poverty and absolute poverty. While relative poverty is measured in terms of inequality in the distribution of income or assets, absolute poverty is reckoned in terms of some kind of notion of subsistence considered necessary keeping in view the socio-cultural and climatic circumstances of the area concerned. In India, the discussions of poverty has tended to concentrate on absolute poverty.

A poor person is one who does not have command over or access to the basic needs of life, both material as well as non-material. On the material plane the basic needs are fundamental physical needs, like, adequate food, clothing and shelter, etc. The non-material needs include basic social services, like, education and health, etc. Almost all Indian studies on poverty have taken into account poverty in terms of material needs only. The usual procedure has been to translate certain minimum nutritional requirements into a specific food basket, such as cereals, pulses, sugar, milk, vegetables and oils, and by valuing this food basket at rural and urban retail prices separately a figure is arrived at for each area which represent per capita expenditure within which the minimum normative diet could be accommodated. Different authorities, such as FAO, the Indian Council of Medical Research (ICMR) and the Second Pay Commission for Central Government Employees (1957-59), have suggested different yardsticks for minimum nutritional requirements. Roughly speaking these have varied between 2,100 and 2,400 calories per person per day.

In 1962, a distinguished working group, consisting of Prof. D.R. Gadgil, Dr. B.N. Ganguli, Dr. P.S. Lokanathan, Mr. M.R. Masani, Mr. Ashok Mehta, Mr. Pitambar Pant, Prof. V.K.R.V. Rao, Mr. Shriman Narayan and Mr. Anna Sahib Sahasrabudha, recommended the minimum per capita expenditure of Rs. 20 per month in rural India and Rs. 25 per month in urban areas at 1960-61 prices. This figure, however, does not include expenditure on health and education, both of which were expected to be provided by the State according to the Constitution and in the light of its other commitments. This estimate is also not related to any nutritional norm and by using various and equally plausible nutritional norms different authors have arrived at a fairly wide range of estimates where the line should be drawn.

Adopting a nutritional norm of 2,250 calories per day, Dandekar and Rath (1971) estimated the consumer expenditure that secures an adequate diet at Rs. 15 per capita per month in rural and at Rs. 22.5 per capita per month in urban areas at 1960-61 prices.[47] They also found that in different States the desired caloric level is reached by different expenditure classes and that the proportion of the rural population living below the desired level varies greatly from State to State. By applying the State-wise estimates of the proportion of the rural and the urban population living on inadequate diets to the State-wise rural and urban population in 1960-61, they found that in 1960-61 nearly 13.5 crore rural people, i.e., about 38 per cent of total rural population, and 4.2 crore urban people, i.e., about 54 per cent of the total urban population, lived on inadequate diets.

At a per capita annual income of Rs. 240 at 1960-61 prices or slightly lower figure of Rs. 200 per annum (roughly Rs. 17 per capita per month), Minhas (1970) estimated that between 1960-61 and 1967-68 there has been a steady decline in the proportion of people below the poverty line.[48] The number of poor decreased from 16.4 crore in 1960-61 to 15.4 crore in 1967-68 or from 56 per cent to 37 per cent. He found that the number of poor tended to rise in bad harvest years.

Using the Second Pay Commission's norm of 2,100 calories and 55 grams of protein per day, Bardhan (1970) put the estimate in 1960-61 prices at Rs. 15 in rural areas and Rs. 18 in urban areas as the desired minimum.[49] He has also estimated rural poverty line for each State in 1960-61 corresponding to all-India rural poverty line of Rs. 15, Contrary to Minhas' Findings, Bardhan's estimates, however, indicated a sharp rise in the proportion of rural people below the poverty line. This proportion, according to Bardhan's findings, almost doubled between 1960-61 and 1967-68.

Taking an income level of Rs. 132 per year to denote poverty, which is roughly half the national average for 1960-61 and is considerably lower than the range of Rs. 170 to Rs. 240 used by others, Vaidyanathan (1974) finds that 15.7 per cent of the rural population were then living in poverty, i.e., about 4.6 crore.[50] He also points out that the NSS data give a higher estimate of the population living in poverty, for both 1960-61 and 1967-68, than the national accounts data and that NSS data indicate an increase in the incidence of poverty over time, whereas the later data indicate a more or less stagnant level of poverty.

Bhatty (1974) using a sample survey data for the year 1968-69 finds the extent of rural poverty with different levels of income representing the poverty line. His estimates of the proportion of population below the poverty line are lower than those of Bardhan, Dandekar and Rath and Minhas and for the lowest poverty level of

Rs. 150 per capita they correspond roughly to Vaidyanathan's.[51] Bhatty has also calculated the extent of poverty by using Sen's *P* measure.

Another study which is interesting from our point of view is the one by Indira Rajaraman (1975), because it is related to Punjab which, along with Haryana, is the area of our study.[52] Using linear programming techniques she arrived at a figure of Rs. 16.36 per capita per month at 1960-61 prices as a poverty line for rural Punjab. Using this as a cut off point, she finds that, while there is an improvement in the mean per capita consumption of the population, there has been significant rise in the percentage of people below the poverty line in rural Punjab from 18.40 per cent in 1960-61 to 23.28 per cent in 1970-71. In fact, she found a significant deterioration not only in terms of relative distribution of total consumption but more seriously in the absolute consumption levels of the poorest 25 per cent of the population, the new entrants joining the 'poor' category coming almost entirely from agricultural labour households.[53] Whereas the share of agricultural labour households in total rural population rose from 17.45 per cent in 1960-61 to 27.16 per cent in 1970-71, their share among households below the poverty line rose sharply from 22.56 per cent to 40.51 per cent during this period.

Ahluwalia (1978) examined NSS data for 14 different years spanning the period 1956-57 to 1973-74 and had tried to find the trend in rural poverty and its relationship with the process of agricultural growth.[54] Following Bardhan, he takes Rs. 15 per capita per month as the poverty line at 1960-61 prices and, using the Consumer Price Index for Agricultural Labourer as the deflator, translates this figure into State specific poverty line for each State. His poverty figure was 53.4 per cent in 1957-58, the proportion went down to 42 per cent in 1960-61 and thereafter rose steadily to 57.9 per cent in 1967-68 but declined to 47.6 per cent in 1973-74. Thus, Ahluwalia finds no increase or decrease trend in the incidence of poverty but observes a pattern of fluctuation with the incidence of poverty falling in periods of good agricultural performance and rising in period of poor performance.

Sukhatme (1978), however, has questioned the procedure followed by Dandekar and Rath and many others of taking average energy to define under-nutrition and argues that keeping in view the large intra-individual variations in energy requirements, a person should be defined under-nourished only if this intake is so low as to be below lower limit of the confidence interval for the chosen level of significance.[55] Using average energy requirements as the norm for determining the poverty line would exaggerate greatly the dimensions of poverty. After taking into account the standard deviation, he came out with an estimate which worked out to about 70 per cent of the estimate of average requirement. Thus, using his alternative definition, Sukhatme worked out that about 33 per cent people were below the poverty line in 1970-71 in urban Maharashtra and not 67 per cent as one would obtain if average caloric requirement were taken as cut off point. Similarly, he obtains a figure of less than 10 per cent below the poverty line for rural Punjab and not 20 per cent that one would obtain using the average requirement criterion.

Using Sukhatme's norms, Rudra (1974) estimated that rural and urban poverty lines would be at Rs. 22.73 and Rs. 27.33, respectively, on 1960-61 prices. In his calculations, adoption of the FAO norms resulted in Rs. 28.60 for rural and Rs. 33.73 for urban areas in 1960-61.[56] Rudra is of the view that the entire procedure of estimating the number below a poverty line is invalid if such a line were to be based on one single dietary pattern valued at one set of national price averages. Rudra's point is very well taken. Panikar (1980), for example, estimates that on a per capita consumer expenditure of Rs. 20.72 per month at 1970-71 prices, it would have been possible for a person in Kerala to get all the estimated nutrients in sufficient amounts as recommended by the ICMR.[57] On the other hand, according to Dandekar and Rath, which are based on the all-India pattern, the requisite caloric level is met in Kerala only when per capita consumption expenditure at 1960-61 prices reached Rs. 34.43 per capita in rural and Rs. 43.55 in urban areas.

Thus, it is clear that within the range of available technical yardsticks, judgments are inevitably involved as to where the line should be drawn and where it is actually drawn could make a great deal of difference to the estimates of the number of the 'poor' whose consumption falls below the chosen limit.

For the purpose of studying changes in the number of those under the poverty line in different States over time, the use of appropriate price indices or deflator becomes inevitable. Different researchers have made different choices. Dandekar and Rath and Minhas have used the National Income Deflator. Bardhan, however, argues that prices of coarse cereals usually consumed by the poor, have gone up in this period at a higher rate and, therefore, uses Consumer Price Index for Agricultural Labour (CPIAL). Analysing the trends in Punjab between 1960-61 and 1970-71, Indira Rajaraman found that :

> "for every commodity group, except cereals, the price rise faced by the poorest groups was greater than, or equal to, that faced by the upper fractile. Indeed, for any pair of substitute item from any non-cereal commodity group, the inferior or cheaper commodity faced the higher price rise".[58]

As might be expected, different deflators have yielded different conclusions as to the extent and even as to the direction of changes in the number of poor in different time periods in different States. Thus, Minhas and Bardhan came to opposite conclusions on trends during 1960-61 to 1967-68. Poverty having considerably declined according to the former, while, according to the latter, it has increased sharply.

In the present study, following Bardhan, we have taken consumer expenditure of Rs. 15 per person for 30 days at 1960-61 rural prices as our poverty line. According to Bardhan the expenditure level of Rs. 15 in 1960-61 rural prices correspond to Rs. 20 per person at all-India 1960-61 prices, which is the minimum level originally adopted by the Planning Commission in 1962, and subsequently became a nationally accepted poverty line. As noted earlier, Dandekar and Rath had also adopted this line for measuring rural poverty on the ground that it corresponded to expenditure level at which food consumption, on an average, provided the norm of 2,250 calories per day. However, we shall not try to justify it in terms of some independently measurable real living standard nor we shall try to interpret this line as corresponding to any nutritional minimum. Suffice it to say that this level of expenditure represents an extremely low level of living and the one that has been most commonly used in Indian studies.

Commodity prices vary significantly across States so that the same real consumption level requires different levels of nominal consumption. Bardhan estimated rural poverty line for each State in 1960-61 corresponding to all-India rural poverty line of Rs. 15. It works out to Rs. 15.90 for rural Punjab including Haryana. Since we are dealing with wage labour and other non-cultivating rural households we have used Consumer Price Index for Agricultural Labour (CPIAL) to arrive at the poverty line corresponding to the year of our study, i.e., 1975-76. The Consumer Price Index for Agricultural Labourers for Punjab (including Haryana) during 1975-76 stood at 308.[59] By multiplying our poverty figure with a factor of 3.08 we obtained a poverty line figure of Rs. 48.97 per capita on current prices for 1975-76. Using Rs. 48.97 per capita as our cut off point, the district-wise and State-wise percentages of rural wage labour and other non-cultivating households below the poverty line for Punjab and Haryana are given in Tables 6.9 and 6.10, respectively.

TABLE 6.9: Percentage of Non-Cultivating Households Below the Poverty Line in Punjab

(Poverty line Rs. 48.97 Per Capita per month at 1975-76 prices)

District/State	Wage labour	Other non-cultivating households	Productivity per acre (Rs.)	Productivity per male agricultural worker (Rs.)
(0)	(1)	(2)	(3)	(4)
Amritsar	60.65	39.53	1,849	3,182
Bhatinda	48.00	34.28	1,336	3,415
Faridkot	42.17	59.25	1,721	3,993
Ferozepur	46.15	45.45	1,900	5,076
Gurdaspur	60.17	40.00	2,050	3,641
Hoshiarpur	42.27	29.63	1,647	3,064
Jalandhar	49.45	20.93	2,243	4,250
Kapurthala	40.54	7.14	2,122	4,158
Ludhiana	28.15	14.28	2,166	4,832
Patiala	62.96	45.83	2,016	4,669
Ropar	37.78	21.43	1,856	3,086
Sangrur	45.65	50.00	1,869	4,564
Punjab	48.10	34.85	1,864	4,030

A look at these tables will reveal that even in Punjab and Haryana, which are considered to be the heartland of India's Green Revolution, a very large proportion of wage labour and other non-cultivating households are living below the poverty line. About 48 per cent of wage labour and 35 per cent of other non-cultivating households were below the poverty line in Punjab during 1975-76.[60] The magnitude of poverty prevailing among non-cultivating rural population of Haryana is even larger than that of Punjab, the corresponding figures being 63 per cent for wage labourers and about 50 per cent for other non-

TABLE 6.10: Percentage of Non-Cultivating Households Below the Poverty Line in Haryana

(*Poverty line Rs. 48.97 Per Capita per month at 1975-76 prices*)

District/State	Wage labour	Other non-cultivating households	Productivity per acre (Rs.)	Productivity per male agricultural worker (Rs.)
(0)	(1)	(2)	(3)	(4)
Ambala	48.98	37.50	1,860	2,055
Bhiwani	80.00	42.86	732	989
Gurgaon	64.70	59.26	1,094	1,094
Hissar	73.56	56.14	1,101	1,300
Jind	64.58	48.84	1,261	1,743
Karnal	67.18	51.78	1,922	2,450
Kurukshetra	54.90	48.27	1,932	2,778
Mohindergarh	29.41	47.50	785	1,120
Rohtak	63.41	53.85	1,175	1,596
Sonepat	63.83	44.90	1,673	2,050
Haryana	63.43	49.69	1,270	1,634

cultivating households.[61] Within each State, however, there are large inter-district variations in the incidence of poverty e.g. in the case of wage labourers in Punjab it varies between as low as 28.15 per cent in Ludhiana to as high as 62.96 per cent in Patiala. Incidentally, both are high agricultural productivity districts. In Haryana, it varies between as low as 29.41 per cent in Mohindergarh and as high as 80 per cent in Bhiwani.[62] Once again both these districts are low productivity districts. In fact, within each State there appears to be no systematic relationship between the incidence of poverty prevailing among wage labourers and the level of agricultural development of the district. For example, in Punjab, districts which have lower proportion of wage labour households below the poverty line as compared to the State average include Bhatinda, Faridkot, Hoshiarpur and Ropar which are low productivity districts as also Ferozepur, Kapurthala, Ludhiana and Sangrur which are high productivity districts. On the other hand, districts where the incidence of poverty among wage labourers is relatively higher include Amritsar, which is a low productivity district, as well as Gurdaspur, Jalandhar and Patiala which are high productivity districts. A more or less similar picture emerges from

Table 6.10 for Haryana. For example, the districts where the incidence of poverty is below the State average include Ambala and Kurukshetra which are high productivity districts as well as Mohindergarh and Rohtak which are low productivity districts. On the other hand, a very high incidence of poverty prevails in Bhiwani, Gurgaon Hissar and Jind which are low productivity districts as well as Karnal and Sonepat which are high productivity districts.

If, however, all the districts of Punjab and Haryana are considered together then there appears to be an inverse relationship between the incidence of poverty prevailing among wage labour households of a district and the level of agricultural development of the district defined as productivity per acre. For example, the proportion of households below the poverty line is low in most of the Punjab districts and some agriculturally well-developed districts of Haryana as compared to the agriculturally backward districts of Haryana, like, Bhiwani, Gurgaon, Hissar and Jind, etc. In fact, the proportion of households below the poverty line is the lowest in Ludhiana which is one of the most developed districts in both Punjab and Haryana. On the other hand, it is the highest (80%) in Bhiwani which incidentally is also the most backward district amongst the 22 districts of Punjab and Haryana. To test out hypothesis whether there is any relationship between the proportion of household below the poverty line and the level of agricultural development of the district (defined as productivity per acre) we have calculated correlation between the two, for a cross section of 22 districts of Punjab and Haryana. The correlation coefficient works out to be -0.391 which is statistically significant at five per cent level of significance. Similarly, the correlation between the proportion of wage labour households below the poverty line and the level of agricultural development of the district defined as productivity per male agricultural worker works out to be -0.496 which again is significant at five per cent level of significance. Thus, there is a negative relationship between the level of agricultural development of the district and the extent of poverty prevailing among wage labourers, in Punjab and Haryana, whether we take productivity per acre or productivity per male agricultural worker as an index of the level of agricultural development.

As in the case of wage labourers, similarly in the case of other non-cultivating households, there are very large inter-district variations in the proportion of households below the poverty line. For example, in

Punjab it varies between as low as 7.14 per cent in Kapurthala to as high as 59.25 per cent in Faridkot. Similarly, in Haryana it varies between 37.50 per cent in Ambala to as high as 59.26 per cent in Gurgaon. Incidentally both Kapurthala and Ambala are high productivity districts in their respective States whereas both Faridkot and Gurgaon are low productivity districts. Within each State incidence of poverty among other non-cultivating households is lower in agriculturally more developed districts as compared to less-developed districts and between the two States, it is lower in Punjab districts which are at a higher level of agricultural development as compared to Haryana districts which are at a lower level of agricultural development. There emerges a clear-cut negative relationship when all the 22 districts of the two States are considered together. The correlation between the proportion of other non-cultivating households below the poverty line and the level of agricultural development of the district defined as productivity per acre for a cross-section of 22 districts of Punjab and Haryana works out to be -0.51 which is statistically significant at one per cent level of significance. Similarly the correlation between the proportion of other non-cultivating households below the poverty line and the productivity per male agricultural worker of the district works out to be -0.452 which is statistically significant at five per cent level of significance. Therefore, like wage labourers, in the case of other non-cultivating households also there is a negative relationship between the percentage of households below the poverty line and the level of agricultural development of the districts howsoever defined.

Thus, we find that when we tested trickle-down hypothesis with income data in Chapter 5 we found a positive and weak relationship between per capita income of wage labour and other non-cultivating households and the level of agricultural development of the region. We had pointed out there that income figures of wage labour and other non-cultivating households are not very stable and reliable and the trickle-down hypothesis should more appropriately be tested with consumption data which are more stable and reliable. Now when we test this hypothesis with consumption data we find that there in fact exists a negative relationship between the proportion of households below the poverty line and the level of agricultural development of the region for both wage labourers as well as other non-cultivating households. Thus, from the analysis of consumption data it appears that

8. *Ibid.* pp. 28-29, Engel also asserted that the wealthier a nation, the smaller the proportion of food to total expenditure.
9. For a partial list of studies, see the bibliography by James N. Morgan, "A Review of Recent Research on Consumer Behaviour" in L.H. Clark (ed.) (1958). *Consumer Behaviour and Research on Consumer Reactions*, New York, pp. 93-219.
10. Del Veechio (1912). *Relazioni fra entrata consuno girnale degli economisti*, 3d ser XMV, as quoted in G.J. Stigler (1954): *Op. cit.*
11. William Ogburn (1916). "An Analysis of the Standard of Living in district of Columbia in 1916", Publication of American Statistical Association, XVI, 1918-19.
12. R.G.D. Allen and A.L. Bowley (1935) *Family Expenditure: A Study of its Variations*, London.
13. Henry Schultz (1938) *The Theory and Measurement of Demand* Chicago.
14. Herman Wold and Lars Jureen (1953) *Demand Analysis: A Study in Econometrics* New York, John Wiley & Sons. Inc.
15. Richard Stone, (1954) *The Measurement of Consumer Expenditure and Behaviour in the United Kingdom*, 1920-38.
16. S.J. Prais, H.S. Hauthakker (1955) *The Analysis of Family Budgets*, Cambridge University Press.
17. H.S. Hauthakker and S.J. Prais (1952) *"Les Variations de qualite dans budgets de famille", Economic Appliques*, No. 1, Jan-March, pp. 1-14.
18. H.S. Hauthakker (1952) "The Econometrics of Family Budgets", *Journal of the Royal Statistical Society*, Series A (Gen.) CXV, Part-I, pp. 1-28, especially section 4.
19. H.S. Hauthakker (1953) "Compensated Changes in Quantities and Qualities Consumed", *Review of Economic Studies*, XIX (3) 5, pp. 55-64.
20. H. Theil (1953) "Quantities, Prices and Budget Enquiries", *Review of Economic Studies*, XIX (3), 50, pp.129-147.
21. S.J. Prais and H.S. Hauthakker (1955) *Op. cit.*
22. H.S. Hauthakker (1957) "An International Comparison of Household Expenditure Patterns, Commemorating the Centenary of Engel's Law", *Econometrica*, 25, October, pp. 532-51.
23. M.G. Reid (1958) "Capital Formation in Residential Real Estate", *Journal of Political Economy*, 66, April, pp. 131-53.
24. On clothing, see Dorotthy S. Brady, "Quantity and Quality of clothing Purchases", in Irwin Friend and Robert Jones, (ed) 1960 *'Proceedings of the Conference on Consumption and Savings'*, 2, Philadelphia pp. 137-42, and also articles by Morris Mamburg; "Demand for clothing" in the same book pp. 311-58, on house furnishing see Vernon Lippitt, "Determinants of Consumer Demand for House Furnishing and Equipment, Service Expenditure at Mid Century", I. Friend & R. Jones, *Op.Cit*, pp. 436-60; on housing, see Sherman Maigel and Louis Winnick, "Family Housing Expenditure; Exclusive Laws and Intrusive Variances", *ibid*, pp. 359-435.
25. Government of India (1957). *A Report of the Foodgrains Enquiry Committee*, p. 55.

26. Ravi Verma (1959) "Income Elasticity of Demand for Foodgrains: A regional Approach", *Artha Vijnana* 1, 4, pp. 271-81.
27. A.K. Biswas and D.K. Bose (1962) "Consumption Projections of Selected Items over the period of Third Plan", in V.K.R.V. Rao (ed); *Papers on National Income and Allied Topics*, II.
28. P.N. Mathur (1962). "Short Term and Long Term Effects on Foodgrains Consumption due to change in Total Expenditure", *Artha Vijnana*, 4, 4, pp. 358-64.
29. S.N. Balota (1964). "Bias in Income Elasticity Estimates Derived from Expenditure per Family Data - A Note", *Artha Vijnana*, VI.
30. P.R. Sinha (1966). "An Analysis of Food Expenditure in India", *Journal of Farm Economics*, 48, November, pp. 113-23.
31. N. Sreenivas Iyengar, (1967). "Some Estimates of Engel Elasticities Based on NSS Data", *Journal of Royal Statistical Society*, Series A (General), 130, pp. 84-97.
32. Balvir Singh (1968) "Consumption Functions in India", an Unpublished Ph.D. Thesis of Delhi University.
33. Ashok Rudra (1969) "Demand Elasticity of Foodgrains", *Economic and Political Weekly*, 4, November.
34. T. Maitra (1969) "on Regional and Temporal variations in Engel Curves in Rural India", *Technical Report No. Econ 12/69*, I.S.I. Calcutta.
35. N. Bhattacharya and T. Maitra (1970) "An Analysis of Engel Curves Based on NSS Household Budget Data for 7th to 22nd Rounds", *Paper Presented at the 10th Indian Econometric Conference* (Mimeo).
36. Devendra B. Gupta (1973) '*Consumption Patterns in India - A Study of Inter-Regional Variations*', Tata McGraw-Hill Publishing Co., Bombay, New Delhi.
37. R. Radhakrishna (1977) "Approximate Determination of Indifference Surface from Family Budget Data", *Artha Vijnana*, 19, 3, pp. 247-58.
38. B.M. Mahajan (1980) '*Consumer Behaviour in India - An Econometric Study*', Concept Publishing Co., New Delhi.
39. B.M. Mahajan and H. Mahajan (1981) "Effect of Grouping of Observation on Coefficient of Determination in Engel Curve Analysis", *Artha Vijnana*, XXIII 4, pp. 352-65.
40. P.A. Samuelson, (1948) *Foundations of Economic Analysis*, pp. 374-75.
41. C.E.V. Leser, (1963) "Forms of Engel Curves", *Econometrica*, 31, pp. 684-703.
42. Richard Stone (1954) *Op. cit.*
43. H. Wold and L. Jureen (1953) *Op. cit.*
44. S.J. Prais (1953) "Non-linear Estimation of the Engel Curves", *Review of Economic Studies*, 20.
45. J. Aitchson and J.A.C. Brown (1955) "A Synthesis of Engel Curve Theory", *Review of Economic Studies*, 22, pp. 35-46.
46. We are aware of the fact that R^2 obtained from various relationships are not strictly comparable. For example, in function (7) R^2 measures the proportion of variation of the logarithms of Y, that has been explained for, which is not the same thing as the proportion of variations in Y implied by function (1). To make R^2 of log-linear form comparable to linear form we should take anti-logarithm of

calculated values of *Y* and then we can find out their coefficient of determination with observed values of *Y*. But D.C. Murphy finds that this adjustment has only negligible effect. Therefore, we have ignored this aspect in our study. See, for example, D.C. Murphy; 'Econometric Analysis of Family Budgets in Ireland' Unpublished Thesis of National University of Ireland.

47. V.M. Dandekar and Nilkantha Rath (1971) "Poverty in India", *Economic and Political Weekly*, Bombay, VI 1 and 2, January 2 and 9.
48. B.S. Minhas (1970) "Rural Poverty, Land Redistribution and Development Strategy: Facts and Policy", *Indian Economic Review*, V (New Series), April, pp. 97-128.
49. Pranab K. Bardhan (1970) "On the Minimum Level of Living and the Rural Poor", *Indian Economic Review*, V (New Series), April, pp. 129-36.
50. A. Vaidyanathan (1974) "Some Aspects of Inequalities in Living Standard in rural India", in Srinivasan T.N. and P.K. Bardhan (ed) *Poverty and Income Distribution in India* (1974), Statistical Publishing House, Calcutta.
51. I. Z. Bhatty (1974) "Inequality and Poverty in Rural India" in Srinivasan and Bardhan (ed), *Op. cit.*
52. Indira Rajaraman (1975) "Poverty, Inequality and Economic Growth: Rural Punjab, 1960-61 — 1970-71", *Journal of Development Studies*, XI, July, pp. 278-90.
53. *Ibid.*, p. 282.
54. Montek S. Ahluwalia (1978) "Rural Poverty and Agricultural Performance in India", *The Journal of Development Studies*, XIV, III April, pp. 298-323.
55. P.V. Sukhatme (1978) "Assessment of Adequacy of Diets of Different Income Levels", *Economic and Political Weekly*, XIII, Special Number, August, pp. 1373-84.
56. Ashok Rudra (1974). "Minimum level of Living - A Statistical Examination", in T.N. Srinivasan and P.K. Bardhan (ed.) (1974), *Op. cit.*, pp. 281-90
57. P.G.K. Panikar, (1980) "Inter-regional Variations in Caloric Intake", *Working Paper No. III* Centre for Development Studies, Trivandrum.
58. Indira Rajaraman, *Op. cit.*, p. 281.
59. *R.B.I. Bulletin*, July 1977, p. S415.
60. The percentage of cultivating households below the poverty line of Rs. 48.33 per capita per month at 1974-75 prices in Punjab was 16.48. See G.S. Bhalla and G.K. Chadha (1983) *Op. cit.* Table 5.18, p. 154.
61. Taking a poverty line of Rs. 48.67 per capita per month at 1974-75 prices, Sharma finds that during 1974-75 the percentage of cultivating households below the poverty line in Haryana was 30.80. See R.K. Sharma (1983) *Impact of New Technology on Income Distribution among Cultivating Households in rural Haryana: A Regional Study*, An Unpublished Ph.D. Thesis of J.N.U., New Delhi, Table VII. 10, p. 284.
62. One possible reason for an unusually low percentage of wage labour households below the poverty line in Mohindergarh district may be the small size of the sample. There are only 16 households of this category in our sample from this district, of which five are below the poverty line.

7

UNEMPLOYMENT POVERTY NEXUS AMONG WAGE LABOUR HOUSEHOLDS

IN THE preceding three chapters we discussed the impact of agricultural growth on employment/unemployment, wage rates and levels of living of wage labour households in Punjab and Haryana. In Chapter 4, we came to the conclusion that while agricultural growth adversely affected the rates of female participation and tended to shift the attached-casual composition of wage labour in favour of attached labourers, but it has not significantly effected the overall employment prospects of wage labourers. Consequently, the agricultural growth for various reasons discussed earlier does not seem to have effected the rate of unemployment, howsoever measured, prevailing among wage labourers of various districts of Punjab and Haryana. In Chapter 5, we discovered that although there is no systematic relationship between the wage rate of attached labourer and agricultural productivity, the wages of casual workers, which is a much better index of the demand and supply position prevailing in the rural labour market, are positively and significantly related with the level of agricultural development of the region. Thus, it is clear that increased agricultural productivity does help to some extent in improving the overall wage rates of rural wage labourers. This is also confirmed in Chapter 6 where we find that proportion of wage labour households below the poverty line and level of agricultural development of the region are negatively related with each other thereby reinforcing earlier finding that accelerated agricultural growth does help to some extent in alleviating the problem of absolute poverty among wage labourers. The extent of poverty prevailing among wage labourers is still quite substantial. This indicates that though the income levels have risen as a consequence of agricultural growth, the rise has not been substantial enough to make a significant dent on their poverty.

But so far we have not explored the question of relationship between poverty and unemployment. The question is, whether poverty is largely a consequence of unemployment, as the conventional wisdom would have us believe, or alternatively the reasons of poverty lie somewhere else? If poverty and unemployment are two sides of the same coin, which the first proposition implies, then one would expect a positive relationship between poverty and unemployment. If, however, seemingly equally plausible argument that poor cannot afford to remain unemployed and they are compelled to seek work irrespective of the level of reward, and consequently the excess labour supply in this situation finds expression in 'distress wage' rather than open unemployment, is accepted then one would expect a negative relationship between the extent of poverty and the level of open unemployment prevailing among wage labourers. This is the question being discussed in this chapter and we shall try to explore it with the help of our data relating to wage labour households of Punjab and Haryana. This chapter is divided into two sections. In Section I, we shall first briefly discuss the two strands of thought regarding the relationship between poverty and unemployment and then briefly review the available evidence on the subject in the existing literature. We shall try to find with the help of our data whether unemployment-poverty nexus exists or not. In Section II, we shall try to explain variations in poverty prevailing among wage labour households of different districts of Punjab and Haryana.

I

Unemployment Poverty Nexus: The Existing Evidence

The extent to which poverty and unemployment in the developing countries are associated with each other has, of late, been a subject of considerable debate. The conventional belief has been that poverty in these countries is the result of the prevalence of widespread unemployment and under-employment. It was assumed that poverty and unemployment are two sides of the same coin and any effort to resolve the one would hit at the other and vice versa. This view began to be suspected when successive labour force surveys in developing countries reported very low levels of open unemployment. It was argued that perhaps the poor are too poor to remain unemployed and that their low levels of income compel them to work irrespective of the level of reward. For example, a survey article by Berry and Sabot reported that :

> "the openly unemployed are not primarily drawn from low income groups; on the contrary they are disproportionately from relatively high income families and are well educated."[1]

Similarly Turnham (1970) provides evidence from Puerto Rico to the effect that family income tended to be higher than average for the families to which unemployed workers belong and that such families on an average included more working members. Turnham also finds that people who want additional work are often quite numerous among those already working long hours.[2] This has been interpreted in two ways. First, the intensity of work per unit of time is so low that they have the capacity to undertake additional work. Second, because even after working long hours their realised income is inadequate and they want to add a little more to their meagre earnings by working for still longer hours. This point was also highlighted by Sinha (1968). Sinha argued that in low wage low productivity States wages at the peak appear too low to leave any surplus for the off season so that workers are compelled to seek work in the off season at very low rates of remuneration. Excess labour supply in this situation finds its expression in the prevalence of what Sinha calls 'distress' wage rate and not in open unemployment. In relatively prosperous areas, however, workers can afford to wait so long as the wages offered to them remain below the reservation price.[3]

More recently, on the basis of data on consumption levels from the 25th round of NSS and data on rates of unemployment from the 27th round, Lakdawala (1978) observed : "In many poor regions of the country unemployment rates are comparatively low."[4] He further observed : "In many parts of the country low standard of living of landless labourers is associated with fairly low unemployment rates."[5] By taking agricultural output per hectare data for NSS regions from JNU-PPD study and person-days unemployment rate data from 27th round of NSS, Lakdawala finds a correlation coefficient between the two as 0.30 (significant at five per cent level) and concludes that higher agricultural productivity is associated with higher unemployment. Thus, Lakdawala concludes that "agricultural growth is no solution by itself to the problem of poverty in India, though it is a necessary prerequisite for effective tackling of the rural poverty problem. The extent of rural unemployment does not vary inversely with the level of consumption in rural areas" and "although unemployment and under-employment are grave problems, poverty is a more severe problem and mere achievement of full employment at the current wage rate may not take us far towards the reduction of poverty."[6]

About the same time, Sinha (1978) observed that "full employment, at prevailing rate of remuneration, may widen income disparities among regions and classes and, even worse, leave a sizable fraction of the people below the poverty line."[7] In a subsequent article, Sinha (1979) vindicates his earlier position that "poverty and unemployment are different problems and further that there is a large zone of trade off between the two."[8] Sinha argues : "Chronic poverty and chronic unemployment are mutually exclusive categories. Persons who remain unemployed for continuously long periods have a minimum reservation price below which they refuse to offer their services in the labour market, and they can afford to do so, in the absence of unemployment benefits, only if their families have a margin over and above the minimum, necessary for maintenance, which is used to sustain them during the period of unemployment. Persons who are chronically unemployed are thus ordinarily above the poverty line, if we consider their actual consumption regardless of the source of its finance. At the same time, the crushing burden of chronic poverty forces people to accept whatever work they can lay their hands on regardless of the rate of return; they thus cannot remain unemployed for long."[9]

By taking person-days rate of unemployment data from 25th round of NSS for non-cultivating wage earners and Monthly Per Capita Expenditure (MPCE) data for 48-crop regions of NSS, Sinha finds that regression coefficient of per capita expenditure on unemployment bears the expected sign but is statistically insignificant. The level of expenditure bears a positive relationship with wage rate at high level of statistical significance. He, however, finds that the parametric estimates of the coefficients of regression of level of per capita consumption expenditure on wage employment and wage rates are both significant. This he interprets as showing that unemployment in less-developed countries is a multi-dimensional phenomenon which cannot be meaningfully reduced to a single number. By contrast, wage employment is a relatively firm variable representing work of a certain duration at the given wage rate and thus it gives positive association with per capita expenditure at a statistically significant level. In yet another exercise, Sinha, taking Rs. 34 per capita per month as the cut off poverty line, regresses households below the poverty line, taken from 27th round of NSS, on unemployment rate, taken from the same round, and wage rates, and finds that association between the incidence of poverty and that of unemployment is positive but weak, whereas one per cent increase in wage rates in observed to contribute to an equi-proportionate reduction in poverty.[10] Thus, Sinha concludes that employment policy which is just focused on eliminating unemployment, disregarding level of wage rates, will widen regional and, by the same token, class disparities in levels of living.[11]

Ranjit Sau (1978) commenting on Lakdawala's observation, that in many poor regions of the country unemployment rates are comparatively low and that standard of living of landless labourers is associated with fairly low unemployment rates, argues "if poverty seems to be co-existing with low rates of unemployment it only means that employment there is not worth the name."[12] Sau, however, puts Lakdawala's data to a closer scrutiny and finds that in 15 out of 26 regions which have per capita monthly consumption expenditure of less than Rs. 27 for the non-cultivating wage earners who are mostly landless labourers, the unemployment rate is above the national average of 7.83 per cent. If anything, poverty and unemployment are thus closely associated. Similarly, he points out that out of 23 regions which have high rates of unemployment (more than 7.83 per cent), as many as 15 are marked by extreme poverty. Therefore, Sau argues that Lakdawala's data does not indicate that regions of acute poverty have a rather low rate of unemployment. The data only show that poverty and high unemployment co-exist in many places. Sau finds a correlation of -0.214 between monthly per capita consumption expenditure of non-cultivator wage earners and the rate of unemployment. He points out that although this correlation is very poor, yet the relationship between the two is certainly not one of positive association as Lakdawala would have us believed. Similarly, Sau finds a positive association between monthly per capita expenditure of non-cultivating wage earners and output per hectare. He concludes, "it appears that the incidence of acute poverty is associated with the high rate of unemployment which in turn goes with low productivity of land."[13]

In his presidential address to the Indian Labour Economics Conference, Dantwala (1979) has been at some pains to indicate that unemployment and poverty are directly related. Citing evidence from Parthasarthy (1979)[14] and Visaria (1980)[15], Dantwala proves his point which is contrary to that of Lakdawala's observation. Commenting on Lakdawala's findings, Dantwala argues : "Perhaps, when household data gets aggregated at the level of an NSS region, the relationship between poverty and unemployment gets blurred."[16]

Following Dandekar and Rath, Parthasarthy (1979) adopts expenditure level at which the minimum diet of 2,250 calories is reached for drawing the poverty line and finds that the relationship between poverty and rates of unemployment at the State level is positive. He concludes :

> "States with higher percentage of population below the poverty line are generally States with higher rate of unemployment – with only three exceptions, Bihar and Karnataka with higher than average rate of unemployment but lower level of percentage of persons below the poverty line and vice versa for Assam."[17]

In a recent articles, Visaria (1980) has attempted to ascertain the relationship between poverty as indicated by monthly per capita consumption expenditure (MPCE) and incidence of unemployment according to three measures of unemployment, i.e., usual activity criterion, current activity criterion and person-days rate of unemployment. He finds :

> "While the incidence of unemployment in terms of usual or current activity do not show a clear and consistent relationship with MPCE decile of households, a more or less steady inverse relationship is evident between MPCE decile and the incidence of unemployment in terms of person-days. Except for some erratic deviations, the labour force in the bottom deciles of households clearly suffer from a significantly higher incidence of unemployment and/or under-employment".[18]

The evidence so far discussed from existing studies is far from clear. However, there is near unanimity on one point that poverty is a much bigger problem than unemployment and that mere removal of unemployment at the existing wage rate will not eradicate poverty. In what follows we shall try to analyse with our data whether unemployment-poverty nexus does exist or not.

To test which one of the two propositions discussed above holds good in the case of wage labour households of Punjab and Haryana, we shall first see whether there is any association between poverty prevailing among wage labourers, defined as percentage of households below the poverty line and person-days rate of unemployment. Tables 7.1 and 7.2 contain information on poverty (column 1) and unemployment (column 3) for different districts of Punjab and Haryana, respectively. A look at these tables confirms the finding of most of the earlier studies that poverty prevailing among wage labourers is a much bigger problem than unemployment in either of the States. Thus, the magnitude of poverty is about three times larger than unemployment in Punjab and about five times larger than unemployment in Haryana. Thus, it is likely that removal of unemployment at the prevailing wage rate may not eradicate poverty which appears to be a more gigantic task. Any attempt to identify the two by definition will only further confound the confusion already existing at the policy-making level.

TABLE 7.1: Poverty and Unemployment Among Wage Labour Households (Punjab)

District/State	Percentage of households below the poverty line (Rs. 48.97)	Per capita monthly expenditure (Rs.)	Person-days rate of unemployment (PDUR)
(0)	(1)	(2)	(3)
Amritsar	60.65	50.82	5.84
Bhatinda	48.00	60.69	10.53
Faridkot	42.17	59.78	12.33
Ferozepur	46.15	54.17	11.31
Gurdaspur	60.17	44.62	19.64
Hoshiarpur	42.27	63.92	28.48
Jalandhar	49.45	52.58	22.17
Kapurthala	40.54	51.22	24.37
Ludhiana	28.15	62.65	10.92
Patiala	62.96	47.88	26.53
Ropar	37.78	58.25	17.36
Sangrur	45.65	51.98	13.89
Punjab	48.10	51.40	16.58

An analysis of our data shows that as far as the relationship between poverty and unemployment is concerned there appears to be no clear-cut relationship. For example, in Punjab there are districts, like, Gurdaspur, Jalandhar and Patiala, where poverty is high and so is unemployment. On the other hand, in districts, such as Bhatinda, Faridkot, Ferozepur, Sangrur and Ludhiana, low poverty is associated with low unemployment. This gives the impression that poverty and unemployment are positively related. But then there are exceptions too. For example, Amritsar has the lowest rate of unemployment in the State (5.84%) but the percentage of wage labour households below the poverty line (60.65%) in this district is the second highest in the State next only to Patiala. Similarly, Hoshiarpur, Kapurthala and Ropar have above average rate of unemployment but the poverty figures for these districts are well below the State average.

TABLE 7.2: Poverty and Unemployment Among Wage Labour Households (Haryana)

District/State	Percentage of households below the poverty line (Rs. 48.97)	Per capita monthly expenditure (Rs.)	Person-days rate of unemployment (PDUR)
(0)	(1)	(2)	(3)
Ambala	48.98	52.55	7.89
Bhiwani	80.00	49.69	23.87
Gurgaon	64.70	45.49	12.69
Hissar	73.56	44.60	5.71
Jind	64.58	44.12	14.26
Karnal	67.18	43.13	7.83
Kurukshetra	54.90	44.01	17.42
Mohindergarh	29.41	69.43	13.19
Rohtak	63.41	44.07	9.26
Sonepat	63.83	39.98	34.74
Haryana	63.43	43.20	13.32

A more or less similar picture emerges from Haryana. There are districts, like, Bhiwani, Jind and Sonepat, where high incidence of poverty is associated with high rates of unemployment prevailing among wage labourers and others, like, Ambala, Rohtak and Mohindergarh, where low poverty is associated with low unemployment. Once again this gives the impression that poverty is positively associated with unemployment. But this impression vanishes when we look at the figures for Gurgaon, Hissar and Karnal where this relationship is reversed. In fact, Hissar and Karnal have the lowest rate of unemployment in the State (the figures being 5.71% and 7.83%) but in terms of wage labour households below the poverty line they rank second and third from above. Taking all the districts together the correlation between the percentage of households below the poverty line and the person-days rate of unemployment for a cross section of 22 districts of Punjab and Haryana works out to be 0.028. This means that there is virtually no relationship between poverty and unemployment.

In the second exercise, instead of percentage of households below the poverty line we take average monthly per capital expenditure (MPCE) of wage labour as an index of their level of living and try to test its relationship with unemployment prevailing among wage labour households of different districts of Punjab and Haryana. The average monthly per capita expenditure figures for various districts of Punjab and Haryana are given in column 2 of Tables 7.1 and 7.2, respectively. A positive relationship between MPCE and the rate of unemployment would mean a negative relationship between poverty and unemployment and *vice versa.* Once again there appears to be no systematic relationship between the monthly per capita expenditure of wage labour households and the rate of unemployment prevailing among them. For example, in Punjab five districts, i.e., Bhatinda, Faridkot, Ferozepur, Sangrur and Ludhiana, which have a higher than average per capita monthly expenditure (MPCE), also have low rates of unemployment. On the other hand in districts, like, Gurdaspur, Kapurthala and Patiala, low MPCE is associated with high rates of unemployment. It may be recalled that the nature of associations for these set of districts is similar to the one obtained between poverty and unemployment earlier. Thus, the only change which has come about by replacing percentage of households below the poverty line with per capita monthly expenditure (MPCE) in Punjab pertains to Kapurthala and Jalandhar which have interchanged their categories, everything else remaining the same.

A look at Table 7.2 would reveal that in Haryana also there does not seem to be any systematic relationship between the monthly per capita expenditure (MPCE) and unemployment prevailing among wage labour of different districts. For example, except three districts of Ambala, Bhiwani and Sonepat, in all other districts MPCE varies between Rs. 43.13 and Rs. 45.49 only irrespective of the rate of unemployment prevailing in these districts. When we calculate correlation between monthly per capita expenditure (MPCE) and the person-days rate of unemployment prevailing among wage labourers for a cross section of 22 districts of Punjab and Haryana, it works out to be -0.115 which is statistically insignificant. Thus, we find that poverty among wage labourers whether defined as percentage of households below the poverty line or monthly per capita expenditure (MPCE) has no relationship with unemployment whatsoever. Thus, our results do not confirm any of the two hypotheses floating in the air. If poverty is not caused by unemployment, its explanation has to be found somewhere else and this is the question to which we address ourselves in the next section.

II

Some Correlates of Poverty

In the preceding section we tried to explore the relationship between unemployment and poverty defined as percentage of households below the poverty line as well as in terms of monthly per capita consumption expenditure (MPCE) and found that there is no relationship between the two. In this section we shall try to analyse other possible variables which are likely to have impact on poverty prevailing among wage labourers and on their levels of living. The analysis has been carried out with the help of district level data. In the first exercise we shall take percentage of households below the poverty line for 22 districts of Punjab and Haryana and shall regress it on specified variables. In the second exercise instead of percentage of households below the poverty line we shall take monthly per capita expenditure of wage labour households in different districts and regress it on those variables.

We know from Chapter 5 that about 78 per cent of total household income of wage labourers in both Punjab and Haryana originates from wage labour. This part of their annual income is the product of number of days the working members of a wage labour household get work and the wage rate at which they work. We also know from Chapter 4 that agricultural growth has tended to reduce the number of days an average wage labourer gets work in a year. But on the other hand wage rates have been found to be positively related with level of agricultural development. Again, in Chapter 6 we find that agricultural growth and poverty (defined as percentage of households below the poverty line) are negatively related with each other, meaning thereby that poverty is less in agriculturally more developed districts and vice versa. If poverty is less in agriculturally more developed districts despite the fact that agricultural growth has tended to reduce work availability to wage labourers in terms of number of days, then the obvious link between poverty and agricultural growth is the wage rates.

Broadly speaking, it appears that there are two types of variables which are likely to play an important role in the explanations of poverty prevailing among wage labour households. The first category would include those structural, technological and demographic variables which have one way or the other an important bearing on wage rate of rural wage labourers. In this category we can include the productivity per acre (representing the level of agricultural development of the region), the proportion of non-Scheduled Castes in total wage labourers (representing some kind of segmentation of the labour market), proportion of workers employed in non-agricultural activities (representing the extent of alternative employment opportunities available to wage labourers and, thus, determining their bargaining strength) and the ruling wage rate in the rural labour market. The second category of factors would include the demographic characteristics of the wage labour households themselves. The prominent among them are the average size of the household and the number of dependents per male wage earner in the household. This is because level of living of wage labour households does not depend on the level of annual household income alone. It also depends upon the number of people in the household who are to share this income. Thus, for any given level of household income, the level of living of the household will vary inversely with the average size of the family. Besides the size of the household, its inner composition is also an important determinant of the level of living of the household. On the basis of the above discussion we identify the following variables which are likely to have significant impact on the extent of poverty prevailing among wage labour households and their levels of living:

O = Output per acre
P_{Nsc} = Proportion of non-scheduled castes in total wage labourers
N = Percentage of workers employed in non-agricultural activities
W = Wage rate of casual labourers
A_{HS} = Average Household size; and
D = Number of dependents per male wage earner.

Since many of these variables are likely to be highly correlated with each other we shall regress poverty (defined as percentage of households below the poverty line) on all these variables separately. The idea is not to determine the extent of variations in poverty being explained by all these variables taken together but simply to ascertain the direction and quantitative magnitude of the impact of each one of these variables on poverty prevailing among wage labour households of Punjab and Haryana. As already mentioned, the analysis has been carried out with the help of district level data because most of these variables are available at the district level. It will also give us a sufficient number of observations. Before presenting our results, a few words about how the variables have been measured, we define poverty *(P)* as a percentage of households below the poverty line (Rs. 48.97 per capita per month at 1975-76 prices). How O, P_{Nsc} and N are measured have already been discussed in the preceding Chapters and needs no repetition. We take average daily wage of male casual workers as our wage rate *(W)*. Average household size for the district has been arrived at by adding total number of persons in the sample households from the district and dividing it by the number of households from that district in our sample. Average number of dependent per male earner is our dependence ratio D.

We expect poverty to be negatively related with output per acre *(O)*, availability of alternative job opportunities outside agriculture *(N)* and ruling wage rate *(W)*. It should be positively related with percentage of non-Scheduled Castes in total wage labourers (P_{Nsc}), average size of household (A_{HS}) and dependence ratio *(D)*. Our expectation of positive relationship between portion of non-scheduled castes (P_{Nsc}) and poverty is based on the assumption that the higher the extent of segmentation in the labour market, the less the changes of their joining hands together for a common cause to improve their economic lot. The results obtained are presented in Table 7.3.

All the variables are having expected signs. Segmentation in the labour market and dependency ratio are found to be positively related with poverty with highly significant coefficients. The coefficient of average household size is also positive and significant at five per cent level of significance. On an average, addition of one more member to the average household size is likely to push up the poverty percentage by 10 points. Similarly addition of one more dependent on each male wage earner is likely to push up the poverty figure by another 23.87 per cent.

On the other hand, output per acre *(O)* and alternative employment opportunities outside agriculture *(N)* are negatively related with poverty, but are significant only at 10 per cent level of significance. What is the meaning of our results? Other things remaining the same, a hundred rupee increase in output per cropped acre is likely to bring down poverty among wage labourers by about one per cent (the value of β is = -0.011). Similarly one per cent increase in employment opportunities outside agriculture is likely to reduce poverty by about 0.39 per cent. Again one rupee increase in daily wage rate of the wage labourers (at 1975-76 prices) is likely to reduce poverty among them by about 6.5 per cent. On the whole, our results appear to be meaningful. Agricultural growth, availability of employment opportunities outside agriculture and higher wage rate tend to reduce poverty significantly. On the other hand, lack of social cohesion among wage labourers, larger family size and larger number of dependents per male earner tend to increase poverty among wage labourers.

TABLE 7.3: Regression Analysis of Poverty Prevailing Among Wage Labour Households of Punjab and Haryana

(Poverty Line Rs. 48.97 at 1975-76 prices)

Dependent Variable: P (Percentage of Households below the Poverty line)

Independent Variable	Constant	Regression coefficient	T-Value	R^2	F-Value
O (Output Per acre)	71.519	-0.011	1.703***	.1268	2.904
P_{Nsc} (Proportion of non-scheduled castes in total wage labourers)	21.439	+0.895	2.590*	.251	6.709
N (Percentage of workers employed in non-agricultural activities)	67.338	-0.392	1.151***	.062	1.324
W (Wage Rate)	100.011	-6.603	3.885*	.430	15.091
A_{HS} (Average household size)	-4.839	+10.027	1.851**	.146	3.416
D (No. of dependents per male earner)	-23.111	+23.871	2.753*	.275	5.575

DF = 20

* Significant at one per cent level of significance.

** Significant at five per cent level of significance.

*** Significant at ten per cent level of significance.

In the second exercise instead of percentage of households below the poverty line we take monthly per capita expenditure (MPCE) which is more direct measure of the level of living of wage labour households as our dependent variable. The results obtained are presented in Table 7.4.

TABLE 7.4: Regression Analysis of Determinants of Per Capita Monthly Expenditure (at 1975-76 prices) of Wage Labour Households of Punjab and Haryana

Dependent Variable: Monthlty Per Capita Expenditure (MPCE)

Independent Variable	Constant	Regression coefficient	T-Value	R^2	F-Value
O (Output per acre)	48.689	0.0015	0.361	.006	.131
P_{Nsc} (Proportion of non-scheduled castes in total wage labourers)	70.818	-0.551	2.659*	.261	7.071
N (Percentage of workers employed in non-agricultural activities)	46.535	0.130	0.618	.018	.383
W (Wage Rate)	24.297	3.805	21.829*	.392	12.913
A_{HS} (Average Household Size)	92.192	-7.066	2.231**	.239	6.305
D (Number of dependents per male earner)	99.779	-15.171	2.962*	.372	11.857

DF = 20
* Significant at one per cent level of significance.
** Significant at five per cent level of significance.

Once again we find that all the variables are having expected signs. As expected, monthly per capita expenditure (MPCE) of wage labourers is higher in those districts where ruling wage rate is high. It is lower where wage labourers do not constitute a socially homogeneous group. It is also lower where average family size is large or number of dependents *vis-a-vis* earning members is high. The effect of large proportion of workers in non-agricultural activities indicating alternative employment opportunities outside agriculture on MPCE is positive but it is statistically insignificant. Unlike in the previous exercise, the impact of output per acre on monthly per capita expenditure of wage labourers, though positive, is insignificant.

To sum up, our results show that agricultural growth does help, to some extent, in alleviating the problem of absolute poverty prevailing among wage labourers but its impact on raising their levels of living is not as important as that of higher wage rate. Higher wage rate is the single most important factor in alleviating the problem of absolute poverty and improving the standard of living of rural wage labourers. Creating more employment opportunities outside agriculture also has a similar effect. On the other hand, segmentation in the labour market, by reducing the chances of joint action by labourers, weakens their bargaining strength and acts as a factor responsible for perpetuating poverty. A large family size and more number of dependents per earner have a harmful impact on the level of living.

We have tested only the impact of social homogeneity or division among wage labourers on their poverty and levels of living but unity among them can also be fostered by making them class conscious. We are stressing this point at the cost of repetition because we feel that it has some important implication for both peasant leaders as well as policy-makers. If high wages are the best guarantee against absolute poverty among rural wage labourers, as results suggest, then the primary task before rural labour organisations should be to make the labourers class conscious and fight for better wages. In future, the struggles of landless labourers have to be on the issue of better wages rather than fighting for getting them postage stamp sized plots in some remote and inaccessible corner of the village land if, at all, the 'surplus land' exists in the village. First of all, not all landless labourers can be given land for cultivation for the simple reason that substantial surplus quantity of land just does not exist. Secondly, even those of the landless labourers who are lucky enough to get it allotted, out of the 'surplus land', may not be able to get its actual possession for years together in the face of opposition from vested landed interests. This is not to suggest that wage labourers should not fight for their right to have access to productive resources and opportunities, but only to bring out the socio-economic hurdles that face them.

At the governmental or policy-making level, fixing realistic minimum wage rate and its strict enforcement will have to be taken seriously. The best guarantee that such laws are enforced is that there exist labour organisations which make rural labourers aware of their rights and provide them guidance. Thus, the apathy and, in some cases, positive hostility, which at present exist towards the political organisations and conscious individuals who try to organise rural wage labourers has to be replaced by positive support to their efforts. Organising rural, mostly illiterate, labourers is a gigantic task and government must supplement the efforts being made by some peasant organisations and individuals if the transformation of our society to a more egalitarian and just social order is to be achieved through peaceful means.

NOTES

1. A Berry and R.H. Sabot *Labour Market Performance in Developing Countries: A Survey of World Bank*, Reprint Series No. 85, p. 1211.
2. O. Turnham (1970) *Employment Problem in Less Developed Countries*, OECD, Paris.
3. J.N. Sinha (1968) The Concept of Unemployment in Developing Economy, *Indian Journal of Agricultural Economics*, XXIII, 2, pp. 15-24.
4. D.T. Lakdawala (1978) "Growth, Unemployment and Poverty", *The Indian Journal of Labour Economics*, XXI, 1 & 2 , April-July, p. 4.
5. *Ibid.*, p. 4.
6. *Ibid.*, p. 15.
7. J.N. Sinha (1978) "Rural Employment Planning: Dimensions and Cnstraints", *Economic and Political Weekly*, XIII, 6 and 7, Annual Number, p. 295.
8. J.N. Sinha (1979) "Unemployment Poverty Nexus Reconsidered" (Mimeo), p. 2.
9. *Ibid.*, p. 11.
10. *Ibid.*, p. 32.
11. *Ibid.*, p. 33.
12. Ranjit Sau (1978) "Growth Employment and Removal of Poverty", *Economic and Political Weekly*, XII, 31, 32 & 33, Special Number, August, p. 1280.
13. *Ibid.*, p. 1280.
14. G. Parthasarthy (1979) "Inter-State Variation in Unemployment and Growth of Agriculture", *The Indian Journal of Labour Economics*, XXII, 1 & 2, April-July, pp. 45-50.
15. Pravin Visaria (1978) "Poverty and Unemployment in India: An Analysis of Recent Evidence" (Mimeo) later on published as *World Bank Staff Paper No. 417*, October 1980.
16. M.L. Dantwala (1979) "Rural Employment: Facts and Issues", *The Indian Journal of Labour Economics*, XXII, 1 & 2, p.9.
17. G. Parthasarthy (1979) *Op. cit.*, p. 46.
18. Pravin Visaria (1980) *Op. cit.*, p. 13.

8

SUMMARY AND CONCLUSIONS

AGRICULTURE IN certain areas of the country, like, Punjab and Haryana, has undergone revolutionary changes since mid-60s with the evolution of high yielding varieties of crops and adoption of modern and improved farm practices. The new agricultural technology consists of two components, i.e., bio-chemical and mechanical. The bio-chemical component consisting of irrigation-seed-fertilizer innovation is normally considered to be land augmenting and labour using in nature. Thus, it is thought to be capable of generating large increases in employment. However, the mechanical component of the new technology, consisting of mechanical tilling, sowing and harvesting, is labour saving in nature and, thus, modify the effect of bio-chemical innovation on employment. The net effect of the new technology on employment will depend on the relative strength of the two components.

To achieve good results from new agricultural technology, timeliness of each operation has become important. Given the short maturing nature of the new varieties and the importance of timeliness of each operation, the new technology is also likely to increase the bargaining power of wage labourers at crucial points of time. Thus, the new technology is expected to have significant positive impact on wage rates. To avoid high cost of hiring labour during peak seasons and to have some kind of assured supply of labour, the employer's preference in this situation is likely to be biased towards more long-term contract, thus, changing the attached-casual composition of wage labourers. What the actual changes have been like? Do the Agricultural labourers in these areas, where new technology has been more successful, have more availability of work in terms of number of days? Has the new technology significantly effected the attached-casual composition of wage labourers? Do they get higher wages in such areas? If so, does it reflect in their income levels, consumption patterns and levels of living? In other words, have the gains of agricultural growth in such areas trickled down to agricultural wage labour and other non-cultivating households or not? These are some of the questions answers to which are explored in the present study.

The study is based on a primary survey of 1,029 wage labour and 330 other non-cultivating households of Punjab spread over 333 villages which were covered by the 30th round of NSS. Similarly, we also have data for 484 wage labour and 485 other non-cultivating households from 329 villages of Haryana. The sampled households are spread over all the 22 districts of Punjab and Haryana. The data relates to the year 1975-76. To analyse the impact of agricultural development of the district on rates of work participation of males and females, their work availability, employment/unemployment, attached-casual composition of wage labourers, their income levels, wage rates, consumption patterns and extent of poverty prevailing among wage labour and other non-cultivating households a cross-section of 22 districts of Punjab and Haryana was taken to see the association between these variables and the level of agricultural development of the district defined as productivity per acre or productivity per male agricultural labour. For this purpose, simple correlation coefficients are used. Wherever the association was found to be statistically significant, we pursued it further by using the method of regression analysis. In such cases, not only the role of agricultural development in explaining the inter-district variations in these variables is quantified but also the impact of other theoretically plausible variables on the dependent variable is explored.

Productivity per acre as index of agricultural development takes into account how much is being produced in an acre of land but does not take into account the other aspect, i.e., how many persons are producing it. In other words, it takes into account the demand aspect of agricultural growth but ignores the supply side. To overcome this problem at certain places in our study particularly where we have tried to test the impact of agricultural growth on level of income and poverty prevailing among wage labour and other non-cultivating households we used productivity per male worker as an index of the level of agricultural development rather than productivity per acre.

To study the variations in wages, a wage determination model in terms of supply and demand factors has been evolved and tested with the help of district level data. Consumption patterns have been studied by fitting Engel Curves to consumer expenditure for different items of consumption that commonly constitute family budget of wage labour and other non-cultivating households. On the basis of elasticities thrown up by most plausible Engel Curve for each item, the relative importance, which the wage labour and other non-cultivating households attach to each item of expenditure, has been discussed. To take care of the regional differences, if any, elasticities have been calculated separately at the regional level as well as State level for both Punjab and Haryana.

By using Rs. 15.90 per capita per month at 1960-61 prices as poverty line and using the Consumer Price Index for Agricultural Labourers (CPIAL), the estimates of the extent of poverty existing among wage labour and other non-cultivating households among various districts of Punjab and Haryana have also been made. The question of unemployment-poverty nexus, if any, has been explored. Finally, an attempt has also been made to find out the factors which explain inter-district variations in the extent of poverty prevailing among wage labour households of Punjab and Haryana.

Summary of Findings

1. Our study shows that about 86 per cent of all male adults in Punjab and about 85 per cent in Haryana participate in work. The corresponding figures for working age group of 15-59 are expectedly higher, being 89.24 per cent for Punjab and 88 per cent for Haryana. Inter-district variations in rates of work participation in the case of males are rather small. Unlike male labourers, in the case of female labourers, however, there are wide variation in the rate of work participation between the two States as well as across districts within each State. Whereas in the case of Punjab the rate of female work participation is only 10.22 per cent, in the case of Haryana it is roughly three times higher as compared to Punjab. Agricultural growth has not affected the rate of male participation but it has adversely affected the rate of female participation. Thus, the rate of female participation as hypothesised by us turns out to be negatively related to the level of agricultural development of the area. Our study also shows that open unemployment prevailing among male workers and preponderence of wage labourers in

total agricultural workers adversely effect the rate of female work participation. It appears that when females do not perceive much work for themselves, the potential female workers simply drop out of the labour force.

2. Our results regarding attached-casual composition of wage labourers show that about two-fifth of all male workers are working as attached labourers in both Punjab and Haryana. The rest three-fifth are casual workers. The proportion of attached to total wage labourers and the level of agricultural development are positively correlated but the relationship is statistically insignificant. Thus, our study, though not conclusive, tends to confirm the results of some earlier studies, like, Bhalla (1976) and Bardhan and Rudra (1981), that new technology has some bias in favour of attached labourers. However, there is a definite negative relationship between the proportion of attached labourer and the level of unemployment. Thus, contrary to the common belief that it is the need for insurance against unemployment, which primarily determines the incidence of tied labour contracts, it appears that it is the tighter labour market conditions which lead to more tied labour contracts. So, it is primarily the demand conditions which have led to predominance of long-terms labour contracts.
3. Our analysis of the unemployment prevailing among wage labourer of Punjab and Haryana shows that whether we go by weekly status unemployment of persons-days rate of unemployment, under various assumptions, the incidence of unemployment is marginally higher in Punjab as compared to Haryana. An average wage labourer gets work for 289 days in a year in Punjab and for 303 days in Haryana. Strangely enough, there seems to be no relationship between the availability of work for the average labourer and the level of agricultural development of the district. Thus, new agricultural technology does not seem to have significantly affected the employment prospect of wage labourers. But analysis of unemployment prevailing among casual workers shows that an average casual worker gets work only for 241 days in a year in Punjab as compared to 258 days in Haryana. There is a negative relationship between the number of days a casual worker gets work and the level of agricultural development of the region. It appears that new agricultural technology has changed the

periodicity of crop rotation in such a way that most of the work has been concentrated in a few peaks of relatively shorter duration. This situation, on the one hand, appears to have changed the employers-labour mix in favour of attached labourers to have some kind of assured supply during the peak seasons and to avoid high cost of casual labourers during the busy peaks and, on the other, it has simultaneously reduced the work availability for casual workers in terms of number of days, although, it has not significantly affected the overall employment prospects of all the wage labourers.

4. Contrary to the results given by NSS, the incidence of unemployment among female labourers in both Punjab and Haryana is quite high. In fact, it is higher than those among male workers. Between the two States it is higher in Punjab as compared to Haryana. An average female worker gets work for 163 days in a year in Punjab and for 197 days in Haryana.
5. Our regression results show that unemployment among wage labourers is positively related with demographic pressure on land, inequality in land holdings, proportion of Scheduled Caste labourers among total wage labourers and the extent of mechanisation, whereas it is negatively associated with alternative employment opportunities outside agriculture and wage rate. But it is only the proportion of Scheduled Castes among total wage labourers, employment opportunities outside agriculture and prevailing wage rate that are statistically significant within the acceptable confidence limits. Thus, our results show that alternative employment opportunities outside agriculture do help to some extent in bringing down the unemployment prevailing among rural wage labourers. But more important than this is the finding that the type of agricultural growth, taking place in Punjab and Haryana (accompanied by large scale mechanisation), tends to aggravate the problem of unemployment among wage labourers. The relative preponderance of Scheduled Castes among total wage labourers (suffering from special social and economic disadvantages) further reinforces this tendency. Concentration of land in a fewer hands by pushing more and more people into the ranks of rural wage labourers swell their number. Whenever increasing number of wage earners compete for limited number of jobs in the rural labour market, unemployment is bound to go

up.

6. Our analysis of the income data shows that for an average wage labour household income from wage employment constitutes about 78 per cent of its total income in Punjab and about 79 per cent in Haryana. The second and third major source of income in Punjab for this category of households is income from other sources (including income from pension, remittances, rent and interest) and income from 'dairying'. In Haryana, however, the order is reverse. Income from dairying constitutes the second major source of income followed by income from other sources. Thus, an average wage labour household in Haryana is better off than its Punjab counterpart in terms of animal wealth. Income from land or cultivation is not an important source of income in either of the State.
7. In the case of other non-cultivating households the pattern of income generation is vastly different from that of wage labour households. In their case about 50 per cent of the total income comes from household enterprises. Income from wage employment constitutes about one-fifth of their total income in both the States. The third major source of income for the other non-cultivating households is pensions and remittances (in Punjab) or dairying (in Haryana). Income from land is an important source for this category of households in Punjab, but it is insignificant in Haryana. Thus, on an average a household belonging to the category of other non-cultivating households in Punjab is better off than its counterparts in Haryana in terms of landed assets.
8. On an average a household belonging to the category of wage labour as well as 'other non-cultivating households' is better off in Punjab as compared to its counterparts in Haryana. In Punjab, the per capita income of a wage labour household is about 15 per cent higher as compared to its counterparts in Haryana. Similarly, in the case of other non-cultivating households, the average per capita income is higher by about 16 per cent in Punjab as compared to Haryana. In fact, there is a positive (though statistically insignificant) correlation between the per capita income of wage labour as well as other non-cultivating households and the level of agricultural development of the district defined as productivity per male agricultural worker. Thus, there appears to be some trickle down of the benefits of

agricultural growth to wage labour and other non-cultivating sections of rural population also, though it is not quite established with income data.

9. There is no relationship between the proportion of non-wage income in total income of wage labour households and the level of agricultural development of the district. In case of other non-cultivating households, however, there is a positive and statistically significant relationship between the proportion of non-wage income in their total income and the level of agricultural development of the district. It appears that the new agricultural technology has created some opportunities for self-employment outside agriculture in allied activities, such as machinery repairing and servicing and supply of various other agricultural inputs. Increased income of farmers as a result of agricultural growth has also created demand for new urban produced goods and new kind of services within the village. That section of rural population which is catering to the demands of modern agriculture in these areas has experienced a shift in their pattern of income generation away from wage employment. As a result, the proportion of non-wage income in their total household income has become stronger in these areas.
10. Wages of both attached as well as casual labourers are higher in Punjab as compared to their counterparts in Haryana. These are generally higher in more developed districts as compared to less-developed districts. The correlation between the wage rates of attached agricultural labourer and the level of agricultural development of the district is positive though it is statistically insignificant. In case of casual labourers, however, the relationship is positive and highly significant. The correlation works out to be 0.616 which is statistically significant at one per cent level of significance. Thus, our hypothesis that wages are positively related to the level of agricultural development of the district is, by and large supported by the empirical evidence.
11. About 46 per cent of the wages of attached agricultural labourers in both Punjab and Haryana is paid in cash and the rest in kind. Generally, the wage rates are lower where the proportion of wages paid in cash is higher. In fact, there is a negative relationship between the proportion of wages paid in cash and the wage rate. The correlation between the two works out to be -0.396 which is statistically significant at five per cent

level of significance. Thus, our hypothesis that wages are negatively related to the proportion of wages paid in cash is also supported by empirical evidence.

12. The results of the regression analysis show that demand and supply factors explain more than 75 per cent of inter-district variations in wage rates. Wages are found to be positively related to output per acre, inequality in land holdings and relative numerical strength of wage labour in total agricultural workers as hypothesised by us. It appears that the proportion of wage labour in total agricultural workers is generally higher in areas where, due to rapid technological changes, the demand for labour and also the wage rates are relatively higher. As expected, wage rates are negatively related to demographic pressure on land and segmentation in the labour market. However, only demographic pressure on land, segmentation in the labour market, output per acre and inequality in the distribution of land holdings are statistically significant within the acceptable confidence limits.
13. Our analysis of consumption data shows that the pattern of consumption of both wage labour as well as other non-cultivating households is heavily food-oriented. In the case of wage labour households, about 75 per cent of the total expenditures in Punjab and about 82 per cent in Haryana are on food items only. In case of other non-cultivating households, these figures are slightly lower being 72.6 per cent in Punjab and 77.1 per cent in Haryana. In both Punjab as well as Haryana, the single most important item in the food budget of wage labour households is cereals followed by 'milk and milk products' and 'sugar and gur'. Within the category of non-food items, priorities differ in Punjab and Haryana. In the case of Punjab, it is 'miscellaneous goods and services' which include expenditure on medicines, education, conveyance, laundry and toilet goods, etc., which account for the highest proportion of expenditure on non-food items followed by clothing and fuel and light. In the case of Haryana, the order is clothing, followed by fuel and light and 'miscellaneous goods'. In case of other non-cultivating households, the pattern of priorities, in both Punjab and Haryana, is exactly the same as in the case of wage labour households, only exception being that 'milk and milk products' replaces 'cereals' as the most important item in their

budgets in Punjab. Region-wise analysis of their consumption pattern shows that their behaviour is by and large in accordance with the postulates of consumption theory.

14. Both wage labour as well as other non-cultivating households are heavily dependent on market purchase for their food requirements. In the case of wage labourers of both the States, more that 80 per cent of their cereal requirements are met through market purchases. For total foods, about two-thirds is the cash purchase component and the rest one-third is either home grown or represents wages received in terms of grains and perquisites of the working members. Dependence of the other non-cultivating households on market purchase for their food requirements is only marginally less than that of labourers. About 63 per cent of their total food requirements are met through cash purchases in both States. Thus, both wage labourers as well as other non-cultivating households, because of their greater dependence on market for food, are more vulnerable to inflationary pressure than the better off rural sections of cultivating households.
15. Our analysis of expenditure elasticities for various commodities of wage labour households of various regions of Punjab and Haryana indicates that, except for absolutely basic necessities, like cereals, pulses, sugar and gur, salt and spices and fuel, everything else ranging from superior foods to other non-food items is luxury for them in all the regions of Punjab and Haryana. Even for basic necessities, the expenditure elasticities are quite high. The magnitude of elasticity for cereals is in the range of .7 to .8. More than 70 per cent of increase in income, if and when it takes place, goes to buy food items only. Some food items, like, milk and milk products, edible oils, vegetable, fruits and nuts, are still in the nature of luxuries for these households. One consequence of this phenomenon of very high elasticities for food items is that not much is left to be spent on non-food items.
16. Our analysis of consumption elasticities at the regional level shows that the pattern of consumption and the relative importance attached to each item in various regions is virtually similar. If the elasticity is less than one for a commodity in one region, it holds true for all the regions. The same is true for most of the items whose elasticity is more than one. Thus there

are no significant differences in the consumption pattern of labour households among various regions of Punjab and Haryana.

17. The pattern of consumption of other non-cultivating households of Punjab and Haryana is broadly the same as that of labour households. There are no significant differences between the two categories except those which are implied by the relatively higher per capita expenditure of other non-cultivating households compared to wage labour households in all the regions of Punjab and Haryana.
18. Using a poverty line figure of Rs. 15.90 per capita per month at 1960-61 rural prices and taking Consumer Price Index for Agricultural Labourers (CPIAL) as price deflator, we obtain a figure of Rs. 48.97 per capita per month as poverty line for the year 1975-76. Taking this poverty line figure, our study shows that in Punjab about 48 per cent of wage labour households and 35 per cent of other non-cultivating households were below the poverty line during 1975-76. The magnitude of poverty prevailing among non-cultivating rural population of Haryana is even larger than that of Punjab. The corresponding figures being 63 per cent for wage labourers and about 50 per cent for other non-cultivating households. Generally the percentage of households below the poverty line is low in agriculturally more developed districts and *vice versa*. There is a negative and statistically significant relationship between the percentage of wage labour as well as other non-cultivating households below the poverty line and the level of agricultural development of the district as measured by productivity per acre or productivity per male agricultural worker. Thus, the trickle down hypothesis, which could not be unambiguously established when we tested it with income data, is more or less confirmed when we test it with more stable and reliable consumption data. It appears that accelerated agricultural growth even within the existing institutional set-up does help, to some extent, in alleviating the problem of absolute poverty prevailing among wage labour and other non-cultivating households.
19. Our study, fails to confirm the much talked about nexus between poverty and unemployment. According to our data there is virtually no relationship between poverty and unemployment prevailing among wage labour households of

Punjab and Haryana. However, our study tends to confirm the findings of most of the earlier studies that poverty among wage labourers is on a much larger scale than the existence of unemployment in either of these States. The statistical relationship between the two, though positive, turns out to be highly insignificant. It appears that the factors responsible for the existence of poverty are far too complex and cannot be explained by a single factor, like, unemployment.

20. The results of our regression analysis show that segmentation in the labour market and dependency ratio are positively related with poverty with highly significant coefficients. The average household size is also positively and significantly related with poverty. On the other hand, as expected, prevailing wage rate is negatively and highly significantly related with poverty. Again, output per acre and alternative employment opportunities outside agriculture are also negatively related with poverty but are both significant only at 10 per cent level of significance. Thus, our results show that agricultural growth, availability of employment opportunities outside agriculture and higher wage rate tend to reduce poverty significantly. On the other hand, segmentation in the labour market, larger family size and larger number of dependents per male earner tend to increase poverty among wage labourers.

Implications

It is important to spell out the implications of our results. First of all it is clear that if our results regarding the impact of agricultural growth on employment/unemployment of wage labour households represent the true picture then agricultural growth of the type which is taking place in Punjab and Haryana (accompanied by large scale mechanisation of most farm operations) cannot solve the problem of unemployment prevailing among rural wage labourers. Although the average availability of work of 289 days in a year to a wage labourer in Punjab and 303 days in Haryana is fairly satisfactory by almost any standards, yet our finding that availability of work to an average casual worker in terms of number of days is negatively related to the level of agricultural development of the region is quite disturbing and needs some explanation.

It may be pointed out that our's is not a unique finding, as some earlier studies have also shown similar results.[1] Thus, many scholars have tried to give a convincing rationale for the lack of relationship between agricultural growth and employment. It is also possible that our finding could be the consequence of some limitations in our employment data. For example, we did not have the hourly time disposition data with us and hence we took a day as a unit to measure employment/unemployment. Consequently, it was not possible to convert days into standard days of eight hours as is usually done in employment studies. It is none of our contention that new technology has decreased total amount of work. All available evidence suggests that perhaps it has increased it. Our contention is that the new technology has effected the periodicity of crop rotation in such a way that most of the work has been concentrated in a few peaks of relatively shorter duration. Now, if the same or more amount of work has to be completed in a fewer number of days then there are two possibilities of doing it. One is that the existing workers work for longer hours than before during these busy seasons and second, is that more number of workers are made to share work during the peak seasons. It appears that both these phenomena are operating in Punjab. For example, it is a well established fact that large number of migrant workers come to Punjab from eastern U.P., Bihar and Rajasthan to seek work during wheat harvesting and rice transplanting seasons. Workers from urban informal sector from within the State also join the ranks of rural wage earners to take advantage of high wages in rural areas during the busy seasons. At the same time, however, regular local workers also work for longer hours during these busy seasons. In this situation taking unstandardised day as a unit to measure employment/unemployment is likely to underestimate the work availability to local labourers and consequently will over-estimate unemployment prevailing among them. Therefore, our results regarding the employment effects of agricultural growth should be interpreted with caution.

Our results regarding effects of agricultural growth on wages, incomes, consumption and rural poverty of wage labourers are, however, on expected lines. We expected that the concentration of work in a few peaks of relatively shorter duration is likely to give, at least temporarily, a greater bargaining power to casual labourer during the peak seasons. This is likely to push up wages of casual workers during the peak seasons and hence their overall wage rates are likely to increase. This is exactly what has happened. The correlation between the wage rate of male casual workers and the level of agricultural productivity per acre for a cross-section of 22 districts of Punjab and Haryana works out to be 0.616 which is statistically significant at one per cent level of significance. The coefficient of output per acre also turns out to be positive and significant in the regression equation. Thus, it is clear that increased agricultural productivity does help in improving wage rates, but more important is the finding that demographic pressure on land and segmentation in the labour market significantly depress wages. The implications are clear. If wage rates of agricultural labourers are to be improved, agricultural growth alone cannot do it. Population pressure on land has to be relieved to some extent and some people have to migrate out of agriculture and seek jobs in other sectors.

Another implication of our results is that, other things remaining the same, the greater the homogeneity or sense of oneness among wage labourers, the better the chances of their coming together and joining hands for a common cause. We tested only the impact of social homogeneity of division among wage labourers but unity can also be fostered by making them class conscious. This brings out clearly the important role which rural labour organisations and conscious individuals can play in uniting the labourers and getting them their due share in the increased agricultural productivity.

The importance of alternative employment opportunities outside agriculture and segmentation in the labour market is once again brought out clearly in Chapter 7 where we find that segmentation in the labour market is positively and highly significantly related with poverty among wage labourers. On the other hand, other things remaining the same, one per cent increase in employment opportunities outside agriculture is likely to reduce poverty among wage labourers by as much as 0.39 per cent. Demographic pressure on land and segmentation in the labour market are also important determinants of wage rates and high wages, in turn, are the single most important factor which can make a dent on poverty prevailing among rural wage labourers. The policy implications of our results are clear. Agricultural development alone cannot solve the problem of unemployment or rural poverty. Demographic pressure on land has to be relieved to some extent. This can be done by creating alternative employment opportunities outside agriculture. Thus, at the policy-making level industrial development of an area has to be simultaneously undertaken along with agricultural development if a significant dent is to be made on unemployment and rural poverty. At the political level, major thrust of organised struggles of wage labourers in future has to be on the issue of better wages.

Small sized families and low dependency ratio can also play a significant role in improving the lot of rural poor. Dependency ratio can be brought down if women start participating actively in economically productive non-agricultural activities. This brings out the need for providing the rural poor with some income generating assets on which women can work or even men can also spend their surplus time productively. That would require radical changes in socio-economic set up. In the mean time, however, programmes, like, food for work, if implemented properly, can go a long way in alleviating the problem of absolute poverty among rural poor to some extent. The experience of Maharashtra and some other States shows that wage rates of agricultural workers tend to rise where the food for work programmes have been implemented properly.

The fixing of realistic minimum wage rate and its strict enforcement will have to be taken seriously. The best guarantee to enforce these laws, in the face of opposition from vested landed interests, is the unity of labour and the existence of labour organisations which make wage labourers aware of their rights and fight for the same. Thus, the apathy and, in some cases, positive hostility, which at present exist towards the political organisations and conscious individuals who try to organise rural and mostly illiterate wage labourers must go if the transition of our society to a more egalitarian and just social order is to be achieved through peaceful means.

NOTE

1. For example T.N. Jha (1980), on the basis of his survey data collected from four developed villages of Bhojpur district and four backward villages of Madhubani district of North Bihar, finds that on an average an adult worker gets work for 192.8 days in a year in Bhojpur which is at a higher level of agricultural development as compared to 196.5 days in Madhubani which is at a lower level of agricultural development. By applying Z-test he also finds that two means are significantly different from each other. See T.N. Jha (1980). *Employment in Rural Economy: A Case Study of a Developed and a Less Developed District in North Bihar*, A Ph.D. Thesis submitted to the School of Social Sciences, Jawaharlal Nehru University, New Delhi, Table IV, 10, p. 107. Similarly Lakdawala (1978) also observes that in many poor regions of the country unemployment rates are comparatively low. See D.T. Lakdawala (1978): "Growth, Employment and Poverty", *Indian Journal of Labour Economics*, XXI, 1 & 2, April-July.

TABLE 5.A-1: Data Profile for Wage Determination Model

District	Wage rate (W)	No. of workers per cropped acre (St)	Index of land holding inequality (I)	Output per acre in (Rs.) (O)	Person-days unemployment rate among casual labourers (U)	Proportion of non-scheduled castes (P_{Nsc})	Proportion of wage labourer in total agri. workers (E)
1	2	3	4	5	6	7	8
Amritsar	7.61	0.47	0.573	1,849	9.23	33.83	36.53
Bhatinda	8.83	0.34	0.532	1,336	26.26	30.59	28.71
Faridkot	8.82	0.36	0.537	1,721	24.13	33.46	35.61
Ferozepur	8.69	0.32	0.556	1,900	25.20	33.46	30.07
Gurdaspur	6.81	0.46	0.572	2,050	31.03	48.49	32.68
Hoshiarpur	8.12	0.44	0.626	1,647	32.09	28.34	29.09
Jalandhar	7.89	0.45	0.557	2,243	29.45	20.92	35.53
Kapurthala	8.42	0.43	0.557	2,122	28.11	25.14	25.02
Ludhiana	9.10	0.39	0.502	2,166	20.00	25.49	35.32
Patiala	7.58	0.37	0.532	2,016	45.52	38.96	32.32
Ropar	8.00	0.49	0.622	1,856	34.81	34.90	25.62
Sangrur	8.12	0.36	0.532	1,869	35.11	32.05	28.69
Ambala	6.05	0.39	0.569	1,860	25.74	49.35	32.48
Bhiwani	4.94	0.21	0.488	732	27.10	38.94	16.14
Gurgaon	5.05	0.41	0.545	1,094	18.27	45.55	18.57
Hissar	6.35	0.27	0.488	1,101	10.05	36.24	25.39
Jind	5.62	0.34	0.515	1,261	32.00	37.20	22.89
Karnal	6.20	0.37	0.483	1,922	17.29	46.24	34.57
Kurukshetra	6.42	0.32	0.473	1,932	39.54	46.26	29.20
Mohindergarh	5.79	0.29	0.478	785	19.05	32.00	16.54
Rohtak	5.77	0.33	0.531	1,175	11.98	33.83	22.41
Sonepat	5.16	0.43	0.500	1,673	50.33	33.83	29.59

TABLE 6.A-1: Number of Households in Each Expenditure Class (*Punjab*)

Category (Per capita monthly consumption in Rs.)	Region-I		Region-II		Region-III		Punjab	
	Labour	Others	Labour	Others	Labour	Others	Labour	Others
Below 25	20	2	5	1	9	1	34	4
25 - 30	27	4	17	4	19	2	63	10
30 - 34	23	7	20	1	18	6	61	14
34 - 38	37	7	31	14	22	2	90	23
38 - 42	38	7	36	15	22	2	96	24
42 - 45	34	7	17	9	17	3	68	19
45 - 48	26	5	21	6	13	5	60	16
48 - 51	29	8	16	9	11	1	56	18
51 - 55	33	8	23	11	16	2	72	21
55 - 60	29	8	29	6	23	5	81	19
60 - 65	24	10	34	4	14	8	72	22
65 - 70	23	18	29	6	15	3	67	27
70 - 80	35	15	15	6	16	2	66	23
80 - 100	36	19	29	8	23	8	88	35
100 and above	20	27	18	12	17	16	55	55

TABLE 6.A-2: Number of Households in Each Expenditure Class (*Haryana*)

Category (Per capita monthly consumption in Rs.)	Region-I		Region-II		Region-III		Haryana	
	Labour	Others	Labour	Others	Labour	Others	Labour	Others
Below 25	12	8	20	12	14	8	46	28
25 - 30	29	10	23	14	9	15	61	39
30 - 34	12	15	30	12	7	6	49	33
34 - 38	29	10	23	8	5	10	57	28
38 - 42	10	13	9	15	6	12	25	40
42 - 45	18	18	12	10	7	5	37	33
45 - 48	11	16	6	9	4	7	21	32
48 - 51	10	18	10	7	7	4	27	29
51 - 55	15	15	7	7	6	1	23	28
55 - 60	13	13	8	5	2	7	23	25
60 - 65	11	10	8	6	7	7	26	23
65 - 70	10	9	4	5	2	6	16	20
70 - 80	16	17	9	11	5	12	30	40
80 - 100	8	15	13	17	7	9	28	41
100 and above	7	24	3	14	5	8	15	46

BIBLIOGRAPHY

Acharya, S.S. "Green Revolution and Farm Employment", *Indian Journal of Agricultural Economics*, 28 (3), pp. 30-45, 1973.

Aggarwal, Bina, *Mechanisation in Indian Agriculture : An Analytical Study Based on the Punjab*, Allied Publishers, New Delhi, 1983.

Ahluwalia, Montek S., "Rural Poverty and Agricultural Performance in India", *The Journal of Development Studies* 14(3), pp. 298-323, 1978.

Ahuja, Kanta, 'Measurement of Rural Labour surplus' : A. Ph. D. Thesis of the University of Rajasthan, 1975.

Ahuja, Kanta *Idle Labour in village India*,Manohar, 1978.

Aitchson, J. and J.A.C. Brown, "A Synthesis of Engel Curve Theory", *Review of Economic Studies*, 22, pp. 35-46, 1955.

Alagh, Y.K., "Indian Planning in the Eighties", *Economic and Political Weekly*, 14, Special Number, pp. 1273-82, 1979.

Allen, R.G.D. and A.L. Bowley, *Family Expenditure : A Study of Its Variations*, London, 1935.

Balota, S.N., "Bias in Income Elasticity Estimates Derived from Expenditure per Family Data: A Note", *Artha Vijnana*, 6, 1964.

Bardhan, K., "Factors Affecting Wage Rates for Agricultural Labour", *Economic and Political Weekly*, 8(26), (Review of Agriculture), 1973.

Bardhan, K., "Rural employment, Wages and Labour Markets in India – A Survey of Research", *Economic and Political Weekly*, 12, 1977.

Bardhan, P.K., "On the Minimum Level of Living and the Rural Poor", *Indian Economic Review*, 5 (New Series) pp. 129-36, 1970.

Bardhan, P.K., "The Green Revolution and Agricultural Labourers", *Economic and Political Weekly*, 5 (29-31) 1970.

Bardhan, P.K., 'On the Incidence of Rural Poverty in India in the Sixties", *Economic and Political Weekly*, 8, 1973.

Bardhan, P.K., 'Size, Productivity and Returns to Scale : An Analysis of Farm level Data in Indian Agriculture", (Mimeo), 1973.

Bardhan, P.K., "Variations in Agricultural Wages: A Note", *Economic and Political Weekly*, 8, 1973.

Bardhan, P.K., "Determinants of Supply and Demand for Labour in a Poor Agrarian Economy : An Analysis of Household Survey Data from Rural West Bengal", in Binswanger, H.P. and M.K. Rosenzweig, (ed.) 1984. *Contractual Arrangements, Employment and Wages in Rural Labour Market in Asia*, Yale University Press, pp. 242-62, 1979.

Bardhan, P.K., "Wages and Employment in a Poor Agrarian Economy: A Theoretical and Empirical Analysis", *Journal of Political Economy*, 87 (3), pp. 479-500, 1979.

Bardhan, P.K., "Poverty of Agricultural Labourers and Trickle-Down in Rural India", in *Land, Labour and Rural Poverty Essays in Development Economics*, Oxford University Press, Delhi, pp. 188-99, 1984.

Bardhan, P.K., *Land labour and Rural Poverty Essays in Development Economics*, Oxford University Press, Delhi, 1984.

Bardhan, P.K. and A. Rudra, "Terms and Conditions of Labour Contracts in Agriculture : Results of Some Survey in West Bengal, 1979", *Oxford Bulletin of Economics and Statistics*, 43, 1981.

Barna, T., *The Distribution of Income Through Public Finance*. Oxford University Press, London, pp. 21-24, 1978.

Bell, C., "The Acquisition of Agricultural Technology: Its Determinants and Effects", *Journal of Development Studies*, 9(1), pp. 123-59, 1972.

Berry. A. and R.H. Sabot, *Labour Market Performance in Developing Countries: A Survey of World Bank* Reprint 85.

Bhalla, G.S., *Changing Agrarian Structure in India – A Study of the Impact of Green Revolution in Haryana*, Meenakshi Prakashan Meerut – Delhi, 1974.

Bhalla, G.S. and G.K. Chadha "Structure of Institutional Set-up of Rural Punjab in the Year 2000", FAO, Rome, (Mimeo) 1980.

Bhalla, G.S. and G.K. Chadha, "Green Revolution and Small Peasant: A Study of Income Distribution in Punjab Agriculture", *Economic and Political Weekly*, 17 (20,21), 1982.

Bhalla, G.S. and G.K. Chadha, '*Green Revolution and the Small Peasant*, Concept Publishing Company, New Delhi, 1983.

Bhalla, Sheilla, "New Relations of Production in Haryana Agriculture", *Economic and Political Weekly*, 11, 1976.

Bhalla, Sheilla, "Real Wage Rates of Agricultural Labourers in Punjab, 1961-77 – A Preliminary Analysis", *Economic and Political Weekly*, 14 (26), Review of Agriculture, pp. A57-A68, 1979.

Bhatty, I.Z., "Unemployment: Questions of Measurement and Mitigation", *Yojna*, 17(1), pp. 71-80, 1973.

Bhatty, I.Z., "Inequality and poverty in Rural India", in Srinivasan T.N. and P.K. Bardhan (ed.): *Poverty and Income Distribution in India*, Statistical Publishing Society, Calcutta, 1974.

Bhattacharjee, J.P., "Underemployment Among Indian Farmers : Analysis of its Nature and Extent Based on Data for Bihar", *Artha Vijnana*, 3(3), 1961.

Bhattacharya, N. and T. Maitra, "Analysis of Engel Curves Based on NSS Household Budget Data for 7th to 22nd Rounds", *Paper Presented at the 10th Indian Econometric Conference* (Mimeo), 1970.

Bhattacharya, Sudhir "A Note On Employment and Unemployment Concepts Adopted in the National Sample Survey", *Report of the Committee of experts on Unemployment Estimates*, Planning Commission, Government of India, Appendix 1, pp. 33-38, 1970.

Billings, M.N. and A. Singh "Mechanisation and Rural Employment – With Some Implications For Rural Income Distribution", *Economic and Political Weekly*, 5, Review of Agriculture, 1970.

Billings, M.N. and A. Singh, "The Effect of Technology on Farm employment in India", *Development Digest*, 10(2), 1971.

Biswas, A.K. and D.K. Bose 'Consumption Projections of Selected Items over the period of Third Plan' in V.K.R.V. Rao (ed); *Papers on National Income and Allied Topics*, II, 1962.

Brady, D.S., "Quantity and Quality of Clothings Purchases", in Friend, I and R. Jones (ed.). *Proceedings of the Conference on Consumption and Savings*, 2, Philadelphia, 1960.

Buck, J.L. *Chinese Farm Economy*, The University of Chicago Press, Chicago, 1930.

Byres, T.J., "The Dialects of India's Green Revolution", *South Asian Review*, 5(2), pp. 99-116, 1972.

Chadha, G.K., *Dynamics of Rural Transformation : A Study of Punjab 1950-80* (Mimeo), J.N.U., New Delhi, 1983.

Chandra, N.K. and Associates, *Survey of Peasant Organisations in West Bengal*, (Mimeo), 1975.

Chandra, R.C., Female Working force of Rural Punjab – 1961", *Manpower Journal*, 2(4), pp. 47-62, 1967.

Chopra, Kusum, "Tractorisation and Change in Factor Inputs – A Case Study of Punjab" *Economic and Political Weekly*, 9(52), pp. A119-A127, 1974.

Dandekar, V.M. and N. Rath, '*Poverty in India*', Indian School of Political Economy, Pune, 1971.

Dandekar, V.M. and N. Rath "Poverty in India", *Economic and Political Weekly*, 6(1 and 2), 1971.

Dantwala, M.L., "Approaches of Growth and Employment", *Economic and Political Weekly*, 7(51), 1972.

Dantwala, M.L., "Rural Employment : Facts and Issues", *Indian Journal of Labour Economics*, 22 (1 and 2), pp. 1-24, 1979.

Davies, D., *The Case of Labourers in Husbandry*, Bath, 1795.

Duepetiaux' E., *Budgets Economiques des classes ouwieres on Belgique Brassels*, quoted in, G.J. Stigler "The Early History of Empirical Studies of Consumer Behaviour", *The Journal of Political Economy*, 62(2), pp. 95-113, 1954.

Eckaus, R.S., "Factor Proportions in Underdeveloped Countries", *American Economic Review*, 45, pp. 539-65, 1985.

Eden, *The State of the Poor*, London, 1797.

Engel E., "*Die Productions – and consumptions verliaitnisse des konigreichs sachsen*" originally in '*Aeitschrft des Statistischen Bureau des Koniglich sachsis Ministerium des Innaen.* 8 to 9, 1857, reprinted with separate pagination as an appendix to *Engels Die Lebenskosten Belgischer Arbeitter Famillien* Dresden, 1895.

Evanson, Robert E. and Hans P. Binswanger: "Estimating Labour Demand Functions for Indian agriculture", in Binswanger and Rosenzweig (ed.); *op.cit.*, pp. 263-79.

Falcon, P. Walter, "The Green Revolution: Generations of Problems", *American Journal of Agricultural Economics*, 52, pp. 698-710, 1970.

Frankel, Francine R., "India's New Strategy of Agricultural Development", *Journal of Asian Studies,* August, 1969.

Frankel, Francine R., "Agricultural Modernization and Social Change", *Mainstream*, 1970.

Gnansekharan, K.S., "Labour Force Projection for India 1951-76", *Artha Vijnana*, 2(1), pp. 1-13, 1960.

Government of India, *A Report of the Foodgrains Enquiry Committee*, 1957.

Government of India *Sarvekshana*, 11 (4), pp. 135-39, 1979.

Griffin, Keith and A.K. Ghose, "Institutional Structure, Technological Change and Growth in Poor Agrarian Economies: An analysis with reference to Bengal and Punjab", *World Development*, 7(4/5) pp. 385-96, 1979.

Griliches Z., "Productivity and Technology", *International Encyclopaedia of Social Sciences*, Macmillan, New York, 1968.

Hansen, B., "Marginal Productivity Wage Theory and Subsistence Wage Theory in Egyptian Agriculture", *Journal of Development Studies*, 2, 1966.

Harrison, J.G., *Agricultural Modernisation and Income Distribution* a Ph.D. Thesis submitted to the Princeton University, 1972.

Hauthakker, H., "The Econometrics of Family Budgets", *Journal of the Royal Statistical Society*, Series A (Gen.) 115, pp. 1-28, 1952.

Hauthakker, H., "Compensated Changes in Quantities and Qualities Consumed", *Review of Economic Studies*, 19(3), 5, pp. 55-64, 1953.

Hauthakker, H.S., "International Comparison of Household Expenditure Patterns: Commemorating the Centenary of Engels Law", *Econometrica*, 25, pp. 532-51, 1957.

Hauthakker, H.S. and S.J. Prais, *"Les variations de qualite dans budgets de famille", Economic Appliques*, (1), pp. 1-14, 1952.

Hayami, Y. and V.W. Ruttan, "Factor, Prices and Technical Change in Agricultural Development: The US and Japan 1880-1900", *Journal of Political Economy*, 1970.

Iyengar, N.S., "Some Estimates of Engel Elasticities Based on NSS Data", *Journal of Royal Statistical Society*, Series-A (General), 130, pp. 84-97, 1967.

Jha, T.N., 'Employment in Rural Economy: A Case Study of a Developed and Less-Developed District of North Bihar', An Unpublished Ph.D. Thesis of the School of Social Sciences, Jawaharlal Nehru University, New Delhi, 1980.

Jorgenson, D.W., "Surplus Agricultural Labour and Dual Economy", *Oxford Economic Papers*, 1967.

Jose, A.V., "Trends in Real Wage Rates of Agricultural Labourers", *Economic and Political Weekly*, 9 Review of Agriculture, 1974.

Kahlon, A.S., *Modernisation of Punjab Agriculture*, Allied Publishers, New Delhi, 1984.

Khan, N.A., "Some Reflections on the Census of 1961", I and II, *Indian Economic Journal*, 10 (3 and 4), 1963.

Khaund, H.P., "Changes in Income Distribution Pattern and Their Significance in a Society in Transition", *Indian Journal of Agricultural Economics*, 25, Conference, 1972.

Khusro, A.M., *Economic Development With No Population Transfers* Asia Publishing House, Bombay, 1962.

Krishnaji, N., "Wages of Agricultural Labour", *Economic and Political Weekly*, 6(39), Review of Agriculture, 1971.

Ladejinsky, Wolf, "The Green Revolution in Punjab A Field Trip", *Economic and Political Weekly*, 4, pp. A73-A83, 1969.

Ladejinsky, Wolf, "Green Revolution in Bihar – The Kosi Area: Field Trip", *Economic and Political Weekly*, 4, 1969.

Lal, Deepak, "Agricultural Growth, Real Wages and Rural Poor in India", *Economic and Political Weekly*, 11 pp. A47-A61, 1976.

Lakdawala, D.T., "Growth, Unemployment and Poverty", *The Indian Journal of Labour Economics*, 21 (1 and 2), 1978.

Leibenstein, H., *Economic Backwardness and Economic Growth*, John Wiley and Sons, New York, 1957.

Leibenstein, H., "The Theory of Under-employment in Backward Economies", *Journal of Political Economy*, 65, pp. 91-103, 1957.

Leser, C.E.V. "Forms of Engel Curves", *Econometrica*, 31, pp. 684-703, 1963.

Lewis A.L., "Economic Development with Unlimited Supplies of Labour", *Manchester School of Economics and Social Studies*, 22, 1954.

Lewis, A.L., *The Theory of Economic Growth*, George Allen and Unwin Ltd., 1955.

Lewis, John P., "Wanted in India: A Relevant Radicalism", *Economic and Political Weekly*, 5, 1970.

Lippitt, V., "Determinants of Consumer Demand for House Furnishing and Equipment: Service Expenditure at Mid Century", In Friend, I and R. Jones (ed.) *Op. cit.*, pp. 436-60, 1960.

Lockwood, B., "Pattern of Investment in Farm Machinery and Equipment", *Economic and Political Weekly*, 7, Review of Agriculture, 1972.

Maigel, S. and L. Winnick, "Family Housing Expenditure; Exclusive Laws and Intrusive Variances", in Friend I. And R. Jones (ed.) *Op. cit.*, 1960.

Mahajan, B.M., *Consumer Behaviour in India – An Econometric Study*, Concept Publishing Co., New Delhi.

Mahajan, B.M. and H. Mahajan, "Effect of Groupings of Observation on Coefficient of Determination in Engel Curve Analysis", *Artha Vijnana*, 23(4), pp. 352-65, 1981.

Maitra, T., 'On Regional and Temporal Variations in Engel Curves in Rural India", *Technical Report No. Econ. 12/69*, I.S.I., Calcutta, 1969.

Majumdar, D., "The Marginal Productivity Theory of Wages and Disguised Unemployment", *Review of Economic Studies*, 26, 1959.

Majumdar, N.A., *Some Problems of Under-employment*, Popular Book Depot, Bombay, 1961.

Mamburs M., "Demand for Clothings", in Friend, I. and R. Jones (ed.) *Op. cit.*, pp. 311-58, 1960.

Mathur, P.N., "Short Term and Long Term Effects on Foodgrains Consumption due to change in Total Expenditure", *Artha Vijnana*, 4(4), pp. 358-64, 1962.

Mehra, Shakuntala, "Surplus Labour in Indian Agriculture", *Indian Economic Review*. 1(1), pp. 111-29, 1966.

Mellor, J.W. and U.J., Lee "Growth Linkages of the New Food Grain Technology" *Indian Journal of Agricultural Economics*, 26, 1973.

Mellor, John W. and Robert D. Stevens, "The Average and Marginal Product of Farm Labour in Underdeveloped Economies", *Journal of Farm Economics*, 38, pp. 780-91, 1956.

Minhas, B.S., "Rural Poverty, Land Redistribution and Development Strategy: Facts and Policy", *Indian Economic Review*, 5, (New Series), pp. 97-128, 1970.

Minhas, B.S. and A. Vaidyanathan, "Growth of Crop Output in India 1951-54 to 1958-61: An Analysis by Component Elements", *Journal of the Indian society of Agricultural Statistics*, 1965.

Mirrless, J.A., "A Pure Theory of Under-developed Economies", in Reynold, L.G. (ed.) *Agriculture in Development Theory*, Yale University Press, 1975.

Mishra, V.N., "Labour Market in Agriculture: A Study of Gujarat Districts", *Indian Journal of Agricultural Economics*, 25(3), pp. 8-15, 1970.

Morgan J.N., "A Review of Recent Research on Consumer Behaviour", in L.H. Clark (ed.) *Consumer Behaviour and Research on Consumer Reactions*, New York, pp. 93-219, 1958.

Murphy, D.C., *Econometric Analysis of Family Budgets in Ireland*, An Unpublished Thesis of National University of Ireland.

Myint, H., *The Economics of Developing Countries*, Hutichinson, London, 1964.

Namboodri, N.K., "A Contribution to the Study of Factors Associated with Working Force Participation Rates", *Asian Economic Review*, 9(1), 1956.

Nurkse, R., *Problems of Capital Formation in Under-developed Countries*, Oxford University Press, London, 1953.

Osburn, W., *An Analysis of the Standard of Living in District of Columbia in 1916*, Publication of American Statistical Association, 1918-19, 16, 1916.

Oshima, Harry T., "Under-employment in Backward Economies: An Empirical Comment", *Journal of Political Economy*, 66, pp. 259-64, 1958.

Parthasarthy, G., "Changes in Rice Farming and Their Economic and Social Impact: A Case Study of Delta Village in Andhra" (Mimeo), 1973.

Parthasarthy, G., "Inter-State Variation in Unemployment and Growth of Agriculture", *The Indian Journal of Labour Economics*, 22(1 and 2) pp. 45-50, 1979.

Parthasarthy, G., "Land, Labour and Poverty", *Economic and Political Weekly*, 19, 1984.

Parthasarthy, G. and K. Adiseshu, "Real Wages of Agricultural Labourers in Andhra Pradesh: Two Decades of Stagnation", *Economic and Political Weekly*, 17, 1982.

Parthasarthy, G. and D.S. Prasad, "Response to and Impact of HYV Rice According to Land Size and Tenure in a Delta Village" *Development Economics*, 12(2), pp. 182-98, 1974.

Panikar, P.G.K. "Inter-regional Variations in Caloric Intake", *Working Paper No. 111*, Centre for Development Studies, Trivandrum, 1980.

Planning, Commission, *Implementation of Land Reforms*, New Delhi, 1966.

Prais, S.J., "Non-Linear Estimation of the Engel Curves", *Review of Economic Studies*, 20, 1953.

Prais, S.J. and H.S. Hauthakker, *The Analysis of Family Budgets* Cambridge University Press, 1955.

Prasad, Pradhan, H., '*Growth with Full Employment*', Allied Publishers, Bombay, 1970.

Quayum, A., "Agricultural Under-employment in Uttar Pradesh", *Economic Weekly*, 15, (51 & 52), pp. 1961-66, 1962.

Radhakrishna, R., "Approximate Determination of Indifference Surface from Family Budget Data", *Artha Vijnana*, 19 (3), pp. 247-58, 1977.

Rajaraman, Indra, "Poverty, Inequality and Economic Growth: Rural Punjab 1960/61 – 1970/71", *Journal of Development Studies*, 11 (4), pp. 278-90, 1975.

Raj, K.N., "Some Questions Concerning Growth, Transformation and Planning of Agriculture in Developing Countries" in *Agricultural Development in Developing Countries: Comparative Experience*, Indian Society of Agricultural Economics, Bombay, 1972.

Raj Krishna, "Unemployment in India", *Indian Journal of Agricultural Economics*, 28 (1), pp. 1-24, 1973.

Raj Krishna, "Measurement of Direct and Indirect Employment Effects of Agricultural Growth with Technical Change", in Edwards, E.G. (ed) *Employment in Developing Nations: Report on a Ford Foundation Study*, Columbia University Press, 1974.

Raj Krishna, "Rural Unemployment – A Survey of Concept and Estimates for India", *World Bank Staff Working Paper No. 234*, 1976.

Ranis, G. and J. Fei, "A Theory of Economic Development", *American Economic Review*, 51, 1961.

Rao, C.H. Hanumantha, *Agricultural Production Functions, Costs and Returns*, Asia Publishing House, Bombay, 1965.

Rao, C.H. Hanumantha, *Technological Change and Distribution of Gains in Indian Agriculture*, Macmillan Company of India, Delhi, 1975.

Rao, S.K., "Measurement of Unemployment in Rural India", *Economic and Political Weekly*, 8 (39), Review of Agriculture, pp. A78-A90, 1973.

Reid, M.G., "Capital Formation in Residential Real Estate", *Journal of Political Economy*, 66, pp. 131-53, 1958.

Robinson, Joan, "Disguised Unemployment", *Economic Journal*, 46, pp. 225-37, 1936.

Rodan, P.N. Rosenstein, "Problems of Industrialization of Eastern and South-Eastern Europe", *Economic Journal*, 53, pp. 202-11, 1943.

Rodan, P.N., Rosenstein, "Disguised Unemployment and Under-development in Agriculture", *Monthly Bulletin of Agricultural Economics and Statictics*, 6, pp. 1-7, 1957.

Rodgers, G.B., "Nutritionally Based Wage Determination in the Low-Income Labour Market", *Oxford Economic Papers*, 27(1), 1975.

Roegen, N. Georgescu, "Economic Theory and Agrarian Economics", *Oxford Economic Papers*, 12, pp. 1-40, 1963.

Rosenzweig, Mark R., "Determinants of Wage Rate and Labour Supply Behaviour in the Rural Sector of a Developing Country", in Binswanger and Rosenzweig (ed). *op.cit.*, pp. 211-41, 1979.

Rudra, A., "Demand Elasticity of Foodgrains", *Economic and Political Weekly*, 4, 1969.

Rudra, A., "Employment Patterns in Large Farms of Punjab", *Economic and Political Weekly*, Review of Agriculture, 6, 1971.

Rudra, A., "Direct Estimation of Surplus Labour in Agriculture", *Economic and Political Weekly*, 8, Annual Number, pp. 277-80, 1973.

Rudra, A., "Minimum Levels of Living – A Statistical Examination", in Srinivasan T.N. and P.K. Bardhan 'Poverty and Income Distribution in India' Statistical Publishing House, Calcutta, pp. 281-90, 1974.

Saini, G.R., "Resource Use Efficiency in Indian Agriculture", *Indian Journal of Agricultural Economics*, 24 (2), 1969.

Saith, Ashwani, "Production, Prices and Poverty in Rural India", *Journal of Development Studies*, 17 (1), 1981.

Samuelson, P.A., *Foundations of Economic Analysis*, 1948.

Sanghavi, Prafulla, *Surplus Manpower in Agriculture and Economic Development*, Asia Publishing House, Bombay, 1969.

Sanyal, S.K., "Has there been a Decline in Agricultural Tenancy", *Economic and Political Weekly*, 7, 1972.

Sarkar, N.K., "A Method of Estimating Surplus Labour in Peasant Agriculture in Over-populated under-developed Countries", *Journal of Royal Statistical Society*, 20, 1957.

Sau, Ranjit, "Growth, Employment and Removal of Poverty", *Economic and Political Weekly*, 13, 31, 32, & 33, Special Number, 1978.

Schultz, H., *The Theory and Measurement of Demand* Chicago, 1938.

Schultz, T.W. "The Role of government in Promoting Growth", in White, Leonard D. (ed.) *The State of Social Science*, University of Chicago Press, Chicago, 1956.

Schultz, T.W., *Transforming Traditional Agriculture* Yale University Press, 1964.

Sen, A.K., *Choice of Techniques*, Basil Blackwell & Moth Ltd., Oxford, 1960.

Sen, A.K., "Surplus Labour in India: A Critique of Schultz's Statistical Test", *Economic Journal*, 77 (1), pp. 154-61, 1967.

Sen, A.K., "Rejoinder to Theodore W. Schultz's Reply", *Economic Journal*, 77 (1), pp. 163-65, 1967.

Sen, A.K., "Poverty, Inequality and Unemployment", *Economic and Political Weekly*, 8, pp. 1457-64, 1973.

Sen, A.K., *Employment, Technology and Development*, Clarendon Press, Oxford, 1975.

Sen, B., "Opportunities in the Green Revolution", *Economic and Political Weekly*, 5, 1970.

Sethuraman, S.V., "Measuring Rural Unemployment to Private Guidelines to Policy Makers", *Economic and Political Weekly*, 6, 1971.

Sharma, A.G., Prakash Mehta and J.N. Single, "Impact of High Yielding Varieties of Crops on Pattern of Income Distribution", *Indian Journal of Agricultural Economics*, 25, Conference Number, 1970.

Sharma, R.K., *Economics of Tractor Versus Bullock Cultivation: A Pilot Study of Haryana*, Agro-Economic Research Centre, Delhi, 1972.

Sharma, R.K., *Impact of New Technology on Income Distribution Among Cultivating Households in Rural Haryana: A Regional Study*. An Unpublished Ph.D. Thesis of Jawaharlal Nehru University, New Delhi, 1983.

Sidhu, H.S., "Technological change in Agriculture and Income distribution – A Regional Analysis of Haryana", M. Phil. dissertation of the School of Social Sciences, J.N.U., New Delhi, 1980.

Sidhu, H.S. "Technological Change in Agriculture and The Distribution of Gains – A Case Study of Haryana", *PSE Economic Analyst*, 5 (1 & 2), pp. 114-25, 1984.

Singh, B., *Consumption Functions in India*, An Unpublished Ph.D. Thesis of Delhi University, 1968.

Singh, R. and B.B. Singh, "Farm Mechanisation in UP", *Indian Journal of Agricultural Economics*, 27, 1972.

Singh, Surender, *Transformation of Agriculture in Ganganagar District of Rajasthan*, A Ph.D. Thesis of Punjab University, Chandigarh, 1977.

Singh, Tarlok, *Poverty and Social Change*, Longmans Green & Co. Ltd., Calcutta, 1945.

Sinha, R.R., "An Analysis of Food Expenditure in India", *Journal of Farm Economics*, 48, pp. 113-23, 1966.

Sinha, J.N. "Comparability of 1961 and 1951 Census Economic Data", *Artha Vijnana*, 6 (4), 1964.

Sinha, J.N. "Dynamics of Female Participation in Economic Activity in a Developing Economy", in *Papers Presented by Indian Authors to the World Population Conference*, Belgrade, Yugoslavia, pp. 253-62, 1965.

Sinha, J.N., "The Concept of Unemployment in Developing Economy", *Indian Journal of Agricultural Economics*, 23 (2), pp. 15-24, 1968.

Sinha, J.N., "Rural Employment Planning: Dimensions and Constraints", *Economic and Political Weekly*, 13 (6 & 7), Annual Number, 1978.

Sinha, J.N., "Unemployment Poverty Nexus Reconsidered" (Mimeo), 1979.

Sinha, J.N., "Full Employment and Anti-Poverty Plan. The Missing Link", *Economic and Political Weekly*, 16 (50), 1981.

Sovani, N.V., "Potential Out-Migrants and Removable Surplus Population in three Districts of Orissa (India)", in International Union for the Scientific Study of Population, *Proceedings of the International Population Conference*, Vienna, London, 1959.

Stigler, G.J., "The Early History of Empirical Studies of Consumer Behaviour", *The Journal of Political Economy*, 62(2), pp. 95-113, 1954.

Stiglitz, J.E., "The Efficiency Wage Hypothesis, Surplus Labour and the Distribution of Income in LDC's", *Oxford Economic Papers*, 28, (2), pp. 185-207, 1976.

Stone, R., *The Measurement of Consumer Expenditure and Behaviour in the United Kingdom, 1920-38*, 1954.

Sukhatme, P.V. "Assessment of Adequacy of Diets of Different Income Levels", *Economic and Political Weekly*, 13, Special Number, pp. 1373-84, 1978.

Theil, H., "Quantities, Prices and Budget Enquiries", *Review of Economic Studies*, 19 (50), pp. 129-47, 1953.

Turnham O., *Employment Problem in Less Developed Countries*, OECD, Paris, 1970.

United Nations, *Measurement for the Economic Development of Under-developed Countries*, Department of Economic and Social Affairs, New York, 1951.

Vaidyanathan, A., "Some Aspects of Inequalities in Living Standard in Rural India", in Srinivasan T.N. and P.K. Bardhan (ed), *op. cit.*, 1974.

Vaidyanathan, A., "Unemployment and Wages in an Agrarian Economy", *Centre for Development Studies Working Paper No. 120*, 1980.

Vashishtha, P., *An Econometric Study of the Effect of Tractorisation on Farm Output and Employment*, (Mimeo), 1975.

Verma, R., "Income Elasticity of Demand for Foodgrains: A Regional Approach", *Artha Vijnana*, 1(4), pp. 271-81, 1959.

Viner, J., "Some Reflections on the Concept of Disguised Unemployment", *The Indian Journal of Economics*, 38, (148), 1957.

Visaria, Pravin, "Comparability of 1961 and 1951 Census Economic Data: A Comment", *Artha Vijnana*, 7, 1965.

Visaria, Pravin, "Employment and Unemployment in India: A Review of Selected Statistics", *Report of the Committee of Experts on Unemployment Estimates*, Appendix ii, pp. 43-144, 1970.

Visaria, Pravin, "Poverty and Unemployment in India: An Analysis of Recent Evidence", *World Bank Staff Paper*, (417), 1980.

Warriner, Doreen, *Economics of Peasant Farming*, Oxford University Press, London, 1939.

Warriner, Doreen, *Land and Poverty in Middle East*, Royal Institute of International Affairs, London, 1948.

Warriner, Doreen, *Land Reform and Economic Development*, Fiftieth Anniversary Commemoration Lectures, National Bank of Egypt, Cairo, 1955.

Wharton, G.R., (Jr.), "The Green Revolution: Cornucopia or Pandora's Box", *Foreign Affairs*, 47, pp. 464-76, 1969.

Wonnacott, Paul, "Disguised and Overt Unemployment in Under-developed Economies", *Quarterly Journal of Economics*, 76, pp. 279-97, 1962.

Wold H. and L. Jureen, *Demand Analysis: A Study in Econometrics*, New York, John Willy & Sons Inc., 1953.

INDEX